CONFLICT AND CONCORD
The Anglo-American Relationship since 1783

CONFLICT AND CONCORD

The Anglo-American Relationship
since 1783

BY

H. C. ALLEN

COMMONWEALTH FUND PROFESSOR OF AMERICAN HISTORY
IN THE UNIVERSITY OF LONDON

A revised and enlarged edition of Part I of
"Great Britain and the United States: A History
of Anglo-American Relations, 1783-1952"

ST MARTIN'S PRESS
NEW YORK

PRINTED IN GREAT BRITAIN
BY ODHAMS (WATFORD) LTD., WATFORD, HERTS.

PREFACE

It has been thought worth while to publish, as a separate book, the first Part of my longer work, *Great Britain and the United States,* 1954. This has been revised, and a final chapter has been added giving a very brief résumé of the other three Parts, which dealt at length with the diplomatic history of Anglo-American relations. What remains here is, except for this last chapter, general and analytical in character, and may well appeal to a wider public than has the longer work, to which those who seek further information can still refer.

I wish to renew my thanks and acknowledgments to those many persons and organizations who are listed fully in the original work.

H. C. ALLEN

Chesham Bois,
Bucks.
April, 1959

CONTENTS

Map of the Development of the United States and its Boundaries, pages 12-13

ABBREVIATIONS

The following abbreviations have been used in the footnotes:

Am.H.R. *American Historical Review*

Bemis S. F. Bemis, *A Diplomatic History of the United States.* New York, 1942

Brebner J. B. Brebner, *North Atlantic Triangle.* New Haven, 1945

Can.H.R. *Canadian Historical Review*

Eng.H.R. *English Historical Review*

W.A.A.E. Beckles Willson, *America's Ambassador to England, 1785–1928.* London, 1928

W.F.R. Beckles Willson, *Friendly Relations, A Narrative of Britain's Ministers and Ambassadors to America, 1791–1930.* London, 1934

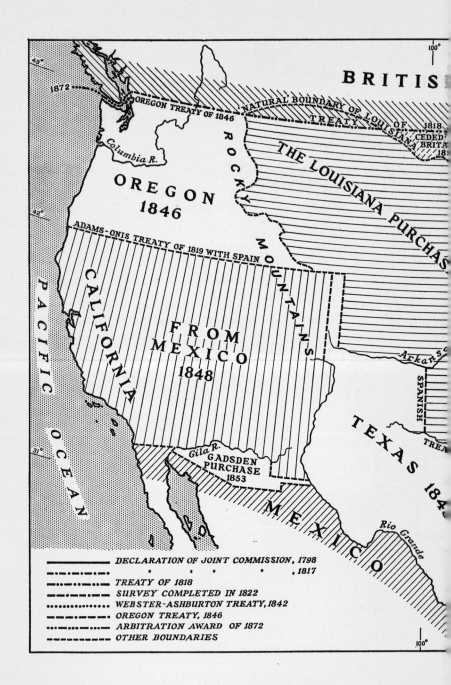

BRITIS[H]

1872

OREGON TREATY OF 1846

NATURAL BOUNDARY OF LOUISIANA TREATY

49°

Columbia R.

ROCK Y

THE LOUISIANA PURCHAS[E]

1818 CEDED BRITA[IN] 18[??]

OREGON
1846

42°

ADAMS-ONIS TREATY OF 1819 WITH SPAIN

M O U N T A I N S

PACIFIC

CALIFORNIA

FROM
MEXICO
1848

Arkans[as]

SPANISH
TREA[TY]

O C E A N

31°

TEXAS 184[5]

Gila R.
GADSDEN
PURCHASE
1853

M E X I C O

Rio Grande

DECLARATION OF JOINT COMMISSION, 1798
. . . . , 1817
TREATY OF 1818
SURVEY COMPLETED IN 1822
WEBSTER-ASHBURTON TREATY, 1842
OREGON TREATY, 1846
ARBITRATION AWARD OF 1872
OTHER BOUNDARIES

100°

100°

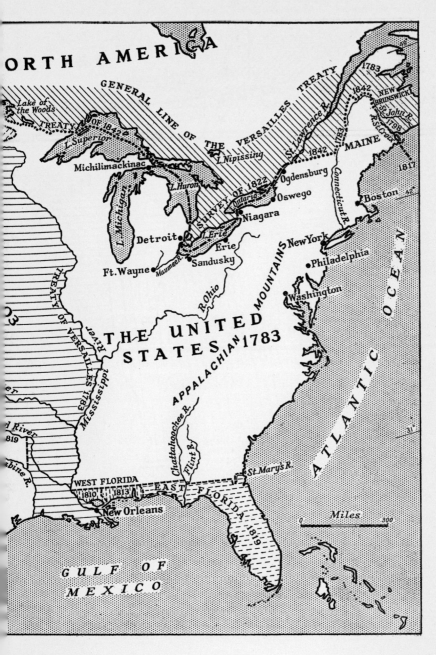

THE DEVELOPMENT OF THE UNITED STATES
AND ITS BOUNDARIES

CONFLICT AND CONCORD

The Anglo-American Relationship since 1783

CHAPTER ONE

INTRODUCTION

I

"THESE two great organizations of the English-speaking democracies, the British Empire and the United States, will have to be somewhat mixed up together in some of their affairs for mutual and general advantage. For my own part, looking out upon the future, I do not view the process with any misgivings. I could not stop it if I wished; no one can stop it. Like the Mississippi, it just keeps rolling along. Let it roll. Let it roll on full flood, inexorable, irresistible, benignant, to broader lands and better days."[1] Winston Churchill's words of August, 1940, embody the confidence with which Americans and Englishmen regarded the future of Anglo-American relations after they had fought together later in World War II. Indeed, Anglo-American friendship until it was subjected, for the first time since 1940, to notable strain by the China crisis which began in 1949, came almost to be taken for granted on both sides of the Atlantic. This was, perhaps, natural. The two peoples had always been conscious, even when serious disagreements existed between them, of their peculiar relationship. In 1843, for example, Dickens heard England referred to as that "unnat'ral old parent", and by 1900 in England, and soon thereafter in America, the idea of war between the two countries had come to be almost unthinkable.

But though it may have become natural by 1945 to take Anglo-American friendship as read, things have not always been thus. Two wars have been fought between the two nations, and, as late as the Venezuela dispute of 1895, Anglo-American disagreements were numerous and sometimes sharp. But by degrees, as the years passed, friendship triumphed over these obstacles, though the triumph was not one of sentiment alone, for only a wide complex of causes, political, economic, social—the totality in fact of Anglo-American intercourse— made it possible. Happily, the intimacy of Anglo-American relations is by no means solely dependent upon the powerful but sometimes

[1] Winston S. Churchill, *War Speeches 1940-1945* (London, 1946), p. 35.

fickle bond of emotion; it has manifold links embedded deep in the lives of both peoples. To see something of those links, and a little of how they came into being, is the object of this book. The first seven chapters deal with their general structure; the eighth and last deals very briefly with the history of Anglo-American diplomatic relations.

The term 'relations' is used in a wide sense. As one student of Anglo-American relations writes, "we talk and write glibly—as we must—about 'international relations'. . . . We are dealing with an immensely complicated web of interactions among human beings. There are relations between governments. . . . There are relations among travellers, students, business men, who have dealings abroad. There are all sorts of transactions conducted by correspondence. International relations are a constant flow of men, goods, and ideas across seas and frontiers."[1] The term 'Anglo-American' also may need precise definition. *American* refers to the United States alone. *Anglo* refers to Great Britain, and, more precisely, after 1921 to the United Kingdom of Great Britain and Northern Ireland.* Of course, the influence of other parts of the British Empire and Commonwealth, and particularly Canada, must be great, but it is primarily with Britain that I am concerned. My aim is the reverse of Brebner's in *North Atlantic Triangle,* for he wished "to get at, and to set forth, the interplay between the United States and Canada—the Siamese Twins of North America who cannot separate and live. . . . The great obstacle to a simple account of this interplay was that . . . the United States and Canada could not eliminate Great Britain from their courses of action".[2] For us Canada is very much the *tertium quid*, and will therefore remain for the most part in the background; our concern is above all with the twofold relationship of Great Britain and the United States.

It is hardly necessary to stress the importance of this subject. How vital Anglo-American friendship is has been understood by the majority of Englishmen since the turn of the century and has become clear to most Americans at least since the entry of the United States into World War II. For a decade now it has been a commonplace of politicians—which has for all that some truth in it—that the future of democracy

[1] Crane Brinton, *The United States and Britain* (Cambridge, Mass., 1945), p. 121.

* I must confess to my Scottish and Welsh readers that I early abandoned any attempt to maintain a consistent distinction between the terms 'England' and 'Britain', and their derivatives. Nor have I endeavoured, because of its complexity, to enter into what is a matter of substance—the distinction between English and, for instance, Scottish influence in Anglo-American relations.

[2] J. B. Brebner, *North Atlantic Triangle* (New Haven, 1945), p. xi.

can only be safe in the hands of an Anglo-American alliance. In view of the tension between the two countries which began in 1949 over the policy to be pursued towards the People's Republic of China, the supreme importance of their friendship has suddenly become to Englishmen even more apparent than before, just because it has come to seem less certain, less safe. From his public utterances it is clear that at that time it remained uppermost, paramount, in the mind of Churchill, the greatest of England's living statesmen. It is significant of the danger of taking Anglo-American friendship for granted that the initial whisper of discord strikes the thinking Englishman like the first faint, but terrible, tremor of an earthquake. Of all historical subjects, it is possibly true that the history of Anglo-American relations is the most important, as well as the most relevant, to the future of Western civilization.

But no study of them will in the long run better Anglo-American relations unless it is an impartial one. Soft words which do not speak the whole truth in judgment will not turn away wrath; partisanship might merely increase danger. It has, therefore, been my aim to write a book for Americans and Englishmen indifferently. In the words of an Anglo-American master, Henry James, "I can't look at the English-American world, or feel about them, any more, save as a big Anglo-Saxon total, destined to such an amount of melting together that an insistence on their differences becomes more and more idle and pedantic. . . . I have not the least hesitation in saying that I aspire to write in such a way that it would be impossible to an outsider to say whether I am . . . an American writing about England or an Englishman writing about America".[1] I have striven to be, in this way, free from national prejudice, intensely difficult though that is. I have found in lecturing on Anglo-American relations in America, that neither I, nor those to whom I talked, were altogether immune from sudden gusts of emotion over contentious issues. But the blood may rush to the head of the best of us, and may as quickly run out again. Even more insidious is the unconscious predisposition which our lifelong habits give us to judge upon any question by our parochial, if well-intentioned standards. It may indeed be impossible for the historian to escape altogether from his environment into impartiality, and since national background constitutes a large part of environment for all of us, the risk of that form of bias is always with us.

[1] *The Letters of Henry James*, Selected and Edited by Percy Lubbock (London, 1920), I, p. 143.

It is worth while to spend a little time on this difficulty, for it still lies at the bottom of much international misunderstanding; certainly it must be a root cause of dissension between two nations who already have so much in common, both in history and principle, as Great Britain and the United States. Even the works of the best of academic historians can seldom wholly escape the taint of national bias, and examples of disagreement on national lines are plentiful among historians writing on Anglo-American relations. One striking example appears in the verdict of two first-class historians, one American, one English, on the Venezuela incident. S. F. Bemis writes in his *Diplomatic History of the United States*:

> A case had now arisen in which a first-class power still possessing colonies on one of the American continents, might, by advancing boundary claims and refusing to arbitrate them, arbitrarily expand its territory in violation . . . of the Monroe Doctrine. . . . Cleveland resolved not to take the rebuff. . . . The country as a whole—despite the chagrin of intellectuals—rallied behind the President.[1]

A glaring contrast is provided by R. C. K. Ensor in his *England, 1870-1914*, who writes of Cleveland's message to Congress on this question:

> This was certainly one of the most unexpected, least warranted, and least excusable steps ever taken in modern times by a Great Power. . . . The message evoked a frenzy of Jingoism throughout the United States; but a chastening influence was exerted by a catastrophic fall in American stocks. British opinion displayed restraint from the start. It became obvious that, while an Anglo-American war would still be the most popular of all wars in America, in England it was viewed as fratricidal.[2]

The effect of national preconceptions is sufficiently obvious.

Yet these books were written between the two world wars, at a time when most intelligent men, and these among them, tended to spurn chauvinist sentiments. Such divergences of judgment occur, of course, between the writers of all nations, but they are peculiarly apt to occur between Americans and Englishmen. Their very closeness, to say nothing of their common tongue, seems to make disagreements more frequent, or, at least, cause them to be noticed more often. We shall have occasion to revert frequently to this theme, the homely one, that

[1] S. F. Bemis, *A Diplomatic History of the United States* (London, 1936), pp. 416-9.

[2] R. C. K. Ensor, *England, 1870-1914* (Oxford, 1936), p. 230.

familiarity breeds family disagreements. Cecil Chesterton wrote in 1915, "what really produces trouble between peoples is when one is quite certain that it understands the other—and in fact doesn't. And I am perfectly certain that that has been from the first one of the primary causes of trouble between England and America."[1] The same analysis has been made and remade by acute observers of Anglo-American relations in this century. What is more, in any case where passions run high on either side, because of identity of language and similarity of ideas, no lack of knowledge of what is being said on the other shore of the Atlantic can long exist, for all is understood, and all is news; there is no veil of language or ignorance to obscure the beginnings of disputes. Thus they have all the bitterness—and happily some of the shortness—of family quarrels.

But not all the misrepresentations of one country by citizens of the other can be pardoned as the results of honest misjudgment or excessive frankness. On the wilder fringe of the literature of Anglo-American history are some authors who cannot be altogether acquitted of malice and all uncharitableness. The relations of no two other nations with so much in common have been so bedevilled by the writings of mischievous publicists, and some brief consideration of a selection of them is, unfortunately, necessary. The harm they have done in the past has been very marked, and beside their misrepresentations the honest differences of academic historians shrink into insignificance. If the passages quoted above are a warning to us in our study of Anglo-American history, those quoted below are a warning to all mankind of how strong is the old Adam of spite within us.

The history of our subject offers us a rich and extensive, if mal-odorous, field of choice in this matter, but I propose to take my specimens from the inter-war years, when the consequences of irresponsibility might have been obvious to anyone on either side of the Atlantic. Probably examples from the early nineteenth century would be as striking, though it is questionable if they would be quite so obviously lacking in taste, but it is a happy indication of the changes wrought in the last decade that bad feeling of this intensity is hardly even conceivable today. Anti-Americanism and Anglophobia both exist indeed (as anyone who has recently resided in both countries will know), but in much more restrained and limited forms. I shall cite

[1] *Literary Digest* 19 June, 1915, p. 1,468: q. H. L. Mencken, *The American Language, An Inquiry into the development of English in the United States* (Fourth Edition, 1946), p. 44.

first some flagrant examples of misrepresentation of the United States by two Englishmen, whose attacks were made more deadly by the fact that they were men of ability who pretended to impartiality and proclaimed the best intentions.

The preface to the first work, if not indeed the very title—C. E. M. Joad's *The Babbitt Warren*—is quite enough to make the hackles of any good American rise: *

> These anecdotes have in every case been taken, usually verbatim, from paragraphs in the daily Press, which presupposes in English readers an inordinate interest in American extravagances. The author has not had the privilege of visiting the United States, and has no means, there-fore, of judging of the accuracy of these reports. His acquaintance with Americans and those who have been to America forces him, however, to the conclusion that the stories given in the text, even if they are not in all respects literally true, possess at least the merit of the inventions of that distinguished author, Mr. Benjamin Trovato; that is to say, if they are not true they ought to be.[1]

The second author—C. H. Bretherton—had spent much time in America and so his preface to *Midas or The United States and the Future* cannot quite reach the level of Professor Joad's, but it is pretty good just the same, notwithstanding its lofty air of impartiality. It ends,

> Some time ago I read in a little volume of poems one by a lady called *Hates*. It recounted the various things the authoress disliked and contains the following lines:
>
> > *'I hate washing dirty plates.*
> > *I hate the United States.'*
>
> Those who hate the United States will get no satisfaction out of this volume. They will much prefer *Babbitt* and *Main Street*. Enthusiasts for the world's biggest republic will hardly be more satisfied but I do not know what antidote to recommend them unless it be the *Saturday Evening Post*.[2]

It is perhaps fair to note that both these books were published in 1926, in the high days of H. L. Mencken and Sinclair Lewis, but citizens of

---

* This passage was written some time before the death of the late Professor Joad, but, after very careful consideration, I have decided that it should stand.

[1] C. E. M. Joad, *The Babbitt Warren* (London, 1926), p. ix.

[2] C. H. Bretherton, *Midas or The United States and the Future* (London, 1926), pp. 7-8.

a country may say many things about it which will not easily, if ever, be forgiven to foreigners, even if they speak the same language. In those two passages of preface is epitomized what is, perhaps, most hateful to Americans in the English, their supercilious assumption of superiority.

But our authors do not content themselves with this. Bretherton proceeds to analyse the future of Midas with an appearance of distaste oddly combined with relish. He knows America and can hit where it hurts most. "The truth is that the modern American has no use for liberty and liberty plays no part in what he conceives to be democracy. He conspues the imaginary tyranny of kings and emperors but earnestly desires to replace them with the very real tyranny of the fifty-one per cent." For American culture, of course, he has nothing but contempt. "American poetry is vile. Nothing so readily reflects the temperament of a people as its poetry and the American passion for *vers libre* is simply a reflection of American superficiality."[1]

Bretherton, however, is a model of restraint beside Joad, who starts off well with a sidelight on American everyday life. "An American will go into raptures about his bath. It is the first thing he will show you when he takes you into his house." But he does not confine himself to light commentary on social habits: weightier topics are discussed, and he concludes an attack on the satisfaction of militarists at a rising population, by turning to America, whose population in 1926 was indeed still increasing, with the words, "Guns and babies, cannons and fodder, with America as usual in the van." It would be hard to imagine, let alone find, such another travesty of the truth about America at that time, but Joad manages it, as we shall see later. Meanwhile he passes to American materialism; perhaps he had some grounds for criticism on this score in 1926, but he did not indulge the British habit of understatement when he pronounced, "The power of money has so permeated every stratum of American society, that to the American no other object of desire seems conceivable."[2] "The rich American's table witnesses the same superfluity of expensive things, the same dearth of good ones, for he is no more of an epicure and no less of a glutton than Trimalchio; pointless jokes and imbecile anecdotes pass for humour, stale platitudes and threadbare clichés for conversation, purse-proud complacency and paunchy self-satisfaction for dignity, rough horseplay and inane catcalls for conviviality." This passage might seem to exceed all bounds of credibility, to say nothing of good taste, were it not for a final grim perversion of the

[1] Ibid, pp. 53, 76.   [2] Joad, pp. 8, 24, 66.

truth: "When we read stories of lynchings in the Southern States, of thousands of cheap excursionists travelling by train to see a nigger's tongue torn out before he is burnt alive, Americans will, I feel sure, forgive us if we fail entirely to subscribe to the view that theories of social change necessarily, and in all cases, require combating in America."[1] On this note let us leave the opinions of these Englishmen on America, and turn to the opinion of one American about the English.

G. H. Payne published his *England: Her Treatment of America* in 1931, five years after Joad and Bretherton had put pen to paper. He, as they had done before him, started with high pretensions of profiting by the lessons of history: "This book is written not with an idea of antagonizing England nor of encouraging anti-English elements in America. It is written with a belief that some portion of the American public may read it with interest but not embitterment. It is written in the belief that it may be read by Englishmen who in all fairness will realize that it is the record of an attitude of mind that is more harmful to England than it is to America."[2] In fact, the Introduction by "George Higgins Moses, President Pro-tem of the U.S. Senate", seems to express the true aim of the book more accurately: "These are the days when the re-writing of history shares public honors with the Tom Thumb Golf Course and when the debunking of historic figures holds literary rank with the crossword puzzles. No one, however, has hitherto attempted the debunking of a nation. It is perhaps an exaggeration to say that this is Mr. Payne's thesis; *but** . . ."[3] The preface concludes in this manner:

Among a great many Americans who have every desire to be fair and who have every wish that there should be friendship on an equal footing, there is a belief that certain basic factors not only act to make the British offensive to Americans but lead them to commit wrongs against our nation. Those factors are:

1. An apparent instinctive and unconscious assumption of superiority by Britons.
2. Their inability to co-operate on an equal basis.
3. Their assumption of propriety of British interests.
4. Their obviously highly organized widespread propaganda.
5. Their refusal to permit trade rivalry.
6. Their unethical and at times immoral diplomacy.[4]

[1] Ibid, pp. 63-4, 219.
[2] G. H. Payne, *England: Her Treatment of America* (New York, 1931), p. xii.
* Authors' italics.　　　[3] Ibid, p. xix.　　　[4] Ibid, pp. xiii-xiv.

Here is all the hyper-sensitivity of American opinion about Britain, with its belief in British conceit, egotism, deliberate propaganda, unscrupulousness in trade, and Machiavellianism in diplomacy.

The body of the work starts well, with a caption drawn from the remarks of that eminent movie character, Trader Horn: "No Englishman's ever a gentleman when it comes to taking what he wants from a foreign country." It continues in much the same vein, and I choose a number of the brighter passages. For a hundred and forty years the English followed "a policy toward America . . . of almost continuous insult."[1] It is "monstrous" that an Englishman, Dean Inge, should declare that in 1812 America was guilty of "stabbing England in the back,"[2] for the truth is that it is "the British opinion that in any war in which England is concerned there should be no neutrals . . . a position . . . that would never be countenanced in this country."[3] Of the Monroe Doctrine he writes, "For over a hundred years England's foreign policy with regards to the American has been a continuous effort to make the Monroe Doctrine inoperative."[4] More and more doubt as to the value of his pretensions to historical scholarship—"I know of only one way of judging of the future and that is by the past"[5]—penetrates the mind of the reader when he sees such statements as, "But recent researches have shown that . . . the Mexican War . . . was largely due to England's secret contempt for the Monroe Doctrine and her interference in Mexican and Texan affairs",[6] and when he refers to a nonexistent eighteenth-century Englishman, Charles Henry Fox,[7] the doubt is confirmed.

In the same way that Joad attacks the Americanized Englishman, so Payne's own countrymen are not immune from criticism: "It is our misfortune that our representatives at the Court of St. James's are so frequently imbued with the English point of view that they forget their duty to their own country."[8] We shall see later something of the chequered history of Anglo-American relations over the project for an Isthmian Canal and shall observe that the English were not without fault in the matter, but Payne goes a good deal too far when he writes, "England has never been more clever than she has in the entire matter of the Panama Canal. Although this Canal was built with American money, made possible by American engineering and American sanitation, England so manipulated the diplomatic negotiations that a special treaty had to be made in order to get her permission to construct this important waterway."[9] More general reflections are also indulged:

---

[1] Ibid, pp. 1, 5. [2] Ibid, p. 36. [3] Ibid, pp. 36-7. [4] Ibid, p. 50. [5] Ibid, p. xiv.
[6] Ibid, p. 75. [7] Ibid, p. 18. [8] Ibid, pp. 144-5. [9] Ibid, pp. 156-7.

25

"In international affairs the English are the leading humorists of the world. This pre-eminence does not arise from a wilful desire to be light or trifling, but from a real appreciation of a good joke; especially if it is on others—as it usually is."[1] Yet even Payne is forced, albeit with obvious reluctance, to admit and comment upon the closeness of the Anglo-American relationship: "The average American has more a liking for England and the English people than he has a dislike."[2] It is in at least lip service to this relationship that his characteristic peroration closes, and on this note we may leave him:

> America and Great Britain, as they stand today, can dominate the world; but they must dominate the world for the benefit of the world and not for the benefit of the English ruling class. . . . The peace of the world may be insured by England and America, but only if England is rid of the carbuncles of two hundred and fifty years of selfishness. . . . Give the British people an opportunity to govern their own country and the prospect of war between America and England will forever vanish. . . . The hate that now smoulders in almost every corner of the earth will be replaced by a toast: "The British people—God bless them!"[3]

We have dwelt long enough in this nightmare world to make us wonder that Anglo-American friendship was ever able to survive such obfuscation and malignity at all, and certainly to put us on our guard against the false witness of some of our sources of information. But let us not, author and reader alike, forget the beam that may be in our own eye; let us be always on our guard against our instinctive partisanship. The responsibility in this respect is certainly more that of writer than reader, and so let me begin by outlining my thesis.

II

Two main themes dominate the history of Anglo-American relations. The first arises directly, and the second indirectly, from the peculiar relationship which has always existed between the two countries, both physically and psychologically. Connected as they are by the great North Atlantic waterway and by the agency of the ever-present British North America, and bound together by a common origin and by much common life and history, they have affinities altogether unusual among nations.

In a sense we can very well look upon them as father and son; at any

[1] Ibid, p. 153. [2] Ibid, p. 284. [3] Ibid, pp. 292-3.

rate the analogy has its uses. In infancy and adolescence, in the seventeenth and early eighteenth centuries, America is born and grows up under the protection of Great Britain. The political family is, if one may use the phrase, rather Victorian in its strictness, but the youth prospers none the less. By 1763, however, he has grown almost to manhood and finds life with father unduly restrictive, so that irritations and ill-will pile up on both sides. In 1776, America comes of age, and in one last glorious 'row' leaves home for ever. In the great world he finds friends to help him resist father's punitive efforts, and after an uncertain start he begins to form his own habits and live his own life. For a period in the first half of the nineteenth century relations remain bad between parent and offspring, with resentment on the one side and hatred on the other, and they even come to indecisive blows in 1812. But as the younger man fills out and makes his way in the world with astonishing rapidity and the older himself prospers as never before, so the mutual sense of filial soreness and aggrieved parental authority dies away. By the end of the century the mistrust has to a large extent subsided, and as the father becomes increasingly conscious of his past faults and his future dangers, and the son gains some of the restraint and confidence of maturity, so friendliness begins to take its place. The international developments of the twentieth century destroyed the isolation of the United States and strongly encouraged the process by which the two countries came to realize how much they had in common. Co-operation was born in World War I and alliance in World War II, and, despite the relapse of the inter-war years, cordiality increased steadily throughout the whole half-century. Between 1941 and 1945 there was a friendship and a unity between them certainly never surpassed since 1783, and hardly even before that date. The Communist China crisis of 1949 served to show that the danger of differences was not over, but, looking back over the whole course of Anglo-American relations from 1783 to the present day, we can see persistent, even steady, progress from mistrust to cordiality. This ripening of friendship is the first theme of this book.

It can be seen very clearly in the diplomatic sphere, but can be observed also in others. It appears in the growing similarity of political ideals and practices which accompanied the development of democracy in both countries, but particularly in Great Britain. It is obvious in social life generally, and the analogy, and indeed connexion, between the great reforming movements of the two nations throughout their history is unmistakable. In the economic sphere, though there is no relative increase in the extent of intercourse, there are manifold, sustained, and intimate contacts. In the subtle and complex emotional relationship of the two peoples there is perhaps most strongly perceptible an advance from the bitter literary battles, the hatred, of the early nineteenth century, to the often deep affection of the present.

The second main theme is concerned, not with the increasing amiability of the relationship, but with its nature, and with the shifting balance of power within it. Pre-eminently is one impressed by the fact that there is a remarkable reversal in the relative position of the two states between 1783 and 1952. In the beginning Great Britain was in every way the superior power: in the end America's strength exceeded hers by quite as large a margin. That this striking inversion might take place had long been apparent to percipient observers, even in the colonial period, because of the vast potentialities of the American continent. By the end of the Civil War it was clear that it was taking place, and by the end of World War I it was obvious that it had done so. In every branch of national life, political, social and economic, we are able to watch this transformation come over the relationship of the two powers.

Yet the change in the material balance of power was only relative: it did not mean any actual decline in the power of Great Britain. Indeed, in the nineteenth century she grew to a height of power far exceeding any in her history, and came to dominate the greatest empire the world has yet known. It was merely that the growth of the United States was even more astonishing; she had the vast vacuum of a virtually empty continent to fill, and she surged through it as if she abhorred the emptiness with an intensity that Nature herself might envy. This combination of unmatched natural resources with unparalleled vigour produced an economic and political development which overshadowed the really quite creditable performance of Great Britain. It is true that the advance of the latter has been checked in the twentieth century; the sceptic might even reflect that the colonial status of 1783 was not very far removed from that of the recipient of Marshall Aid in 1949. But it is to be hoped that the exhaustion of Britain after 1945 was only a temporary condition. She may be an ancient among the nations, but it does not necessarily follow that she is doomed inevitably to the weakness, and ultimately the decrepitude, of senility. There are, most decidedly, limits to the validity of the analogy between the old age of nations and that of individual human beings, and history furnishes many surprising examples of the longevity and resilience of states. So the decline of Great Britain, even in the twentieth century, may still be considered only as relative to the growth of the United States. Although she grew rapidly in the nineteenth century, Britain was already a Great Power in 1783, and the pattern of her development in nearly all aspects of national life was foreshadowed, if not actually predetermined, before that date. In her growth and actions after 1783, therefore, there can be detected a certain consistency: the main principles and interests upon which her policy was based were hardly to change in their broad outlines through the whole period.

The United States, on the other hand, was not a Great Power by 1783; she was in fact a respectable power, but there were those who were pessimistic of her future. Certainly all lay before her, but this future was as yet in the realm of possibility and not in the domain of fact. It follows from this that the whole nature of her progress was dynamic and ever-changing compared with that of Great Britain. Radical as were the alterations in the life of the latter, they pale almost into insignificance beside those which transformed that of the United States. This fact, though it is true of almost every aspect of existence, is perhaps most obvious in the international relations of the two states, for the foreign policy of Britain, as we shall see, followed general principles in 1783 very much the same as those it still pursued in 1951, whereas that of America was markedly different in 1812, in the mid-nineteenth century, and again (even more strikingly so) in 1952. To some extent, therefore, one may visualize the history of Anglo-American relations with Great Britain as a comparatively stable back-cloth, against which the United States moves off and on to the international stage, and it is convenient for the purposes of analysis to concentrate upon the changing policy of the United States and to tell the story from that point of view. We shall in this way watch the emancipation of America from the tutelage of Europe, her withdrawal into isolation during the opening up of the West, and her eventual return to active participation in world affairs as the greatest of the powers. The junior, if not the sleeping, partner in the First British Empire has become the senior partner in an alliance whose second, though not whose only other, member is Great Britain.

The increasing cordiality of the relationship and the increasing preponderance of the United States within it are, then, the two threads of which we shall be repeatedly aware as we follow the complicated pattern of the century and a half of what Franklin D. Roosevelt—even on so American an occasion as the commemoration in 1937 of the signing of the Declaration of Independence—could call "Anglo-American history."

CHAPTER TWO

THE TWO NATIONS

I

W HAT are and have been the basic determining factors in the development of these two nations? What are their main differences and what have they in common?

At first sight in mid-twentieth century their differences are striking. The area of the continental United States is 3,022,387 square miles; that of the United Kingdom of Great Britain and Northern Ireland 93,053 square miles. Within the former are to be found widely varying conditions of terrain and climate; within the latter there is a considerable physiographical uniformity. The population of the United States in 1950 was 150,697,361; that of the United Kingdom in 1951 50,210,472.* In 1950 and 1951 the average population densities of the two countries were 50 and (excluding Northern Ireland) 550 persons per square mile respectively. In agricultural and mineral resources the United States is very rich, even in proportion to her population, while Great Britain is less so. Thus the one is virtually self-sufficient in all the necessities of life, except for a few things such as uranium, chrome, tin, sugar, rubber and coffee, and in most luxuries, except tea, spices and tropical fruits; whereas the other is heavily dependent upon imports for her existence, having only two major raw materials in quantity, coal and iron, and importing, in 1950 for example, no less than 78 per cent of her wheat, 87 per cent of her oils and fats, and 94 per cent of her butter.

In social and political life there are differences nearly as great. The relative homogeneity of the population of Great Britain, which, despite internal racial differences, has remained comparatively unaltered in the composition of its basic constituents for nearly nine hundred years, contrasts strikingly with the racial diversity of the United States, which received within a hundred and twenty-five years, beginning in 1820, no less than 38,461,395 immigrants from many and various lands. Another difference is the lack in the past in America of a central capital like

* Preliminary figures of 1951 Census.

London. Equally vivid, perhaps, is the contrast between the long slow years of English development, stretching back, if not in unbroken continuity, at least with some genuine, though often unconscious, descent of political and social tradition, for more than a millennium, and the swift, and indeed fabulous, growth of the United States. America, founded three hundred years ago by a mere handful of men who clung for their livelihood to the edges of a vast and uncharted wilderness, emerged as a political community somewhat over a century later in a series of acts which were more nearly deliberate acts of political will than those which accompanied the birth of almost any other nation in the world. To these differences must be added the acquisition in the past by Great Britain, and to some extent her retention to this day, of a great colonial and maritime empire, which gave her a tradition markedly different from that of the United States, which has rarely, except at the end of the last century, sought overseas dominions. With this goes—to some extent it arises from it—the fact that Great Britain has been for many centuries heavily involved as a major power in the main current of international affairs, whereas the United States has until recently spent much of her independent existence in a vigorous and vocal isolationism. There must be noted, too, the difference between the republican written constitution of the one and the unwritten monarchical system of the other, and between the unitary compact government of Great Britain and the wide federal organization of the United States. Finally, one must mention, though not in this brief space attempt to define, the often-misleading but none the less significant contrast between the traditional social inequalities of English life and the proud egalitarianism of the American people.

Yet great as the contrasts at first appear, upon closer examination they shrink somewhat in significance, and similarities, some of them frequently overlooked, become more apparent. In the first place, many of these very differences are counteracted by others. Thus the existence of the great British Commonwealth and Empire makes the differences between the United Kingdom and the United States in area, population, terrain, climate and resources much less important than they otherwise would be. Though the population of the United States is three times that of the United Kingdom, that of the British Commonwealth as a whole—539,870,000—is much more than three times that of America, while the land area of the Commonwealth—14,435,060 square miles— is four times bigger and contains within it even greater diversity than America's. Similarly, the American admixture of Negro, Oriental and

Indian stocks is more than outweighed by the fact that only 70 of the 539 millions mentioned above are white men. In much the same way, Great Britain is to some extent able, either directly or indirectly, to make up for deficiencies in natural resources by the existence of the Commonwealth and Empire. So long as control of the sea is not gained by a hostile power, this situation gives her some of the advantages that accrue to the United States from her great internal resources.

There are also positive similarities between the two countries when they are gauged, which is the only possible way, by comparison with other nations or people. Both enjoy, relatively, a very high standard of living; though the average annual British income *per capita* in the years before World War II was estimated at $100 less than the American, which was $525, those of South America, India and China were all between $50 and $90 per head. Both are great industrial powers. Great Britain, of course, led the way in this, but the United States followed, and now stands head and shoulders above all the other nations of the world, producing in 1952 65 per cent of the world's manufactured goods and 52 per cent of its mechanical energy. Great Britain, however, still remains a very highly industrialized country. When the degree of her industrialization is compared even with that of Russia, whose strides in this respect are giant, she still makes quite a good showing. Her *per capita* consumption of steel and electricity, her *per capita* production of coal and pig-iron, and her *per capita* railroad-track mileage are all much less than those of the United States, but they were still, in 1952, greater than those of Russia, despite the rapidity of Soviet development. They are far greater than those of most of the other nations in the world. The nature of a country's armed forces is an interesting reflection of its state of industrialization, and those of Britain, almost alone, approach those of America in the degree of their mechanization.

There are positive, if not always very tangible, likenesses, too, between the two countries in other spheres than the economic. In their political life both are now democracies, a word which, despite slight differences of interpretation and emphasis, both use in sufficiently the same sense to understand one another with some clarity. To get the measure of this likeness it is sufficient to observe that the Russians use the word in an utterly different sense. In fact, the nineteenth and twentieth centuries witnessed a great growing together of the United States and Great Britain in this respect, and in their internal politics their differences became steadily less apparent than their similarities; the British monarchy, for example, seemed of less significance as a

point of difference in a country ruled by a Labour government, and in
the age of the New and Fair Deals the fact that the United States had
a federal and rigid constitution seemed a less important divergence
than it once had. In foreign affairs, too, the differences narrowed as
America became irrevocably committed to active leadership of the
democracies, and as she became aware, though she continued to shun
colonial imperialism, of the need for strategic bases of the kind that
Gibraltar had long been to Britain. In fact, the United States came more
and more to play the part in the world that Great Britain had so long
performed, but which she could no longer adequately execute alone.
In 1945 the two peoples were much closer than they had been since
1776, and in some ways than they had been even before that date. But
this political structure of alliance and friendship rested upon a broad
social base, for, though the racial composition of the United States
became increasingly divergent from that of Britain in the century
1820-1920, it remained true that the British was not only the largest
single group, but also that those of British origin in the United States
exceeded the total of all the rest. What is more, the history of Britain
and the British people, at any rate before 1776, remained almost unconsciously a part of the American experience and background. What
they did not acquire consciously by the reading of history they absorbed
insensibly by their literature, because of the existence of their common
tongue, a bond of great significance at any stage of human development
but of literally inestimable importance in this age of swift communication, mass printing, telephone, radio, cinema, and almost universal
literacy. It, more than any other single factor, has made possible the
symbiosis.

These and other similarities, as well as differences, between the two
nations will become apparent as the study proceeds. Indeed they constitute in some ways a third truth which emerges from the history of
Anglo-American relations. One must add to their increasing cordiality,
and to the reversal of the balance of power between them, which we
have already noted, the fact that from their common heredity, environment, and will, there has developed an increasing similarity, and even
sometimes identity, of opinion and action. It is not merely that they
have grown together with the passage of time, but that they could not
have done so without deep and prior similarities which in part determined the nature of their development. Again and again we shall be
conscious of these likenesses. We shall see them in important things;
in their common tongue; in their belief in a democracy which has its
roots deep in English political thought and history; in their mutual high

degree of industrialization; in the increasing identity of their international roles. We shall see them in seemingly subtle and unimportant, but often notable and sometimes significant, things; in the slightly contemptuous attitude of both Englishmen and Americans towards foreigners; in the corresponding sneers of those foreigners about nineteenth-century Englishmen and twentieth-century Americans, who cared only for the wealth they made in such abundance; in their vanity over such technological pre-eminences as that in plumbing; in the fact that the French still say of the American tourist what they first thought up to apply to his English predecessor; in the disheartening response which they both find greets a nation which steps out over the seas to rescue alien peoples from aggressive national dictatorships, the causes of whose existence it finds so hard to understand. In these and in many other things shall we be repeatedly reminded of the resemblance between the two peoples. But it arises from fundamental facts, chiefly of geography and history, and the chief purpose of this chapter is to examine, first, the geographical basis of Anglo-American relations, and, secondly, some of the effects of it.

II

IN the time-scale of human history, geography is a relatively stable component of man's environment, and in Anglo-American history the geographical background has been fairly constant. This is at least true of what may be called external geography, the geographical position that the nations occupy in the world and *vis à vis* one another, but it is less so of their internal geography, which may best be discussed first.

Within both lands the changes in geography wrought by the hand of man since 1783 are tremendous: the face of each has been transformed. In America the transformation is the more dramatic. In 1783 the United States consisted of a long and relatively narrow strip of populated land stretching along the Atlantic coast from Massachusetts to Georgia, barely cresting the Appalachians except in the centre and seldom more than two to three hundred miles in width. Beyond lay the seemingly illimitable wilderness, whose western shores three thousand miles away had scarcely yet been charted, whose harsh forests, plains and mountains no white man had yet traversed, and in whose vast expanses the feared and hated savages moved and had their being.

There could hardly have been in the wildest imaginings of man a greater transformation than that which the last century and a half has effected. The change in Britain was much slower, but even here the hand of man has altered much, for from a country predominantly agricultural, and to some extent still hedgeless and unenclosed, it has become a land of immense industries and great cities. The industrialization of Britain does not match in rapidity or intensity of achievement the subduing of the vast American continent to the will of twentieth-century industry and agriculture, but in both lands internal geography has altered greatly.

Nevertheless, despite these changes, certain basic geographical factors remain the same in each country, and for the most part they tend to make for diversity in the one and uniformity in the other. The great continental United States—3,000 miles from east to west and 1,500 from north to south—is a land of geographical contrasts even greater than those of one part of Europe with another. Her mountains vary from 6,000 ft. in the Appalachians of the east to 14,000 ft. in the Cordillera region of the west; the great desert between the Rockies and Sierra Nevada has no rival in Europe; the United States contains rivers greater than the greatest that Europe can show. These and many other geographical contrasts mean that America provides not one but several geographical environments for her people. Compared with this diversity, the homogeneity of the British Isles appears extreme. It is true that it consists of two parts, a mountainous north and west of hard rock and an eastern lowland plain of newer and softer rocks, so that the latter is traditionally more fertile and more abundant in easy communications, particularly by water, but its tiny island character binds it tightly together. Within it there are no mountains higher than 4,500 ft., no very large rivers, and certainly no deserts. Thus the uniformity of Britain's geographical environment is considerable compared with that of the United States.

When we look at the facts of climate, the comparison becomes even more notable. The mean annual temperature of the United States is 52 deg. F., varying between an average of 31 deg. in the coldest to one of 73 deg. in the warmest month, a range of 42 deg. F. The mean annual temperature of the United Kingdom is 49 deg. F., varying between 40 deg. and 61 deg., a range of 21 deg. F. The large land mass of the United States means wide extremes of climate, from the sub-tropical Gulf to the extremely cold North Dakota area, and of course a wide diversity of regional temperatures; the climate of the British Isles is much more uniform.

35

But once more the differences appear less if we measure them against a third country, or indeed against many of the countries of the world. The difference in average temperature, for example, is only 3 deg. F., while Ellsworth Huntington gives the most favourable span of temperature for the support of vigorous people as 40-70 deg., and both lands have their average temperatures at around 50 deg. The case of Russia again furnishes a contrast. The mean annual temperature of Russia in Europe is 40 deg. F. and of Russia in Asia 34 deg. The average coldest month temperature of the former is 16 deg., of the latter minus 1 deg.; warmest month temperatures are 65 deg. and 67 deg. respectively. This gives ranges of temperature as wide as 49 deg. and 68 deg., which constitutes a much wider diversity than exists even in America. Here again the contrast of both the United States and Great Britain with Russia is apparent, a contrast which would be even stronger with a largely tropical country like India.

Thus there are marked differences of internal geography between the two; in particular the political and social sectionalism of American life is very different from the compact homogeneity of the British political and social structure. But, though there are clearly great similarities in geography between Russia and America, their vast territory and their great variety of climate and terrain for instance, there are also material resemblances between Britain and America.

Even more manifestly is this true of external geography, where there is a most significant and positive likeness between Britain and America. One is vast and the other is tiny, but both are in their essence islands, and both have played the part of island powers in history. This has not escaped attention in the case of the British Isles, "anchored," as Emerson appreciated, "at the side of Europe and right in the heart of the modern world",[1] but in some respects Britain is much less an island than America, protected as she is by vast oceans, or their equivalent. This important fact, which has sometimes passed unobserved, was noted in 1893 by one well fitted to appreciate its significance, Admiral A. T. Mahan. He wrote in an article on "The Isthmus and Sea Power", "Fortunately, as regards other states, we are an island power, and can find our best precedents in the history of the people to whom the sea has been a nursing mother."[2] This

---

[1] R. B. Mowat, *Americans in England* (London), p. 132. [No date of publication given.]

[2] A. T. Mahan, *The Interest of America in Sea Power, Present and Future* (London, 1898), p. 104.

insularity is now beginning to break down for the United States, as it has already done for Great Britain, through the coming of air power, and it has disrupted her sense of security in much the same manner, except that the change appears much more startling and overwhelming to Americans. The extent of this insularity in the past is clearly reflected politically in the strength of isolationism in American history, but it can be plainly seen also in intrinsic geographical facts.

She is protected to east and west by the two largest oceans of the world, so that it is 4,521 miles from San Francisco to Yokohama and 3,043 from New York to Liverpool. In the south her protection is also formidable, with the barriers of the Caribbean and the Gulf of Mexico, for, while the Panama Canal gives her shipping access from coast to coast, the isthmus on which it is built is even yet hardly a serious means of north-south communication, and is in any case, because of its extreme narrowness, very easily defensible by the power controlling the sea on its flanks. Furthermore, it is worth while noting that it is farther by the direct route from New York to Rio de Janeiro than from New York to Moscow. None the less the barrier to the north is even more effective. The frozen waste lands of northern Canada, huge even if we make allowance for the deceptive effect of Mercator's Projection, and the icy expanse of the Polar Region form perhaps the last effective geographical barrier to man on the surface of the whole earth, and have in the past been a much more formidable obstacle than the ocean. The contacts of the United States with East and West, by the stepping stones of islands, are nearly all in the north where, through the curvature of the earth, the distances are shorter, but in the past this has been to a minor degree compensated by the bad weather and adverse winds of these latitudes.

In this age of the aircraft and the guided missile, the isolation of the island has gone, but it has been of immense significance in history, when it was emphasized by the weakness of her immediate neighbours. By 1783 the United States had, in reality, nothing to fear from her southern neighbour, Spain, and by 1820 the establishment of Mexican independence meant a permanently weak and inferior power upon her southern border. No power arose in Latin America to rival, let alone to threaten her. In the north, the situation has always been more complex, for though Canada was until recently a comparatively weak power, absolutely at first, and relative to the United States later, she was always sustained by the might of Great Britain. This is the reason for the incessant activity of Anglo-American diplomatic relations in the nineteenth century. Canada was a constant bond between the two powers, often a bond which appeared as a chain and chafed accordingly, but, whether pleasant or unpleasant, never absent. Historically this island position of the United States was effective from the beginning of her independent existence, for during the period of her weakness the great wilderness of the West formed as powerful a protection as the Pole or the oceans. If there was any doubt on this score it was removed by the Louisiana Purchase, and the point was made crystal clear after the Mexican War ended in 1848. It is indicated by the fact that in her early years and of late the United States has been a great maritime power. The first period of the Republic saw the great days of the American merchant marine and the Yankee Clipper Ship, but during the nineteenth century her maritime activities diminished in importance, because of the passing of the wooden ship, and, even more, her absorption in the West. With the closing of the frontier, however, and the attainment of the Pacific with its oriental trade, the United States became a two-ocean power, and not only constructed a two-ocean navy, but encouraged a revival in the strength of her merchant marine. This is essentially the story of an insular power, and that insularity goes far to explain the depth of the often unremarked similarity between the fundamental interests of the two peoples.

III

LET us follow this theme into some of the realms of national life arising from the geographical foundations, and discuss briefly what may perhaps, for want of a more elegant term, be described as certain geo-political factors; first population, then military potential, and finally diplomatic principles dictated directly by geographical considerations.

If we are to have an accurate picture in our minds of the changing relations between Great Britain and the United States during the last one hundred and seventy years, we must always be aware that those relations have in large part changed because each of the two nations itself has changed. This is perhaps most immediately illustrated by population figures.

England, Wales and Scotland		The United States	
		1790	3,929,214
1801	10,500,956	1800	5,308,483
1821	14,091,757	1820	9,638,453
1851	20,816,351	1850	23,191,876
1881	29,710,012	1880	50,155,783
1901	36,999,946	1900	75,994,575
1921	42,769,196	1920	105,710,620
—	—	1940	131,669,275
1951	48,840,893	1950	150,697,361

The figures show clearly, not only the startling rapidity of the American increase, but also the alteration in the relative power of the two states, for population is still an indispensable factor in political power. It is, of course, by no means the only factor, for in a world so highly developed technologically, industrial capacity is at least as important. China is certainly not three times as powerful as America, nor India six times as strong as Britain. But the factor of manpower cannot be ignored, and in any case, as between Great Britain and the United States, it is a fairly reliable gauge of their relative power because both are highly industrialized and technically skilled nations. America surpassed Britain in population in the early eighteen-forties, though it is doubtful whether she was her equal in political power until well after the Civil War, because of British industrial superiority.

It is noteworthy that the British increase (which was never greater or more rapid than it was in the first years of the nineteenth century) was comparatively gradual and steady, whereas that of the United States from the eighteen-forties onwards was extremely swift and frequently uneven; the relative flatness of the British curve contrasts with the steep rise of the American. This was because the British growth was due mainly to the increase in commerce and industry, which was comparatively regular, while to this process was added, in the case of the United States, not only the agricultural resources and immense incentives represented by the opening up of the West, but also the unprecedented immigration of the years 1820 to 1920. Of this admixture we shall see more when we discuss the intermingling of the two peoples. But the salient fact which emerges is that in 1783 Great Britain had more than three times the population of the United States, whereas in 1950 the United States had more than three times the population of Great Britain.

It is obvious, however, that throughout these years there has always been a great difference in the density of population in the two countries, that of the United States being, even today, very much sparser than that of Great Britain. But though the density of population in Britain has always been far higher than it has ever been in America, both have increased more or less steadily, except that there is a marked, if temporary, recession in the American figures in 1810 as a result of the Louisiana Purchase, and in 1850 as a result of the vast accession of territory from Mexico in the treaty of Guadalupe Hidalgo (1848). But once again the rate of increase in America has been even swifter than that of Britain. The population density of Great Britain, excluding Ireland, has increased about five-fold since 1801, that of the United States about tenfold since 1790. The figures (of persons per square mile) are as follows:

	United States	Great Britain		United States	Great Britain
1790	4·5	—	1880	16·9	337
1800/1*	6·1	119	1890	21·2	375
1810	4·3	136	1900	25·6	420
1820	5·5	160	1910	30·9	463
1830	7·3	184	1920	35·5	485
1840	9·7	210	1930	41·2	508
1850	7·9	236	1940	44·2	532†
1860	10·6	262	1950	50·7	550††
1870	13·4	296			

It is interesting to observe that the gap in this respect between the two has narrowed quite fast in the twentieth century, for whereas until about 1875 the density of the one was never less than twenty times that of the other, by 1950 it was only about eleven times as great. But these figures are mere averages. Quite obviously, the population density of the American South-west is utterly different from that of the American North-east and yet again from that of the South. Even in Great Britain, where there is more homogeneity, there are marked contrasts; for example, in 1801 the density of England and Wales was 152, but of Scotland 54, and in 1931 the figures were 685 compared with 163. But to the inhabitant of the megalopolis of the twentieth century it does not make much difference, from the point of view of

* U.S. Census in the even, G.B. in the odd years.
† Estimated.
†† Computed from preliminary Census figures for 1951.

cramped conditions, whether he lives in London or New York, and there is little to choose between the population densities of Birmingham and Chicago.

Firmer conclusions may possibly be drawn from figures of relative urbanization in the two countries. Once again we see a disparity between the two, though not quite as marked as before, and we see the United States rapidly overhauling Great Britain. The figures of urban as a percentage of the total population are as follows:

	United States	Great Britain
1800/1	6%	29%*
1850	15%	50%
1890	35%	72%
1910	46%	78%
1930	56%	80%
1950	59%	82%†

In both countries there has been an increasing concentration in great cities, so that in 1930 in the United States there were 93 towns of more than 100,000 inhabitants, containing 29·6 per cent of the total population (in 1950 there were 107 containing 29·5 per cent), while in England and Wales 39·5 per cent of the population lived in such areas. Thus Great Britain is much more urbanized than the United States, but both are relatively rich in city dwellers. The essential difference between them today is the magnificently healthy balance between agriculture and industry which the United States is still able to maintain, and which is a vital element in her strength. But though their development here differs in degree, it does not do so as greatly as it does in the case of other lands. To take Russia once more as an example, neither the density of her population nor the number of her great cities compares with either Britain or the United States, while a recent estimate of her urbanization gives the figure of 33 per cent of the whole, one which was exceeded by Great Britain early in the nineteenth century, and which is not much more than one half of the American figure. Thus, in the extent of their urbanization, as elsewhere, the similarities between the two nations are perhaps as marked as their differences, and those similarities become more marked more rapidly as the twentieth century proceeds. From being in effect primarily a rural, one might almost say colonial, producer of raw materials in the early nineteenth century (which England had not really been since the sixteenth),

* Estimated.   † England, Wales and Scotland.

America has, like Britain before her, become a great urban and industrial nation. It is not, perhaps, entirely coincidental that these later years have, as we shall see, also been the years of swiftly growing brotherhood, instead of traditional rivalry, between the two peoples.

IV

BUT in some ways even more illuminating than a study of population figures is that of what one may call, in a broad sense, military power. Of course, population and industrialization, as we have seen, are the crucial factors, excluding moral ones, in military potential: but in some ways a more satisfactory, because a more direct, way of assessing the power of a nation is by consideration of the history of its armed forces. A comparison of the history of the armaments of Great Britain and the United States produces, despite some contrasts, very interesting evidence of similarity. We can see the outstripping of the one by the other, with which we are already familiar, but we can also see that both naturally concentrate primarily upon maritime power for their defence. The naval power of Great Britain until World War I was more highly developed, largely because of her wide empire and extensive commerce, but as soon as America re-enters the international scene and ceases to be exclusively concerned with the development of the West, she creates a navy at first equal to and later far exceeding in power that of Great Britain. Both nations later concentrate heavily upon their air arms because they are a necessary complement to a great navy. The obverse also is true of both, that their armies were, if not neglected, at least the recipients of much less money and much less attention in time of peace than their other armed forces, though here again the imperial responsibilities of Britain make a difference: in 1848, for example, the United States War Department spent 5 million pounds, the British War Office 15 million pounds. Mahan wrote of the two countries in 1894:

> Partners each, in the great commonwealth of nations which share the blessings of European civilization, they alone, though in varying degrees, are so severed geographically from all existing rivals as to be exempt from the burden of great land armies; while at the same time they must depend upon the sea, in chief measure, for that intercourse with other members of the body upon which national well-being depends. How great an influence upon the history of Great Britain has been exerted by this geographical isolation is sufficiently understood. In her case the

natural tendency has been increased abnormally by the limited territorial extent of the British Islands, which has forced the energies of their inhabitants to seek fields for action outside their own borders; but ... the same tendency, arising from the same cause, does exist and is operative in the United States, despite the diversion arising from the immense internal domain not yet fully occupied, and the great body of home consumers which has been secured by the protective system. The geographical condition, in short, is the same in kind, though differing in degree, and must impel in the same direction.[1]

Largely effect of this, but partly cause, is the mistrust of standing armies in both peoples, a mistrust which has misled not a few other powers as to their efficiency as soldiers. It has also meant that there is a similarity between the inefficiency of the British and American armies at the beginning of every war which would be humorous if it were not so expensive in blood, for both have always inadequate immediate resources and are always, in the nature of things, slow in bringing their great military potential on to the actual field of battle. *The Economist* wrote on 24 June, 1899: "Since our own Crimean muddle there has been no worse instance of military mismanagement than that displayed by the American War Department in Cuba and the Philippines,"[2] while with the sort of defeat that the American armies suffered in the early weeks of the Korean war of 1950 the British have been only too familiar. Examination of a few statistics brings out this neglect of the army in favour of the navy and air force even more clearly.

Perhaps the best way to approach the problem is through the medium of expenditure on armaments as shown in the table on page 44.

What are the conclusions to be drawn from these figures? First, some obvious but none the less interesting facts. Though the population of the United States, as we have seen, overhauls that of Great Britain in the eighteen-forties, and though, as we shall see, her wealth and productivity do so about fifty years later, her total national expenditure does not exceed that of Britain until the nineteen-thirties, until the Depression and the New Deal, by which time her population and national wealth were nearly three times as great. More immediately relevant is the fact that the total annual expenditure on the American army does not surpass that on the British until just after 1910; on the

[1] Mahan, pp. 110-111.
Article on "The American Political Situation," p. 899.

DEFENCE EXPENDITURE OF THE UNITED STATES AND GREAT BRITAIN

In Millions of Dollars* (To the Nearest 1 Million Dollars[1])

Date	Total National Expenditure		Expenditure on the Army		Expenditure on the Navy		Total Defence Expenditure		Naval as Percentage of Total Defence Expenditure		Population (in Millions) at nearest Census		Expenditure on Defence per head of population to nearest $		Ratio of Column O to Column N
A	B U.S.	C G.B.	D U.S.	E G.B.	F U.S.	G G.B.	H U.S.	I G.B.	J U.S.	K G.B.	L U.S.	M G.B.[2]	N U.S.	O G.B.	P
1789[3]	4	51	(-633)	11[4]	(-001)	10	(-634)	21	(-1)	48	4	11	(-2)	2	10
1821	16	226	4	45	3	28	8	73	38	38	10	14	(-8)	5	6¼
1841	27	203	9	44	6	34	15	78	40	44	17	19	(-9)	4	4½
1870	310	341	58	69	22	49	79	118	28	42	40	26	2	5	2½
1879	267	422	40	78	15	52	56	130	27	40	50	30	1	4	4
1890	318	380	45	88	22	71	67	158	33	45	63	33	1	5	5
1903	517	653	119	183	83	177	201	361	41	49	76	37	3	10	3⅓
1912	690	943	184	140	136	222	320	362	43	61	92	41	3	9	3
1923[5]	3,295	3,944	397	290[6]	333	320	730	610	46	52	106	43	7	14	2
1937	8,177	4,235	628	457	557	532	1,185	988	47	54	132	45	9	22	2½
1950	41,860	10,365	8,000[7]	1,232	6,268[7]	914	14,268	2,145	43	43	151	49	94	44	½

[American figures from *Historical Statistics of the United States, 1789–1945* (published by the United States Department of Commerce, 1949), pp. 299–301. British figures from *The Annual Register* (1789, p. 285; 1822, pp. 312, 319; 1841, pp. 377, 385; 1870, p. 234) and from *Whitaker's Almanack* (1881, p. 124; 1892, p. 183; 1905, p. 186-7; 1914, p. 500; 1924, p. 490 and 1925, p. 494; 1938, p. 673 and 1939, p. 653; 1951, p. 590 and 1952, p. 577). American figures for 1950 from *Whitaker*, 1951, p. 821.]

NOTES TO THE TABLE

[1] This produces some apparent discrepancies in columns H and I.
[2] Figures for England, Wales and Scotland.
[3] U.S. figures cover period 1789–91.
[4] Figures for 1789, 1821 and 1841 include Ordnance.
[5] Air Force expenditure for both countries divided between Army and Navy.
[6] British figures for 1923 and 1937 based on Estimates. British and American figures for 1950 based on Estimates.
[7] Approximate figures.

FOOTNOTE

* The problem of finding a satisfactory rule-of-thumb by means of which to convert dollar into sterling statistics throughout Anglo-American history is a formidable one. To follow the detailed fluctuations of the exchange markets is impossible, and some general rule must be found, inaccurate though it is bound to be. There are, however, four main phases in the sterling-dollar exchange rate. From 1783 to about 1830, despite violent fluctuations, the norm was something under $4.5 to the £; in Jay's Treaty, for example, the pound was reckoned at $4.44. During the century which followed the pound was normally worth between 4.8 and 4.9 dollars; the mint par of exchange when both were on gold was $4.86⅔ and treaties in 1848 and 1853 made the conversion at $4.84. During the third period, beginning in 1939, the British Government fixed a rate of $4.03, but in 1949 was forced to devalue to $2.80 to the £. Thus, in round figures, the following conversion table may serve our purpose.

1783–1830	$4.5 to the £
1830–1939	$5 to the £
1939–1949	$4 to the £
1949–1952	$3 to the £

navy until World War I and the period immediately thereafter, when the Washington Conference recognized American and British naval parity; and on Defence as a whole until the same period. Before putting any great weight upon such figures one must appreciate, not only that exchange difficulties may make accurate comparison difficult, but, even more important, that differences of expenditure may to a considerable degree be accounted for by differences in national standards of living and costs of production. Where, as in the army, a substantial portion of the total expenditure goes in pay, the fact that American rates of pay are very much higher than British may explain much of the discrepancy and will not mean that the American army is as much more powerful than the British as army estimates might make it appear. The same argument applies to costs of production, particularly, for example, in naval expenditure, so much of which represents new capital construction. In other words, it is at least possible that in the nineteen-thirties the difference in defence expenditure between the two countries is partly to be explained by high American costs and rates of pay. Similarly, arguments depending on the proportion of total national expenditure spent on defence are very suspect because the total British national budget has usually been, throughout this century, relatively much greater than that of the United States. This is the result of many factors, particularly the heavy services of the vast British National Debt, the greater expenditure on social services, and the fact that in the United States much governmental expenditure is in fact made by state rather than federal authorities. But, even given these reservations, it is perfectly plain that Great Britain has until the inter-war years spent absolutely more on arms than the United States (Columns H and I), and, quite obviously, immensely more relatively. There could be no better illustration of the sense of security (and not merely the sense of it, but the thing itself), which the Americans derived from their insular position, which provided natural defences much better than the British Isles have ever enjoyed.

More conclusive still are the results of assessing the ratio of expenditure on defence to population figures. This is best seen in the form of a calculation of the expenditure annually per head of the population on defence, and the resulting figures are almost startling (Columns N and O). In 1789 the British expenditure was approximately $2 and the American approximately 20 cents; in 1879 $4 and $1 (the 1870 figures of $5 and $2 represent exceptional post-Civil War conditions); in 1912 $9 and $3; and in 1937 $22 and $9. Not until after World War II does the United States regularly spend more on defence per head of the population in peace time than Great Britain, as when in 1950, for example, she reckoned to spend $94 to Britain's $44. The ratio figures bring this out most clearly, and show, with some slight exceptions, a rough progression from ten times the expenditure on the part of Great Britain in 1789 to three and a third times in 1903, two and a half times in 1937, and twice on the part of the United States in 1950. It is abundantly clear from these figures—if proof were needed—how much greater the participation of Britain in world affairs has always been; indeed it is interesting how rapidly American expenditure upon armaments increases at just that crucial period in her history, at the end of the nineteenth century, when she re-enters international affairs as an active participant. It is also apparent how closely these facts in the political world conform to the geographical realities beneath them.

But this can perhaps be demonstrated most conclusively by a third set of facts, the proportion of the whole defence expenditure of the two states spent upon the navy (Columns J and K). Compared with the wide variations between the two in, for example, the proportion of total national expenditure taken by defence, the relative amounts they spend on their navies are not only very similar but very constant. Except for the first years after the formation of the national government in the United States, which were plainly exceptional, the proportion in the case of both is usually somewhat under 50 per cent, a figure to which Britain remains remarkably close through the whole of the century. In 1841, as a typical peace year, 40 per cent of the American defence budget went on the navy, 44 per cent of the British. In 1870 there was a drop in the American figure, which was not recovered till the turn of the century, owing principally in the first instance to the fairly large armies kept in being after the Civil War and later to the fact that this was the height of American isolation from Europe, the period when she felt most secure in her strength and her island position. By 1903, after the rise of American Imperialism, the proportion is back at 41 per cent, relatively close to the British 49 per cent, but shortly before this date Great Britain had begun to be affected by the beginning of the naval armaments race with Germany, and by 1912 was spending over 60 per cent of her defence budget on naval expansion. Her expenditure in the inter-war years continued to exceed 50 per cent. That of the United States increased much more gradually—43 per cent in 1912, 46 per cent in 1923, 47 per cent in 1937—and only in the post-World War II period did it just top that of Great Britain. But though there are discrepancies, the similarity between these figures is more notable than the variation, which is chiefly owing to the similarity between their fundamental positions in the world.

Mahan, as we have seen, pointed this out and, of course, actually formulated a policy for the United States based directly on his observations of the British tradition on the seas, but his influence was by no means confined to his own country; he had perhaps even more effect in England than at home. Lord Wolseley wrote: "Mahan's books have done the country, and the Navy for that matter too, a world of good. It is a sad reflection that it has taken a Yankee to wake up this generation of Englishmen to the meaning and importance of sea power."[1] Not only did his articles in the *Daily Mail* go far to arouse Britain to the German danger, but he even popularized the very term "sea power." He was in a sense the living symbol of the fundamental insularity of the two peoples, which found practical expression in the passage of technical knowledge between the two navies, particularly after the Spanish-American War, which taught, for instance, to both navies the use of electricity in ships and the need of distilling and repair vessels as adjuncts to the fleet. Other examples of this interchange were the American experiments with submarines, and the British introduction in 1902, partly on the American model, of a plan for the preliminary common training of all officers before specialization, in order to secure the interchangeable officer. Even the neglected national armies, small professional bodies of non-conscripts, had sufficient in common for Arthur Lee, one-time military attaché in Washington, to believe, according to Heindel, that "the American Army was the only one in the world which resembled the British Army to any degree."[2] These things arise at bottom from the insular position which the two countries occupy, and which creates a certain sympathy of outlook between them. Right-wing American talk in 1951 of a refusal to send troops to Europe, and the call of a Hoover or a Taft for American concentration on great naval and air strength causes alarm and utterly fails of comprehension on the continent of Europe, but in Britain it can only cause misgivings. She cannot but understand it well enough, since it has always been her own policy.

Once again, a glance at certain of these European powers serves to heighten the effect of similarity between Britain and America. As we have seen, the expenditure of these two on naval as opposed to land defences has normally averaged somewhat under 50 per cent, though

[1] R. H. Heindel, *The American Impact on Great Britain, 1898-1914* (Philadelphia, 1940), pp. 117-8. [2] Ibid, pp. 123-4.

rising in the case of Britain to about 60 per cent in 1912. That of the Continental powers, as is to be expected, was always much less. In 1912, for instance, France spent only 32 per cent of her total defence budget on the navy, while Germany—it was the era of her greatest naval strength—spent only 27 per cent. In 1938 France spent only 24 per cent, and Germany probably less. Even now, in 1952, when Russia's is the second peace-time navy, it would seem doubtful if she spends more than a third of her defence outlay on it.

The same story appears from a cursory review of the relative size of armies, taking as the basis of calculation the number of fully trained reserves.

ARMY STRENGTHS
(*In Thousands*)

Year	U.S.	G.B.	France	Germany	Russia
1890	27	619[1]	2,000	1,492	2,151[2]
1912	212	730	3,120	3,800	2,700
1924	209[3]	517	3,300	100[4]	720
1938	263[3]	518	3,000[5]	2,500[5]	1,600
1948[6]	600	530	600	Nil	4,000

[Figures from *Whitaker's Almanack* (1891, pp. 215, 532, 536, 554, 565; 1913, pp. 105, 481; 1914, p. 694; 1925, pp. 243, 741, 785, 790, 824; 1939, pp. 427, 908, 1,015; 1949, p. 454).]

Even allowing for differences of population, the figures speak for themselves. The United States has always had the smallest of armies prepared for war, and, though Britain has had a larger army than her in peace-time, chiefly because of her imperial responsibilities, she has hardly been better prepared for large-scale war. Thus the latter only most reluctantly introduced peace-time conscription shortly before the outbreak of war in 1939, and the former only during the course of the war itself. The vast peace-conscripted armies of the Continental powers have always put them in a totally different category from the island powers protected by the seas, the oceans and the polar cold.

[1] All British figures include Indian troops.
[2] All Russian figures are unreliable, and those of later years almost certainly too small.
[3] Strength of National Guard estimated approximately at 80,000.
[4] Maximum under Versailles Treaty.
[5] Approximate figures; Germany certainly underestimated if para-military formations included.
[6] In 1946 the British Army had numbered 3 million, the American 8 million, and the Russian more than 10 million.

Thus over the century and three-quarters of their independent relationship, we can see clearly how the power of the United States, whether gauged in terms of population, of military potential or of actual armaments, has overhauled and overtaken that of Great Britain; we can observe that reversal in their relative positions of which we have already taken note. Great Britain is outstripped in potential strength by the end of the nineteenth century and decisively so in actual military strength in and after World War II, though, to prevent an exaggerated perspective in this matter, the present strength of the British Commonwealth of Nations as a whole must not be forgotten. We can see also, to a minor degree, in military affairs evidence of the growing co-operation of the two countries. But most clearly of all we see, what we shall often observe again in other spheres of life, the remarkable and fundamental similarities between the two lands, similarities by no means confined, as is so often assumed, to the possession of the same language and the fact that they are kindred stock, but arising from basic geographical situations surprisingly alike. We see their high degree of urbanization, of industrialization, of wealth; we see their preoccupation with naval, and later, air power; we see also the corollary of this, their neglect of peace-time armies. It is true, certainly, that there are many geographical factors which differentiate the two nations—size and variety of climate and resources, for instance —but they are not more influential than those which tend to identify them. The great land-mass of the continental United States, for example, has not prevented the Americans from being a great sea-faring people. In all these things the influence of geography is apparent.

V

BUT its influence is perhaps most obvious in the diplomatic sphere. It is thus the geographical proximity of Canada to the United States which was the fundamental cause of Anglo-American friction in the nineteenth century. Between these two extensive lands, inseparably conjoined, there were outstanding problems which could not but be a cause of irritation and which tended to counteract the powerful factors making for co-operation. Nearly all the diplomatic *causes célèbres* between the two states arose because of the existence of Canada, or of other indigenous British interests in the Western Hemisphere. The exception to this was the great dispute over the Freedom of the Seas, which arose directly from the fact that both were leading maritime powers:

the interests of the greatest of maritime neutrals and the greatest of maritime belligerents were perhaps bound to clash. Nearly all the Anglo-American issues centred in America or American waters; the western posts; the boundary disputes in Maine, the Great Lakes, Oregon and Alaska; the Caribbean disputes over Honduras and the canal; the perennial bickering over fisheries, seals and even the Navigation Acts themselves, the rub of which was chiefly in the West Indies.

Furthermore, because of this, the affairs always touched the Americans much more closely than the inhabitants of the British Isles, for they concerned issues remote from the interests of the bulk of the British people, interests which in the nineteenth century were scattered widely over the surface of the globe, and some of which, as was inevitable, were from time to time in dispute or jeopardy. Why should the Oregon question be of much deeper significance to the average Englishman than the acquisition of Hong Kong? The Canadians felt the full effect of this fact also, when Great Britain refused to support them in the dispute with the United States over the Alaska boundary, because Anglo-American friendship had become more vital to her in the rising tide of European tension than a Canadian border dispute. But Oregon was on the very doorstep of America, as Alaska was on that of Canada : it was important to her national development, and had it not been for the acquisition of California, would have been even more important. It followed naturally from this that the United States cared a great deal more about most Anglo-American disputes than did Great Britain, and, as Bryce justly observed, the American people were as a result much more bellicose and pugnacious, so that the desire for co-operation appeared somewhat earlier in Britain than in America. But though these irritants, arising from geographical proximity, frustrated for a period the operation of causes making for co-operation, they were not strong enough to do so for long, for there was no deep, inherent antagonism between the two peoples such as that which appeared to exist between France and Germany. There was no difficulty comparable to the "pressure of population on the Rhine" between Canada and the United States, because America had bountiful room for expansion to the west, the normal direction of her growth. The 'safety-valve' theory of the American frontier—that it provided an outlet for the social discontent of the East—may be no longer valid, but it is certainly true that the Westward Movement took the sting out of Canadian-American relations. In 1812 the United States was not strong enough to annex Canada, and in the eighteen sixties and seventies, when she was, it was not possible to arouse sufficient enthusiasm for the project among the American people, because there were still great unoccupied tracts of land in the United States itself. As E. L. Woodward writes, "The United States already held vast territories, and although the addition of certain areas might be desirable for strategic, economic, or sentimental reasons, there was nothing of the acute land-hunger or the desire to approach ice-free waters which affected the policies of European Powers."[1] There was thus no irreconcilable antagonism between Britain and the United States arising from North American geography, and by World War I all their disputes had been settled, in every case except the first by peaceable means. Indeed, the unfortified frontier between the two countries had become the ideal type of frontier in international relations. That this was so was not only the result of a growing cordiality between the peoples, but of the triumph of long-term similarities, arising partly from physiographic facts, over short-term differences arising from the same source.

Finally, geographical factors go far to explain, not simply the increasing warmth of Anglo-American relations in this particular aspect, but also the peculiar history of those relations in the broad theatre of world affairs. America's break from the mother country in the Revolution, her emancipation from Europe in the years up to 1814, her isolation in the nineteenth century, these were plainly influenced by her geographical position. The growth of America's Imperialism, and her slow, reluctant assumption of the leading role in world affairs in the twentieth century, were also forced upon her by the breakdown of her isolation in a world of rapidly developing technology. Geography explains equally clearly the persistent participation of Great Britain in the affairs of Europe and the world; there were periods when isolationism was powerful in Britain, and there were periods also when she was tempted to withdraw within the naval defences of her widespread Empire, but, despite these, she has played much the same part in the crises of world affairs since the sixteenth century. She has never been quite so isolated from the main currents of world affairs as has the United States, even in the age of sailing ships, for it is a mere twenty-two miles across the English Channel, and she has as a consequence been always of Europe, if not in it.

There have invariably been three main forces influential in the making of British policy: her tendency to isolation, her tendency to imperial development in colonies overseas, and her tendency to participate in European affairs. It was the dynamic resolution of these

[1] E. L. Woodward, *The Age of Reform, 1815-70* (Oxford, 1938), pp. 293-4.

forces which conditioned British political actions, and to them in the last fifty years has perhaps been added a fourth, the tendency to closer and closer co-operation with the United States. This last fact has become of increasing importance both to Great Britain and the United States, as well as to the rest of the world, since the surest hope, if not for peace, at least for the safety of the Western world lies still in Anglo-American friendship. This, too, derived much of its impetus from the facts of geography, and there is perhaps no more remarkable instance of it than the way in which the United States has come in the last decade increasingly to assume the role in international affairs which had in the past been played by Britain, but which she could no longer adequately perform. From her secure island base, strong on the sea and in the air over it, the United States has assumed the mantle of Britain and the indispensable task of holding together, as their principal protagonist, the nations of the free world, in their effort to ward off the aggressive domination of a single power entrenched firmly in the heart of the Eurasian continent.

CHAPTER THREE

ECONOMIC DEALINGS

I T IS not surprising to find that the economic relations of the United States with Britain have in general outline been analogous to their political relations. There has, in the first place, been a decisive swing-over in the balance of economic power from the one to the other, which is almost exactly paralleled by the similar change which we have observed in the political sphere. This steady increase in American strength has led to a reversal of the economic roles of the two countries, in the sense that the United States has had thrust upon her in the twentieth century the economic leadership of mankind which had been achieved by Great Britain in the nineteenth. As far as fundamental economic power was concerned, the scales had swung down decisively in America's favour by the turn of the century, though in finance it was not unmistakably clear until World War I.

In the second place, there has been throughout the history of the two countries since 1783, as obviously before that date, a great and remarkable intimacy of economic relations. It will be noted that this is not exactly analogous to the political or emotional development, which showed an increasing and broadening contact and friendliness as the years went by, for it does not seem that, considered relatively, the extent of economic relations grew at all during the latter half of the period; indeed, the reverse appears to be the case. It does not seem very probable that, taking into consideration such factors as national population and national income, Britain and the United States were more closely bound together economically in 1950 than they were in 1830, appearances to the contrary notwithstanding; the burgeoning of Anglo-American cordiality, from war in 1814 to close alliance in 1949, was essentially a political phenomenon. But the continuous economic intimacy from the beginning to the present is none the less of the greatest significance, although it has escaped popular attention. This has not been without unfortunate consequences in recent years, when the dollar gap and associated problems have all too often been thought of as arising from a new and, in some respects, unwelcome economic intercourse between the two countries in World War II. In fact, however new the dollar problem itself may appear, the powerful economic bonds have existed in one form or another since the American colonies were first founded, and their strength was remarkably little affected by the attainment of political independence in 1783; economic independence was much slower in coming. There can, indeed, be little doubt that the peculiar bitterness of certain aspects of Anglo-American relations in the early years and the important place occupied in those relations by commercial questions, and questions of international law concerning trade, owed much to the continued dependence of the American people for their economic development upon their political parent, and to their uneasy consciousness of it. It will be convenient, therefore, to discuss, first this intimacy of economic relations, and later the shift in the balance of economic power across the Atlantic.

I

THE extent of Anglo-American economic relations has always been remarkable. Brebner writes of the economic interplay of the North Atlantic Triangle, in the years 1815-50: "During that period much of what happened in Great Britain was almost as important in the lives of North Americans as what happened at home",[1] and in the period 1896-1940, "the economic triangle of buying and selling, investing and dividend-paying, migration and production, into which Great Britain, the United States, and Canada poured their efforts, became the mightiest thing of its kind on earth and seemed destined to remain so. . . . Interestingly enough this economic co-operation persisted in spite of a curious procession of changes in the economic activity of the members."[2] In this triangle the hypotenuse was the Anglo-American trade, which remained greater than that of Canada and the United States until 1935, and as a result the "so-called world price for wheat, cotton, copper, beef, pork, cheese and wood products were pretty much the price which was set in the world's warehouse which was Great Britain, and if they read no other foreign news, the commodity brokers of Butte, Winnipeg, Chicago, Richmond and Houston never failed to look for certain prices quoted from Liverpool, Manchester, Bristol and London."[3] Goods were the life blood of this relationship. "Their movements, therefore, give the best idea of why the three countries remained locked in an interplay whose vitality could triumph over generations of economic isolationism, depressions, and wars."[4]

[1] Brebner, p. 109. [2] Ibid, p. 225. [3] Ibid, p. 240. [4] Ibid, p. 239.

The flow of goods between the thirteen new-born states and the United Kingdom immediately after the end of the War of Independence showed very clearly that the political rupture was going to have little effect upon the volume of trade on the Atlantic. Though the plans of English liberals for free trade with the new republic failed, as we shall later see, the springs of commerce did not. In 1765, perhaps the last year of quite normal trade before the war, the United Kingdom had exported £1,944,114 of goods to the mainland colonies, and had received £1,151,698 of produce in return.[1] In 1784, the first full post-war year, the total exports from England and Scotland to the United States, including re-exports, had an 'official' value of £3,679,467, and the total imports therefrom of £749,329.* But it is apparent that the American market was positively deluged with British manufactured goods as soon as the War of Independence was over, and contemporary observers commented upon the tremendous flood of goods in these months.

It should be noted that this post-war situation made more pronounced the customarily adverse trade balance of America with Britain, which was also exaggerated by the slowness in the recovery of American exports, due no doubt to the disorganization resulting from the war and the shortage of credit. By 1786 British exports had sunk back to a much lower figure, £1,603,465, while imports from America had only risen to £843,119, largely owing to the severe American slump.

But what is perhaps most interesting to us is the proportion which British imports from and exports to the United States bore to the whole of Britain's import and export trade. In 1784 her total imports from all sources had an official value of £15,272,877 and in 1786 of £15,786,072; her total exports, of £15,101,491 and £16,300,730. Thus, whereas imports from the United States accounted for approximately

---

[1] David Macpherson, *Annals of Commerce* (London, 1805), III and IV, *passim*.

* All figures of trade in these early years must be treated with great caution, for they are unreliable and complicated by such factors as re-exports. Not until 1798 were re-exports distinguished from exports of home products, and until 1854 the values for imports and re-exports were largely 'official' ones. These were based on valuations made for the most part in the seventeenth century, and real values very greatly exceeded 'official' ones—perhaps by as much as fifty per cent on occasion. Not until precise government trade statistics become available after 1854— hitherto there had only been real, or declared, as opposed to 'official' values for *exports* in the years since 1798—can British estimates be relied on for more than quantitative comparisons.

one-twentieth of the whole in both years, exports thereto accounted for almost a quarter of our total exports in the exceptional year 1784 and almost one-tenth in the year 1786. Despite the altered flow of trade during the seven years of war, America had rapidly regained a place of great importance in Britain's economic life, particularly as an export market for British goods.

From the American point of view the importance of the British trade was already considerably greater. Once again the statistics must be treated with caution, but since they are all derived in this section from the same source they are a reasonably sure guide to proportion. The value of American exports to England, Scotland and Ireland in the years 1795, 1798 and 1801 was $6,324,066, $11,978,870 and $30,892,300; in the same years her total exports to all parts of the world amounted to $47,855,556, $61,527,097 and $93,020,513, so that her trade with Britain constituted somewhat under one-seventh, over one-sixth and about one-third of the whole in each of these years. This is an increasing ratio, which reflects America's growing productive capacity, chiefly in agriculture, but the ratio in imports is not only more constant, but very much larger. Total American imports from all sources in the same three years amounted to $69,756,258, $68,551,700 and $111,363,511, and those from Britain to $23,296,591, $17,275,161 and $39,398,620, being about a third, a quarter and a third. Thus already, a third to a quarter of all America's imports, which chiefly consisted in manufactured goods, came from Britain, which is an impressive illustration of the importance of Anglo-American commercial relations. These years, too, set the course which trade was to follow until the American Civil War. It is, however, important to note, when comparing the very great dependence of the United States upon British imports with Britain's relatively (and only relatively) small dependence upon American produce and markets, that the people and economy of the United States as a whole were, and have been ever since, a great deal less dependent upon any kind of external trade than the British. America grew to economic greatness on the foundation of her own great internal free-trade area and her own vast resources; Britain upon the huge foreign trade which her industrial leadership in these early years made possible. Reductions in foreign trade were only of marginal importance in the lives of the American people; proportionate British reductions spread wide and serious misery. It must not, therefore, surprise us that America's dependence upon Britain seems at first sight so great: but though this effect is exaggerated, as it were by an optical illusion, it remains of great importance none the less.

The period of the Napoleonic wars, with its rapid development of economic warfare, makes generalization about Anglo-American trade difficult, particularly in view of the American embargo on British trade in the period prior to the outbreak of war in 1812 and of the actual war itself. Already the hostilities between Britain and Revolutionary France had had considerable effect on British economic life; the American imports from Britain in 1798, for example, which are quoted above, fell well below those given for 1795 when the war was still in its early stages, partly owing to an economic depression in both countries.[1] Now, during the second phase of the conflict such effects of war are even more marked. The combination of French economic measures with the American embargo, and subsequently the Non-Intercourse Act, reduced British exports to the United States from £11,846,513 in 1807 to £5,241,739 in 1808, and from £10,920,752 in 1810—a year when trade was freed to a great degree—to £1,841,253 in 1811.[2] In 1812, 1813 and 1814, during the course of the war, British exports to the United States, of course, virtually ceased, but in 1815 history repeated itself and there was a huge outpouring of British manufactured goods on to the American market, so that they attained in that year the unprecedented value of £13,255,374, which was not surpassed for over a quarter of a century. Again, as in 1784, this made up a quite exceptional proportion, more than a quarter, of our total exports during that year, and was to a great degree responsible for the beginning of American tariff protection in the following year, since the mass of British goods proved too much for many infant American industries which had been encouraged by the cutting off of British manufactures in the war. The tariff of 1816 was certainly one factor causing the sharp reduction in British exports to America in 1817, but that which occurred in 1819 was probably due to a severe depression in that year.

There was also a depression at this time in the United States—there had indeed been no real recovery since that which followed the war—and it is highly suggestive of the intimacy of Anglo-American economic relations that there has usually been a peculiarly sensitive interaction in this respect between the two economies. There is, of course, an international pattern in the trade cycle which becomes increasingly visible as industrialism spreads ever more widely over the surface of the earth, but, partly because one of the two has always been since 1783

[1] A. Achinstein, *Introduction to Business Cycles* (New York, 1950), pp. 168-9.
[2] G. R. Porter, *The Progress of the Nation* (Revised edition, London, 1912), p. 479.

the financial and, in some respects, economic focus of the activities of mankind, there appears to have been a peculiarly long-standing and close coincidence between the troughs of the business cycle in America and Britain. This extends back to the birth of the United States, long before she developed her great industry, and is strong evidence for the closeness and significance of Anglo-American economic bonds. Later, in 1876, the American Minister, arriving in London, wrote: "I am not a little surprised to find the commercial depression in England, so exactly like our own in kind, varying only in degree. The two nations *surely sympathize in trade and finance if in nothing else.*"[1] There were other instances, besides those given below, of depressions in both countries, some of which were partly contemporary, but there were striking examples of correspondence in the beginnings of recessions in the following years: 1796 U.S., 1797 G.B.; 1802 U.S., 1803 G.B.; 1807 both; so too in 1815; 1825; 1828 U.S., 1829 G.B.; 1837; 1847; 1853 U.S., 1854 G.B.; 1857; 1865 U.S., 1866 G.B.; 1873; 1882 U.S., 1883 G.B.; 1890; 1900; 1907; 1913; 1918; 1920. The evidence is from our point of view most compelling in the early years, before the wide international character of the phenomenon was obvious.

Both countries had recovered from the post-war depression by 1821, and during the next thirty years a more stable situation prevailed. American figures for these years prove our contention of intimate economic intercourse most forcefully; they show the trade of the United States with the United Kingdom and all other countries, giving the percentage of it which was with Britain.[2]

The figures, shown in the table opposite, dispense with any further need to emphasize the dependence of the United States upon British trade in these years.

The British figures are still not to be relied upon for precise calculation, but they show clearly enough, as we have already seen to be the case in earlier years and as we should expect, that the proportion of her foreign trade which was with the United States was considerably less than that of the United States with her, though its importance to the national economy as a whole may not have been. Thus in 1825 18 per cent of all her exports went to the United States, and in 1840

[1] Pierrepont: q. *W.A.A.E.*, p. 368.

[2] Statistical Tables, H.R.Mis.Doc. 117, 52nd Congressional Session, 1893, x-xi: q. N. S. Buck, *The Development of the Organisation of Anglo-American Trade, 1800-1850* (New Haven, 1925), pp. 2-3.

Periods of Five Years	The United Kingdom	All Other Countries	Percentage from/to the United Kingdom
	IMPORTS FROM—		
	$	$	%
1821-5	151,346,561	217,885,821	40·39
1826-30	138,667,139	221,589,264	38·77
1831-5	219,976,517	317,452,362	40·93
1836-40	254,414,559	403,363,348	38·68
1841-5	178,359,348	298,895,659	37·37
1846-50	285,730,187	417,962,596	40·60
	EXPORTS TO—		
1821-5	122,154,837	221,828,068	35·51
1826-30	117,569,294	232,758,038	33·56
1831-5	188,287,249	270,533,755	41·04
1836-40	273,849,766	302,831,240	47·49
1841-5	221,175,606	285,131,492	43·68
1846-50	349,495,899	339,746,360	50·71

approximately 10 per cent, while in the same years she received approximately 13 per cent and 27 per cent of her imports thence.[1] One thing of importance should, however, be noted: it was during this period that the balance of trade between the two shifted finally and irrevocably into America's favour. Until probably the year 1829 British exports to the United States regularly exceeded her imports thence; during the eighteen-thirties the balance was in doubt, but by the beginning of the forties, probably by 1837, had swung down on the side of the United States, whose exports to Britain thereafter exceeded, later by great amounts, her total visible imports thence. From this time forward the dependence of America upon British trade diminished, while British dependence upon her American imports tended to increase and the proportion of her whole exports constituted by those going to America to decrease. This revolution was due to many things; fundamentally it was due to the increasing strength of the American economy; in later years it was to be due to the growth of free trade in Britain and of protection in the United States; it was also due latterly to the development of American industry and of Britain's need for

[1] John MacGregor, *Commercial Statistics: a digest of the productive resources, commercial legislation, customs tariffs, and etc. of all nations* (London, 1844-50), III.

American foodstuffs. But in this period it spelled the word cotton.

Since the end of the eighteenth century the Southern states had quite supplanted the West Indies as cotton-growers for the vast expansion of the British cotton industry, the first full fruit of her industrial revolution. This dual process of expanding industry in Britain and swiftly advancing the western frontier of the cotton area in the South soon locked the two countries in what appeared an unbreakable embrace, one indeed upon which the Confederacy based many of its hopes in the Civil War. By the five-year period 1846-50 the United States provided over 80 per cent of Britain's total cotton imports; in the five-year period 1850-4 over 70 per cent of her total cotton exports went to Britain; by 1860 cotton accounted for approximately three-quarters of her total exports of all commodities; and at the time of the Civil War the annual value of British cotton manufactures exceeded the total governmental revenue of the United Kingdom. Not merely was Britain very dependent upon imports of American cotton, but in these early years she exported a considerable quantity of cotton products to the United States. But, supremely important though the cotton link was, it was not the only one.

Americans, short of ready money still, as a frontier society always is, bought British goods, not merely because they were the cheapest, if not the only, ones available, but also because from Britain alone could they get such long terms of credit. The cut-throat competition between British merchants and manufacturers, particularly in the cotton industry, kept down prices, and the ready availability of capital for investment kept down rates of interest. These things applied in many other industries besides the textile; other characteristic British exports to the United States were Birmingham hardware, Sheffield cutlery and, in due course, iron rails. This vast flow of goods was facilitated by the fact that in these years both countries were extremely active in shipping across the Atlantic; they saw not merely the dominance of the American Clipper ship but the beginning of regular transatlantic routes, such as the Black Ball and Cunard lines, the latter being founded in 1840. Since 1814 this flow has never been stopped and only seriously checked, except through economic and natural causes, in the two world wars. Thus in these years the United States was the best of all Britain's customers, better than the colonies had been before the Revolution and better than any other country at the time; British exports to the United States far exceeded those to France and Germany combined, and the French and German trade of the United States amounted to less than half the British.

From the year 1854, when reliable and comprehensive government statistics are for the first time available, we can get a much more precise picture of the relative importance of American trade to Britain, and after 1880, when we have the British government version of American government statistics of American trade, of the comparative importance of the two.[1] The years following the repeal of the Corn Laws and the beginning of free trade in Britain saw, as we have remarked, a great increase in British imports, notably of foodstuffs but also of raw materials. Thus the official figure of £75,953,875 for imports from all sources in 1846 had risen by 1849 to £105,874,607, and though these are unreliable as an index of value, they give an idea of quantitative increase. By 1854 we are on solid ground, and in that year total imports into the United Kingdom amounted to £152 million, of which £30 million, or 19·7 per cent, came from the United States; the total from the whole of the British Empire in the same year amounted to £34 million, or 22·4 per cent, and the next largest single source was Germany, which sent £16 million, or 10·5 per cent of the total. Exports tell a similar tale. In 1854 total British exports amounted to £97 million, of which £21 million, or 21·6 per cent, went to the United States, £34 million, or 35·1 per cent, to the British Empire, and £9 million, or 9·3 per cent, to Germany, our next largest customer. One may already note here in passing the heavy adverse British trade balance in visible exports and imports, and the extent to which it was necessary for her to strike a balance by invisible exports, such as services and interest upon capital invested overseas.

The percentages of British imports from America and British exports to her, in five-yearly averages, until 1908 are set out below.

	Imports	Exports		Imports	Exports
	%	%		%	%
1855-9	19·4	16·4	1885-9	22·5	12·2
1860-4	13·6	10·9	1890-4	23·4	11·0
1865-9	13·7	12·9	1895-9	24·4	8·6
1870-4	18·0	14·1	1900-4	24·3	7·4
1875-9	21·6	9·0	1905-8	20·9	7·0
1880-4	23·7	12·2			

Apart from such obvious incidental effects upon them as that of the Civil War and the Reconstruction period, with their shrinking of cotton

[1] *Statistical Tables and Charts relating to British and Foreign Trade and Industry (1854-1908)* (H.M.S.O., Cd. 4954, London, 1909), passim.

imports, the figures follow a fairly clear pattern—one of relative stability, though with a slight increase in the middle years as far as imports are concerned, and a gradual dwindling in exports as American industry develops and as competition increases from other industrial nations. In the last four-year period the annual average figures were as follows. Total imports, £603 million; total from the Empire, £139 million, or 23.1 per cent; from the next largest supplier after America, France, £52 million, or 8·6 per cent. Total exports, £368 million; total to the Empire, £123 million, or 33·4 per cent; total to Germany, the next biggest customer, £33 million, or 9·1 per cent.

The figures for the United States are, as they have been all along, more telling still. In the five-year period 1880-4 the annual average exports of the United States to all destinations were £165,429,000, less than a half of Britain's, which is what we should expect despite the already great disparity in population; of this total no less than 53·8 per cent, or £88,994,000, went to the United Kingdom. In the period 1905-8 the average total of exports from America was £359,281,000, of which £118,370,000, or 32·9 per cent, went to the United Kingdom. The intervening years show that this was a steady decline: 1885-9, 52·4 per cent; 1890-4, 50 per cent; 1895-9, 45·1 per cent; 1900-4, 39·1 per cent. That this process was primarily the result of the great growth of the American economy and of its search for new markets in fresh areas of the world is suggested by the fact that, as we have seen, this same flow of goods, seen as British imports, played a fairly constant part in Britain's total imports in the same period. With the closing of the frontier and the growth of American imperialism at the end of the century, there was a dramatic increase in American exports from a £213 million average per annum in 1895-9 to one of £292 million in 1900-4; this even produced some criticism of the protective system, under which this had been achieved, from men as internationally minded as Mahan, who wrote in 1898 : "Our self-imposed isolation in the matter of markets, and the decline of our shipping interest in the last thirty years, have coincided singularly with an actual remoteness of this continent from the life of the rest of the world."[1] Great efforts were now put into the American export trade; aggressive American manufacturers replaced foreign—usually British—trading houses by their own export departments and it was to be symptomatic that monopoly agencies, for the export trade only, were to be specifically exempted from anti-trust legislation by the Webb-Pomerone Act of 1918. Whether or not the flag follows trade, American exports certainly

[1] Mahan, p. 19.

followed the Stars and Stripes at this time; in 1895 British exports to Puerto Rico and the Philippines totalled $1,995,854, and American (excluding Guam) $119,000, while by 1913 the respective figures were $4,718,000 and $25,360,000.

The impact of many new American commodities upon Britain was great; machine-made American boots were being worn by three-quarters of a million Britons by 1902, and in 1912 £415,468 worth of American cars were imported. This meant, too, increased competition for British exports, for between 1887-97 American exports to China increased 126 per cent and between 1895 and 1907 those to the British Empire itself increased at a faster rate than Britain's. The British reacted to this in specific ways, such as the defeat of an American effort to capture the retail tobacco trade by the formation of a trust on the American pattern (the Imperial Tobacco Company), and in a general way by supporting such powerful but abortive movements as those for tariff reform and imperial preference.

The pattern of American exports is clear, but reliable figures in terms of sterling for American imports from Britain are not to hand. They are, of course, the obverse of Britain's exports to America, but the latter figures can only be used as the roughest of guides; nevertheless, we can gain from this source an approximate impression of the ratio between her total imports and those from Britain. Thus in 1855-9 British exports to the United States seem to have averaged something like a third of America's total imports for home consumption, which does not disagree too violently with the established American figure, for the years 1846-50, of 40·6 per cent. Figures for later years seem to bear this out by showing the same decline as we have seen in the proportion of exports; in 1885-9 and 1905-8 they seem to have constituted roughly a fifth and a tenth of the whole. There is, therefore, an even more startling reduction in the proportion of the whole provided by Britain in the case of American imports, than in the case of American exports sent to the United Kingdom. This decline is explicable enough.

The great growth of American industry lay behind her increase in exports, and it was natural that these should seek an outlet in areas where they were not subjected, as in Britain, to fierce local industrial competition. Thus, as we have seen, the ratio of American to total imports into Britain remained remarkably constant in the sixty years before World War I, but the ratio of British to total exports from the United States declined, because the increasing flow of American exports was absorbed in other markets. But though Britain still needed

American imports, particularly of foodstuffs and raw materials, America had a decreasing need for Britain's chief exports, manufactured goods, in view of her own industrial development; this situation was exaggerated by the scale of American tariff protection, which was, after all, devised primarily for just this purpose of reducing British imports. There was, therefore, this sharp decline in imports from the United Kingdom. In practice this could be seen in such cases as that of Stanley Baldwin, who, according to G. M. Young, visited the United States in 1892, when a new and higher tariff was coming into operation; the effect of this was never forgotten by Baldwin, whose family business lost its best market within two years, first the cheap stuff, which could be made by anyone, and then the quality goods and specialities. In the case of Britain, as we have seen, this was reflected in an increasing dependence on invisible assets to right her balance of trade; she also tended to rely on types of triangular trade very similar to those by which the New Englanders had come to thrive in earlier days. Thus Britain began to utilize such methods as exports of raw materials, like tin, which America needed, from the British possessions overseas, which themselves had need of manufactured goods from the mother country, in order to pay for American commodities which she herself had to have. What, in the later day of the dollar gap, was to be a characteristic pattern of British trade was already perceptible.

In the case of the United States this situation was simply a reflection of her increasing economic stature, for, though her direct trade balance with Britain had been favourable by the beginning of the eighteen-forties, it was in these years that she had an export trade balance with the whole of the world for the first time, though she was to remain financially a debtor nation until World War I. Until 1873 she had been an immature debtor nation, with an import trade balance, but between 1874 and 1914 she became a mature debtor nation; in those years, except for 1875, 1888 and 1893, she had an export trade balance. In the years 1914-8 she was to become a creditor nation for the first time. It was this revolutionary economic development, which was to prove probably the most important happening in the economic history of mankind since the Industrial Revolution in Britain, that lay behind the great change which came over Anglo-American economic relations in these years.

World War I involved a gross distortion of world trade, and particularly of Anglo-American trade. Both before and, increasingly, after America's entry into the struggle, there was a great and growing flood of goods eastward, and a marked diminution of return traffic; the financial means which were found to make this possible, despite the drop in British exports, ranged from realization of British securities in America to outright American loans. The unprecedented extremity of Britain's economic dependence upon the United States during the war needs no further emphasis, but it is perhaps important to point out that the economic dependence of America upon Britain was decreased rather than augmented. In this respect the great crisis merely increased the swiftness of tendencies which we can see had been at work for a good many years, but this made it harder for Americans to adjust themselves to their new role, particularly towards Britain, who had for so long played that same part towards them. Whether they liked it or not, the United States had become by the end of the war the world's greatest creditor nation, a position which brought with it new economic responsibilities. This difficult adjustment was made even more painful by the fact that it occurred during, and was mixed up with, an upheaval which thrust her into an unwelcome political prominence in the affairs of the nations, and which emphasized her very important political obligations to Great Britain. These things complicated the American and British reactions, but they were never so crystal clear as they were to be in World War II. In 1940 it was becoming plain to Americans that Britain was defending the United States, and it seemed reasonable to repay that debt by unstinted economic aid; indeed this feeling carried enough weight after the war to contribute a good deal to the Anglo-American loan of 1946. In the aftermath of the first war, no such bargain could be struck, and this confusion, arising from America's sudden and bewildering position of economic dominance, combined with reluctance to accept corresponding political obligations, was merely worse confounded by the acrimonious war debts issue. But by the middle of the twenties some form of normality seemed to have returned to the economic affairs of mankind.

Certainly a very familiar pattern reappears in the commercial relations of Britain and America. The figures of relative exports and imports in both cases (see table on page 66) take up the story where we left it and speak for themselves.[1]

The figures show a continued decline in all categories in the twenties, but some sort of an equilibrium in the thirties. There is relatively little change in any category after 1931, but even in the two years before that there is not more than 3 per cent alteration anywhere; it is curious

[1] *League of Nations Memoranda on International Trade*, passim.

	UNITED KINGDOM		UNITED STATES	
	Percentage of whole constituted by :		*Percentage of whole constituted by :*	
Year	*Imports from U.S.*	*Exports to U.S.*	*Imports from U.K.*	*Exports to U.K.*
	(General Trade—Merchandise only)			
	%	%	%	%
1913	18·43	9·37	15·17	23·78
1923	19·22	9·67	10·66	21·17
1924	18·88	8·33	10·15	21·41
1926	18·47	9·49	8·65	20·22
1928	15·8	8·1	8·5	16·5
1929	16·1	7·4	7·5	16·2
1930	14·7	6·1	6·9	17·6
1931	12·1	5·8	6·5	18·8
1932	11·9	5·0	5·7	17·9
1933	11·2	6·3	7·7	18·6
1934	11·2	5·2	6·9	18·0
1936	11·0	7·4	8·3	17·9
1938	12·8	5·4	6·0	16·8

indeed to reflect that these apparently stable figures cover the greatest period of economic collapse in the history of industrial civilization. The total imports of Britain from America sank from £195,980,000 in 1929 to £82,100,000 in 1934 and her exports to America from £62,016,000 to £23,300,000. Anglo-American trade, in other words, was far more than halved in terms of money value, yet the relative dependence of the two peoples upon one another varied very little. In 1934 the United Kingdom was still America's best customer, and was only approached by Canada in this respect, for she still took more American exports than any other nation; on the other hand the United States imported more from Canada and a shade more from Japan than she did from the United Kingdom. Thus already the shape of the dollar gap looms more ominous on the horizon. Britain in the thirties has a consistently adverse balance of trade with the United States, though she is still able to continue the purchases she needs from there by indirect means of payment; thus it is significant that the United States had substantial adverse trade balances with Malaya and India. By such means as these Britain might have kept the wolf from the door for many years.

But World War II, like World War I, though to an even greater degree, speeded the processes already in operation, and by 1945 the wolf had pretty nearly effected an entry. With the details of this desperate situation for the British people and the efforts to remedy it, we shall deal at a later stage, for it had by then become a diplomatic and political matter; after World War II the economic relationship of the two countries thrust itself insistently and irresistibly on to the political plane. There had been a tendency in this direction over the war debts and reparations question in the inter-war years, particularly those of economic crisis, but now it was no mere question of the defalcation of Britain, but of her life and death. Yet, despite the new urgency of the situation and its extreme gravity, it was one with whose general outline we are already familiar. Once more the figures speak for themselves.[1]

| | UNITED KINGDOM | | UNITED STATES | |
| | Percentage of whole constituted by : | | Percentage of whole constituted by : | |
Year	Imports from U.S.	Exports to U.S. (including re-exports)	Imports from U.K.	Exports to U.K. (including re-exports)
Annual Average	%	%	%	%
1934-8	11·6	6·3	7·1	17·4
1943	58·7	7·3	3·1	34·8
1947	16·6	5·1	3·6	7·7
1948	8·8	4·3	4·1	5·1
1949	9·8	3·4	3·4	5·8
July, 1949, to June, 1950	8·8	4·1	3·4	5·4

The war year 1943, when Lend-Lease was approaching full flood, gives some idea of the vast dependence of Britain upon American economic resources, an ample reciprocation for the military dependence of the United States upon Britain in 1940; it also shows how seriously Britain's vital export trade to America dwindled owing to the exigencies of the struggle.

[1] J. M. Cassels (Editor), *The Sterling Area, An American Analysis* (London, 1951), passim.

Once more we see that while Britain needs to keep up her standard of living by maintaining her American imports, she has the greatest difficulty in keeping up her exports to the United States; she has, as always, a heavy adverse trade balance with America. Matters have not been improved by the decline in her invisible exports, and by her heavy indebtedness to the so-called Sterling Area, consisting chiefly of members of the British Commonwealth, upon some of whose dollar-earning capacity the mother country had long relied for her international solvency. Fundamentally, the whole problem arose from the change in the nature, as well as the strength, of the American economy; not only did she become a great creditor, but there was a continuous and marked decrease in the importance of her raw material exports relative to those of manufactures. In 1850 raw materials constituted three-fifths of the whole, but by 1940 they made up less than one-fifth, while finished manufactures rose from 12 per cent to 50 per cent; foodstuffs reached a peak in exports in the last quarter of the nineteenth century and then diminished. But, despite this change, so colossal was the expansion of the American economy that Britain, like the rest of the world, still showed an insatiable desire for American goods. The dollar problem, therefore, is not an entirely new one, but an old one writ exceedingly large by adverse circumstances which came to a head through World War II.

What then is the pattern of mutual Anglo-American commercial dependence during the century and three-quarters since independence? In the first place, naturally enough, it seemed as if British trade was throughout the nineteenth century more important to America than American trade to Britain, but this is an illusion produced by the relative unimportance of all foreign trade in the American economy. In the second place *it appears that it was in the second quarter of the nineteenth century that Britain's American exports were most important to her economy and that of the United States,* a conclusion which is broadly borne out by the financial history of that period which we shall consider later. British exports to the United States constituted approximately 10 per cent of her total exports in 1786. The curve rose to a height of just under 20 per cent between 1825 and 1850, after which a decline set in, and by 1949 they constituted, despite all the efforts to improve the position, only about 3 per cent of the whole. The obverse, American imports from Britain, which were approximately 33⅓ per cent of total American imports in 1795, rose to a plateau of around 40 per cent in the second quarter of the century, and

68

then declined to a similar figure of 3 per cent of the total by 1949.

In the third place, however, *it seems to be in the second half of the century that America's exports to Britain were most important to the life of both countries.* In 1795 they constituted perhaps 14 per cent of her whole exports, had risen to about 50 per cent by 1850 and had remained at or near that level until the first half of the nineties, after which they sank to 5 per cent of the total by 1949. The importance of these goods to Britain, relative to her total imports, was greatest in the same period (though it began a little earlier and lasted a little later) while undergoing a slight decline in the sixties, no doubt a reflection of the significance of cotton, in the earlier, and grain, in the later years, as essential imports for the running of the British industrial machine. It is characteristic that Britain remained dependent upon American imports to a much greater degree until the present time, so that in 1949 they constituted 9 per cent of the total; the disparity between the 3 per cent of her exports and the 9 per cent of her imports is some indication of the dollar difficulty.

Thus it would plainly seem, as far as commercial relations are concerned, that the mutual dependence of the two countries was greatest between approximately 1825 and 1890; and that after this date a decline in the importance of the connexion set in, although it operated much less in the case of Britain, whose relative reliance upon America therefore increased as the years passed. It was during the years when American isolation was at its height and when the two countries were most remote from one another politically that their tangible economic bonds were strongest. It was perhaps a providential dispensation that, when the economic bonds were loosened, political ones, in some ways more powerful, were coming into existence to take their place.

But in some senses it is misleading to talk of a decline in the importance of mutual economic dependence in the twentieth century; certainly the period of the American Loan of 1946 and Marshall Aid seems to belie the very existence of such a decline. Partly, it is true, these things may be discounted as temporary expedients to meet a situation precipitated by World War II and motivated largely by political fears of Soviet Communism, but, even beneath these, there obviously lie economic ties of the greatest strength and sensitivity between the two nations. Perhaps the best analysis would be that the relationship has ceased, since the nineteenth century, to be the unique and exclusive thing it had been, but that it has lost little of its importance. In absolute terms of money value it has not declined at all except for the universal shrinkage, though there has almost certainly been some decline in physical terms.[1]

	American Exports to Britain	American Imports from Britain	British Exports to United States	British Imports from United States
	$	$	£	£
1913	590,732,000	271,955,000	59,453,000	141,652,000
1929	848,000,000	330,000,000	62,016,000	195,980,000
1938	521,000,000	118,000,000	28,900,000	118,100,000
1948	644,000,000	290,000,000	70,900,000	183,200,000

Even given increases in population and national income, if we take triangular trade with the sterling area into account, this does not indicate a marked decline; the hard core of Anglo-American trade has not been too greatly affected in extent. But that is indeed what it has really become. In the nineteenth century it was more than a core, but by 1950 the stupendous growth of the American economy has simply meant that Anglo-American trade is a very similar core of a very much bigger fruit. In 1913 total American exports to all parts of the world were $2,484 million; in 1948 they were $12,653 million. Figures for the development of American national income show an even more remarkable increase. Thus the American domination of the world's economy has grown until it has greatly exceeded even that of Britain in the nineteenth century, and so complex and widespread has the web of that economy become, that changes at its heart can have the most far-reaching effects at its extremities. In this fashion Anglo-American trade has retained its significance. In general terms it remains the most important economic relationship of its kind on earth, one which is greatly enhanced if the Canadian and Commonwealth trade be reckoned in. America is the world's greatest producer, Britain its largest, most influential trader; and in the economic sphere each remains on the whole the best neighbour of the other. So the Anglo-American relationship has lost its peculiar and outstanding character, in that it can no longer be isolated from the broadening pattern of world economic development, but it has not lost its central and supreme position.

Thus our first point, the mutual economic dependence of the two peoples throughout their history, is amply proven. It cannot be described as a *growing* intimacy, parallel to the ripening cordiality in

[1] *League of Nations Memoranda* and *The Sterling Area*, passim.

70

the political sphere, since its unique and exclusive nineteenth-century basis was broadened in the succeeding years, but of its continuous existence and deep importance throughout the whole period from 1783 to the present there can be no question.

II

THUS the economic interdependence of the two peoples is incontrovertible, but it must not be imagined that this always meant an easy interchange of goods; except perhaps for one period, the channels of trade were indeed constantly blocked by obstacles raised by one or other of the two nations in the belief that it was in their interest to do so. In the event, the forces of nature triumphed over those difficulties, but the difficulties were none the less real. Brebner writes: "While it is rank heresy to say so to interested Americans, Britons or Canadians, the whole apparatus of tariffs, quotas and preferential duties . . . has been far less important than the irresistible floods of goods which have flowed through, by, or over those nationalistic locks, dams and weirs":[1] but though this is true, it would give a quite unreal picture of Anglo-American relations if one failed to depict the tariff history of the two countries. Frankland wrote in 1928: "In . . . raw-material resources . . . Britain and the United States mutually compensate one another's deficiencies. . . . Each is the other's greatest customer. The greatest damage either could suffer is to have the other's market shut to him. In international trade these two that one might expect to be rivals are drawn closer together by most compelling interests."[2] This is only true within strict limits—except in the first half of the nineteenth century when it was true almost without limit—and one of the difficulties of the twentieth century has been that it has become less and less true, except in so far as the British Commonwealth can be regarded as an economic unit; and even in that sense it seems possible that the science of synthetics may undermine America's need for raw materials from British possessions, such as rubber from Malaya. For the truth is that, whereas from 1783 to perhaps 1900 and even beyond, the United States was primarily a great raw material, and later food, exporter, from that time onwards she became increasingly an industrial nation exporting manufactured goods. Britain on the other hand was fast

[1] Brebner, p. 239.

[2] J. M. Frankland, *The Influence of International Trade upon British-American Relations* (New Haven, 1928), pp. 99-100.

becoming a great industrial power in 1783, and has remained such ever since, so that it was only in earlier years that the two economies were in a full sense complementary. Yet even then, the commercial policies of the two were not really in accord, except for the space of a very few years.

Let us consider first those of Britain. In 1783 Britain was still a mercantilist, economic-imperialist, and protectionist country, but two great documents published in 1776, the Declaration of Independence and *The Wealth of Nations,* had helped to cause or to symbolize the breakdown of this three-century-old system. Already by the coming of war in 1793, though the enlightenment of men like Pitt and the clamour of the new industrialists like Wedgewood had failed (in face of opposition from those, like Sheffield, imbued with a goodly measure of the old Adam) to implement the far-seeing plan proposed by extreme liberals like Shelburne for free trade with the erstwhile American colonies, it had produced moves in the direction of the freeing of trade, such as the Anglo-French commercial treaty of 1786. The twenty years of war suspended the process of change by encouraging concentration on economic nationalism as a means to victory, and by making the reduction of taxation impossible. Britain emerged from the war in 1815, as before, with a very high tariff wall, including duties, on manufactured goods ranging from 40 per cent to 180 per cent, and on such articles as tea of 100 per cent, while British West Indian sugar was charged 30 shillings per hundredweight and foreign sugar the colossal sum of 63 shillings per hundredweight.

But a revolutionary change was in prospect, for Britain's unrivalled industrial supremacy meant that she had a vast field of expansion if she could import the food and raw materials she needed and enable the producers thereof to buy her manufactured goods. The latter was by no means the less powerful motive; as a traveller of the period declared in a manner strikingly reminiscent of more recent travellers in the opposite direction, "If we persist in refusing to admit her corn into Great Britain, she must of necessity limit her importation of our manufactures; for her consumption is bounded by her means of payment, and by that alone."[1] The great free-trade movement was victorious in three stages, of which the second was the most important. The first included the reductions of duties and the removal of restrictions in the years 1824-7 which was chiefly the work of Huskisson,

[1] Q. J. L. Mesick, *The English Traveller in America, 1785-1835* (New York, 1922), p. 194.

though there were liberal measures after his death, such as the repeal of certain Orders-in-Council, restricting colonial trade with the United States, in 1830. The second, which was the work of Peel under the tremendous pressure of Cobden and Bright with the Anti-Corn Law League, began with great alterations in the protective system between 1842 and 1845, and culminated in the abandonment of the Corn Laws in 1846. The landed interest who supported these laws were the only very powerful political and economic force standing in the way of free trade, and when Peel in the face of Cobden's arguments crumpled up his piece of paper and left others to answer them, he not only broke his own party but symbolized the triumph of free trade. That triumph was finally celebrated by Gladstone, chiefly in 1853 and 1860. This system of virtually free trade, financed by regular income tax, monopolized the English scene for forty years and remained in operation for more than sixty; it became the gospel of the Liberal Party and was accepted by the Conservatives as the basis of the great national prosperity of this period, which indeed it was.

Yet, though it had not been inaugurated hastily, but over a period of at least thirty years, it was in a sense, as Mumford points out, a supreme act of faith. It is true that Britain could only attain greatness as well as wealth on the basis of a world-wide commerce, but the continued existence of that commerce, particularly in the form of free trade, and of the stable political conditions which made it possible, was, on any extensive view of history, problematical. Britain's difficulties in 1950 are more severe because her economic policy in 1850 was unrestrained by doubts, but one must also remember that her wealth and power in the intervening years can be traced to the same source. The voices of doubt began first to be raised in the economic depression of the eighties, but they did not become penetrating until conducted by Joseph Chamberlain in the tariff reform choir after 1903. The movement was precipitated by the agricultural depression produced by the competition of cheap overseas foodstuffs, by the growth of industrialism in other countries under the protection of tariffs, and by the wide revival of the imperialist spirit; it demanded protection of British manufactures, and also imperial preference in foodstuffs, because the latter alone appealed to the Empire as a whole, and this involved a tax on food. The effort failed, partly because of aversion from the idea of food taxes, and partly because it suffered, by association, from the disgrace of its forebear, the imperialism of the Boer War period, but in World War I the issue was kept alive by economic circumstances and by the close imperial association. The Coalition Government in 1920-1 took certain tentative steps in continuation of the measures to protect "key" industries for strategic reasons which had been inaugurated during the war, but when the Conservatives, led by Baldwin, went to the country in 1923 on the full issues of protection and imperial preference, they were soundly defeated.

When they returned to power in 1924 they dared not do more than continue the "safeguarding experiment," as it was called after the Safeguarding of Industries Act of 1921, but the forces of nature were working on their side. The competition of the great new industrial nations was becoming ever more pressing, as the penetrating eye of Cobden had foreseen as early as 1835, after his visit to the United States, "Our only chance of national prosperity lies in the timely remodelling of our system, so as to put it as nearly as possible upon an equality with the improved management of the Americans."[1] The Great Depression made a return to protection almost inevitable; indeed it can be argued that an economic collapse on this scale will not only inevitably defeat any government in power, but almost inevitably reverse any economic policies then in operation. Certainly Great Britain abandoned free trade in 1931 in much the same way as America began to abandon unrelieved protection in 1933. The first importation duties in 1931 were followed in 1932 by the Ottawa Conference and the establishment of a system of imperial preference; there was also a marked tendency in British commercial policy towards conservative bi-lateral trade arrangements, which would ensure Britain a modicum of economic stability.

The Anglo-American Trade Agreement of 1938 ran counter, as we shall see, to this tendency, and was largely signed for political reasons, but World War II was to effect a change, and men even came to believe that they had already seen the light when they signed the agreement in 1938. Chamberlain was to say of it in 1940: "It was the very negation of that too prevalent system of bi-lateralism, of exclusive advantages, of discrimination carried to the pitch which clogs the wheels of commerce, and which promotes ill-feeling among the nations. . . . One of our foremost aims will be the restoration of international trade. . . . That is a policy that we have in mind when the time comes to turn once more from war to peace."[2] This repentance was in fact produced by the war, which is "the supreme destroyer of conventional modes of thought and habits of mind. Under its influence the

---

[1] Richard Cobden: q. Heindel, p. 153.
[2] Q. D. Abel, *A History of British Tariffs, 1923-1942* (London, 1945), p. 134.

outlook of many undergoes transformation. . . ."[1] Certainly during the war years Britain's leaders turned for the most part back towards forms of trade which were more free, partly perhaps in that warm feeling that all will, after victory, be well, which sustains men in time of war. So the new Lend-Lease Agreement of 1942 promised action "directed to the expansion . . . of production, . . . exchange and consumption of goods, which are the material foundations of the liberty and welfare of all peoples; to the elimination of all forms of discriminatory treatment in international commerce, and to the reduction of tariffs and other trade barriers. . . ."[2] Though, as we shall see, these intentions were not to prove easy of fulfilment, they were to remain the intentions of the British Government up to the present time.

The tariff history of the United States was very different; indeed it presents itself for the most part in terms of startling contrast. The first tariff of the Federal Government after its inauguration in 1789, though it was framed under the influence of Hamilton, was so low as to be little, if anything, more than a revenue tariff, but it was to be the foundation on which the later structure of American protectionism would be raised. The natural interests of the American republic, as a neo-colonial power and a prime producer of raw materials, were in free trade, but the fact that virtually the only source of manufactured goods was the hated mother country set up a conflict in the American mind between political mistrust and economic desire, which gave her a natural predisposition towards protection. The wartime blockade, the embargo and the Non-Intercourse Act, and above all the war of 1812 itself, all encouraged this predisposition as well as the domestic industries which alone would make it possible, except with the hardships which had been such a feature of the non-importation boycotts of the Revolutionary period. Thus, when in 1814 the flood of British goods threatened these infant industries, the tariff of 1816, the first truly protective American tariff, was imposed; its highest duties of a permanent nature were those of 20 per cent on textile manufactures and iron. The depression of 1818-19 strengthened protectionist sentiment and resulted in the tariff of 1824, which raised duties on cotton and woollen goods, among others, to $33\frac{1}{3}$ per cent. In 1828 the protectionist interest succeeded in getting yet another tariff through Congress, which raised the duty on most textiles and iron to what was in effect 50 per cent; it doubled the duty on rum and left an average rate of duty, on all commodities taxed, of 41 per cent.

[1] Ibid, pp. 133-4.   [2] Article 7: q. Abel, p. 145.

But there had been a rising tide of protest against this policy, particularly in the South. Henry Clay's original "American policy" of tariffs and internal improvements had been intended to promote national unity, and had been supported even by John C. Calhoun of South Carolina, but this new "tariff of Abominations" threatened to disrupt the Union itself. The South, in the increasing grip of cotton culture, came to realize that excessive protection was directly contrary to its interest, which was in as free an exchange as possible of its raw material exports for the cheap manufactured goods of Britain; the demand for protection became increasingly a Northern and sectional one. South Carolina, which was suffering an economic decline, became the leader of opposition, and when it became clear from the passage of a new tariff in 1832, which, though it made some reductions, retained a considerable degree of protection (a 34 per cent average), that the Administration would not keep the protectionists in check, she precipitated the Nullification Crisis by refusing to accept this piece of legislation. The result was the "Compromise" tariff of 1833, which decisively reversed the protectionist trend. It provided for a gradual reduction of the high rates over the next nine years, which would result in the restoration of the 20 per cent level of the 1816 tariff by the year 1842. This policy was put into effect and was a measure of that influence of the South in the national government which was such a marked feature of this pre-Civil War period of Democratic ascendancy. But the economic crisis of 1837 and the accident of a Whig Administration enabled the protectionists to gain the passage of the measure of 1842, when the process of reduction was complete; this was, broadly speaking, a return to the rates of 1832 with some slight modifications, which produced an average rate of 30 per cent on dutiable articles. The return of the Democrats, however, led to the liberal Walker tariff of 1846, which, "though often described as a 'free-trade' measure . . . was really one of qualified protection, not much superior to the English system before Peel's reforms."[1] It completely reorganized the system, enlarging the "free list" and making eight schedules of goods each with a different rate; the duties varied from 5 per cent to 100 per cent and averaged about 25 per cent, with iron and wool at 30 per cent and cotton goods at 25 per cent. In 1857 there was a further relaxation which reduced the average rate to 20 per cent.

The triumph of the Republicans on a protectionist platform in 1860 and the secession of the chief opponents of a high tariff produced a

[1] C. F. Bastable, *The Commerce of Nations* (Ninth Edition (Revised), London, 1923), p. 75.

sharp change in American commercial policy, and this new trend was to remain dominant during what were in effect the next seventy years of Republican and Northern domination. It was under this régime of high protection that the giant of American industrialism was to be reared.

The first move made by the Senate, soon after the secession of the Southern Congressmen, was the Morrill tariff of 1861, which raised certain duties; it was followed by the Act of 1862, with an average rate of 37 per cent, and, in the flush of victory in 1864, by one with an average rate of 47 per cent. In 1867, in the post-war depression, wool was granted further protection, but by 1870 there was a mild reaction, and in 1872 this went as far as a general reduction of 10 per cent. A slump, however, began in 1874 and the 10 per cent was accordingly added again in 1875. The period until 1897 was complicated by differences as to the nature of reform demanded, and by changes in the structure of the tariff, and though efforts were made to effect reductions, particularly in 1883 and 1893-4 (the latter a serious attempt by the Democrat President Cleveland), they were obstructed in Congress and did not produce very decisive results. The legislation of 1883 was revised by the Republicans in 1890 and that of 1894 by the Dingley tariff of 1897, which was a distinct high-water mark in American protection to date; the average rate of the McKinley tariff of 1890 had been 49·5 per cent, and that of the Democratic tariff of 1894 39·9 per cent, but that of 1897 was 57 per cent. It was not altered for twelve years, after which President Taft obtained the passage of certain mild reductions, though against considerable opposition, by the Payne-Aldrich tariff, but it was not until the advent of Wilson and the Democrats to power in 1912 that any serious measure of reform was undertaken. This took shape as the Underwood tariff of 1913, which made certain reductions and which considerably enlarged the free list, but a great part of it consisted in the abolition or reduction of obsolete or nominal duties. It certainly left the United States a highly protectionist country compared with Great Britain, and a protectionist country by any standard.

But the return of the Republicans in 1921 on a surge of American isolationist nationalism resulted in an enthusiastic adoption of even more extreme protectionism than that of 1897. An emergency tariff in 1921 extended protection to agricultural produce and took strong measures against "dumping," which figure much in contemporary English legislation under the "safeguarding system." The Fordney-McCumber tariff of 1922 was the highest enacted to date, and not merely raised a number of basic duties, but gave the President discretionary powers of a wide order to raise these still further, in certain circumstances by as much as 50 per cent. The initial reaction of Congress to the economic collapse of 1929 was, contrary to the advice of economists, to pass the Hawley-Smoot tariff of 1930, which raised these unprecedented rates yet higher. But with the New Deal came an inevitable reaction; under the Trade Agreements Act of 1934 the President was authorized for three years to negotiate trade agreements with the consent of the Senate, and to raise or lower tariff rates by not more than 50 per cent, an interesting adaptation of the precedent of 1922, for there was certainly little idea now of *raising* them. The life of this Act was repeatedly extended throughout the next twenty years of Democratic rule, and until the end of that time America's face was set in the direction of the liberalizing of world trade. But the steps she was able, or willing, actually to take were by no means revolutionary. This was partly due to the occasional restiveness of Congress, and to the fact that all America's instincts were protective; even the Act of 1934 was in form an amendment to the Smoot-Hawley Act, which remained the basic tariff of the country. Furthermore, it should be noted that the continued pressure for the reduction of tariffs came primarily not from the Treasury or Commerce Departments, but from the State Department under Cordell Hull. This is perhaps significant, for it may indicate that the main desire in America was to induce other nations to lower their tariffs and thus facilitate American exports. The United States was willing to make reciprocal reductions and did so in the many trade treaties which she signed in the next twenty years, but she showed no ardent desire to lower drastically, let alone to abolish, her protective tariff walls. Between 1842 and 1860 Britain had gone the whole hog to free trade because her industrialists wished, not merely to gain markets by the economic and political inducements which a free-trade Britain offered to the exports of foreign lands, but also to gain tax-free food and raw materials. The situation in America, which had vast natural resources of her own, was different (though with the exhaustion of such American supplies as timber, petroleum and iron it was rapidly becoming less so), and she remained until 1952 a strongly protectionist country. One of the most critical questions at the close of 1952 was what the attitude of the new Republicans would be on this matter, for if they continued to move, however slowly, in the direction of free trade, there was a chance that Britain and America might, for almost the first time in their history, be facing the same way on tariff policy.

For the impressive fact which this résumé of Anglo-American tariff history reveals is that, except for the period of Southern ascendancy between 1832 and 1861 (discounting the years 1842-4) and for brief Democratic spells, such as those beginning in 1893 and 1913, the commercial policies of the two Governments have always, until World War II and the succeeding years, been moving in opposite directions. From 1783 to 1816 America's interest was in and her policy was in effect one of free trade, but Britain was still a highly protected imperial area on traditional mercantilist lines, whose severe restrictions on American trade with the colonies and the mother country undoubtedly made it more difficult for Americans to earn the money with which to pay for imports of British manufactured goods. In the twenties there began the trend in Britain towards free trade which was accomplished by 1860, but by the time her first reforms were inaugurated, the United States had embarked upon a policy of protection. In 1832, however, this policy was checked by the determined opposition of the South, and, broadly speaking, during the next eighteen years both countries moved in the direction of free trade; Britain virtually reached this goal by 1860, but America was still far from a free trade state even after the enactment in 1857 of her lowest tariff since serious protection had begun. It was one of the great ironies of the defeat of the Confederacy in the Civil War that it signified the weakening of the strongest single strand that has ever existed in the rope of Anglo-American economic relations, that woven of cotton. But there can be little doubt that this weakening was inevitable in any case; it was no more than a dream that, as Stephen Vincent Benet has it, the Civil War buried:

> "And with these things, bury the purple dream
> Of the America we have not been
>
> .   .   .   .
>
> The pastoral rebellion of the earth
> Against machines, against the Age of Steam,
> The Hamiltonian extremes against the Franklin mean,
> The genius of the land
> Against the metal hand,
>
> .   .   .   ."[1]

No one can doubt that America was destined to become a great industrial nation. Already, almost before the Southern supremacy had entered its prime, Cobden had published his first important work,

[1] S. V. Benet, *John Brown's Body* (New York, 1928), pp. 374-5.

which was on the subject of the United States. Supreme representative of the new industrial middle class, unhampered by Tory prejudices, he had prophesied the rise of American industrial might. But while the agricultural ascendancy of the South and West remained, it proved the perfect complement of the rising dominion of the British industrial interest; it was natural enough that there should follow a period of harmonious commercial policies.

But with the Civil War and the triumph of the Northern industrial section, there came the sharp change to severe protectionism which we have noted; restrained at first—for nearly forty years—by the agricultural interests which the North also contained, and by Britain's demand for grain, it reached new heights after 1897, while contemporary British tariff reform movements proved abortive. World War I twisted the effects of the Wilsonian reductions, and the Conservative move towards protection in the twenties, which might have put both countries on a protectionist basis, did not gain the support of the British electorate until the coming of the Great Depression. But by this time America's tariffs were higher than ever, and so in the great crash both countries sharply reversed their commercial policies and found themselves as a result facing once more in opposite directions. It is true that though they faced opposite ways they came gradually to stand closer together, since Britain was moving from free trade to moderate protectionism and America from extreme protectionism to the same stand, but this was counterbalanced by the contrast between America's new demand for the removal of restrictions upon trade and Britain's tendency to multiply them. The opposition between American protectionism and British free trade between 1860 and 1931 was, it must be remarked, natural enough; Britain was a developed industrial power dependent on the outside world for markets, food and raw material; the United States was a developing industrial power largely sufficient unto itself. But the policies of the thirties in both countries were overshadowed by what Churchill calls the "economic blizzard."

By 1945, however, the interests of the two nations were much more akin than they had perhaps been before; in the second quarter of the nineteenth century they had been complementary, but now they were very much alike. Both were highly urbanized industrial societies; both, though America to a less degree, needed export markets for their manufactures; both, though America to a less if increasing degree, needed imports of food and raw materials. Both, therefore, seemed to have a plain interest in the freeing of international trade and its consequent rapid expansion, and the realization of this appears to be reflected in their policies, for during and after World War II these were the causes to which they both paid at least lip service. Britain might still have balance of payments problems, America might still retain a high tariff, but both powers did at least seem, for the first time in nearly a hundred years, to be facing in the same direction on tariff policy.

III

THERE could no longer, however, in 1952 be any possible doubt whatever as to which was the paramount economic power; the United States had long since moved into that position. And this is our second thesis, that there is the same swing over in the mutual balance of power in the economic as in the analogous political field. This is apparent enough to anyone living in the nineteen-fifties; there is little need to emphasize it, and no need to prove it. What is not so often remembered is the long period during which the reverse was true, for it was only just before the end of the nineteenth century that supremacy passed unquestionably into American hands. It is true that her population passed that of the United Kingdom in the middle of the eighteen-forties, but it was not until the decade after 1890 that her total production of coal and pig-iron exceeded Britain's. The figures of industrial output make the acceleration in American development crystal clear. Indices of industrial output, from a base of 100 in 1860, when Britain's economy was already highly developed are as follows:[1]

	Great Britain	The United States	Germany
1860	100	100	100
1880	156	213	179
1900	232	675	464
1913	294	1,250	714

This surpassing of Britain by the United States had long been foreseen in America, with its boundless optimism and sense of power; Franklin had prophesied it, Lincoln had made an over-sanguine estimate of its rapidity. Henry Adams put his finger on it after the turn of the century with the uncanny accuracy of the Adamses; "The power of the railway system had enormously increased since 1870. Already the coal output of 160 million tons closely approached the 180 millions

[1] Howard S. Ellis, *The Economics of Freedom, The Progress and Future of Aid to Europe* (New York, 1950), p. 88.

of the British Empire, and one held one's breath at the nearness of what
one had never expected to see, the crossing of courses, and the lead
of American energies."[1] In England, too, the best heads had foreseen it.
Gladstone wrote in 1879 in *Kin Beyond The Sea*:

> I do not speak of the vast contributions which from year to year,
> through the operations of a colossal trade, each makes to the comfort
> and wealth of the other, nor of the friendly controversy, which in its
> own place it might be right to raise between the leanings of America to
> Protectionism and the more daring reliance of the Old Country upon
> free and unrestricted intercourse with all the world, nor of the menace
> which in the prospective development of her resources America offers
> to the commercial supremacy of England. On this subject I will only
> say that it is she alone who, at a coming time, can and probably will
> wrest from us our commercial supremacy. . . . We have no more title
> against her than Venice or Genoa or Holland has had against us. . . .[2]

As much as twenty-eight years earlier *The Economist* had put it far
more unequivocally: "The superiority of the United States to England
is ultimately as certain as the next eclipse."[3]

Yet contemporaries, even when they perceived the revolution, were
often slow to see its implications. Sir Norman Angell writes of the
growth of the United States, "If, in 1910, a prophet had ventured to
predict that there would take place in twenty years what has actually
taken place, his forecast would have provoked contemptuous
derision."[4] Brooks Adams saw much of what this entailed in the decline
of Britain, and even what it might involve if the Anglo-American
rapprochement of his day could be perpetuated:

> Friends and enemies now agree that an Anglo-Saxon alliance, directed
> to attain certain common ends, might substantially make its own terms;
> but how it would stand, if opposed by a power capable of massing troops
> at pleasure in the heart of China, is less clear. . . . Supposing . . . China
> to be closed, the centre of exchanges might move east from the Thames;
> and then London and New York could hardly fail to fall into geographical
> eccentricity. Before the discoveries of Vasco de Gama Venice and
> Florence were relatively more energetic and richer than they. On the

[1] H. B. Adams, *The Education of Henry Adams, An Autobiography* (London, 1919), p. 330.

[2] Q. J. D. Whelpley, *British-American Relations* (London, 1924), p. 166.

[3] 8 March, 1851: q. Heindel, p. 138.

[4] Norman Angell, "An Englishman's Point of View," in *American Policies Abroad, The United States and Great Britain* by Carl R. Fish and C. L. Hussey (Chicago, 1932), p. 85.

other hand, if an inference may be drawn from the past, Anglo-Saxons have little to fear in a trial of strength. . . . Exchanges would then move strongly westward. . . . Probably human society would then be absolutely dominated by a vast combination of peoples whose right wing would rest upon the British Isles, whose left would overhang the middle provinces of China.[1]

Neither of the future worlds glimpsed so starkly by this second seer of the Adams clan in 1900 has quite materialized, but the prophecy was pregnant enough.

Yet the change was perceived by many Englishmen at the crucial turning point of the end of the century, however much some of them may have desired to ignore it. As the historian of *The American Impact on Great Britain, 1898-1914* declares, "We helped to produce a fit of self-depreciation current in England at the turn of the century, a more receptive mentality, a desire to overhaul industry, and a blow to British complacency as effective as the German competition of the early nineties."[2] The impact is obvious to the historian. At the time of the Civil War, for example, there had been perhaps a dozen American enterprises in Britain; in 1900 there were about 75; and by 1929 there were to be 389. Again, American inventiveness, as gauged by patents, seems to have produced results equal to Britain's between 1876 and 1900, while between 1901 and 1908, they were three times as great; the first American industrial exhibition in Britain was held at Earl's Court in 1909. In many and various aspects of economic life, the impact of American methods and ideas was felt; American salesmanship and advertising methods were adopted by such men as Sir Thomas Lipton; Selfridge's was founded on the American model in 1909; Rotary, the mail order system, roll top desks, filing cabinets, and Westinghouse brakes, to take but random examples, were flourishing by 1914; and American influence was apparent in the development of engineering (particularly bridge building), steel production, the use of electrical power, automatic telephones, tramways, and all forms of standardization and specialization. What Britain's example had been to the world in the first phase of the Industrial Revolution, America's was now becoming. Not that there were no things in which Britain could make headway against the tide—though American insurance companies had eighty thousand policy holders in Britain in 1906, there were no less than eighty-three British companies operating in the United States by

[1] Brooks Adams, *America's Economic Supremacy* (New York, 1900), pp. 23-5.

[2] Heindel, pp. 138-9.

1934—but it was set irresistibly in an easterly direction. It was, however, one in which Britons could swim without too much difficulty; the economist Marshall wrote that "the Americans are the only great people whose industrial temper is at all like that of the English, and yet even theirs is not very like".[1] The American system with its freedom from certain forms of monopoly, whether in the form of restrictive land tenures or municipal and national corporativism, and its constant economic pressure upon, combined with its great incentives for, the individuals of society, had a freedom and yet a sometimes harsh immunity from governmental restraint, which came to be lacking in the British system; but the two remained very close in many ways. Yankee ingenuity, although it had impressed even early nineteenth-century observers, was merely a more uninhibited version of the spirit and skill which had been associated in Britain with the birth of industrialism. The parallel between America in 1900 and Britain in 1800 is very close; Arkwright and Ford were not so far apart, and the Englishmen of the earlier era demanded the same *laissez faire* as did the Americans later. One is repeatedly reminded in this respect of that other basic fact of which we have been aware, that the similarities between Britain and America are still, when all is said and done, more striking than the differences.

The swing over of economic leadership to the United States at the turn of the nineteenth century can be seen clearly in these evidences, but in none is it so compelling as in the financial history of the two countries. This topic requires some consideration because it brings out more clearly than anything else the importance of Britain's economic domination of America in the far off days of a century ago. While we consider it, however, we might also note that it illustrates, even more clearly than do trade and commerce, the intimacy of the economic relationship, whichever partner was dominant at the time. As Hacker writes, "English capital—poured into America with a generous hand . . .—helped to put the young republic on its feet. . . . This is one of the ties between the two countries American historians have been blind to. . . . British funds . . . made possible the expansion of the American foreign trade. . . . In effect, an English private revolving fund was set up which protected the American dollar. . . . (Need I mention the modern-day parallel?)"[2]

[1] Ibid, p. 201.
[2] L. M. Hacker, *England and America, the Ties that Bind* (Oxford, 1948), pp. 20-1.

84

America began life, as was natural in a colonial economy, as a debtor, and in the financial sphere this remained her status until World War I; her demand for capital was, indeed, insatiable, "The New World soaked up this flow of capital like blotting paper, for that was its oldest economic habit. . . ."[1] In the first years of the Republic it seems that nearly as much, if not more, of these funds came from Holland than from Britain, partly because of British mistrust of American investments after the confiscations of the war, but Britain's contribution was already great, and after 1814 began, slowly at first but later hugely, to exceed that of any other power. Even so, already by 1803, according to Hacker, total security issues came to $129,700,000, of which $59,250,000 was in foreign and $34,700,000 in British hands; of the bond issue of $11,250,000 for the Louisiana Purchase $9,250,000 came from Britain. "What was true" of "long-term requirements was even truer in the case of short-term financing."[2] British investment in the United States rose to a great crescendo in the second and third quarters of the century, and by 1875 American domestic investment had expanded hugely, while America was replaced by other foreign fields for British capital, so that these middle years show the same intimacy in the financial as we have observed in the commercial sphere, which is no more than we should expect, for "Money, of course, was little more than the symbol of the . . . economic relationship."[3] By 1837, it has been estimated, there was $200 million of long-term foreign investment in the United States, mostly British; by 1914 $7,090 million, of which $4,250 million was British.

But already America had begun to prepare herself gradually, and for the most part unconsciously, for the change in her financial status from a debtor to a creditor country. After 1873 Americans began to replace the representatives of foreign banking houses in New York City by their own branches in foreign cities. By the turn of the century Americans were beginning to buy back their own railroad investments from foreigners on a large scale for the first time. It was the vast American expenditures in World War I and the corresponding need of the European powers for money which decisively turned the scale. Prior to the spring of 1917 Great Britain borrowed about £200 million in the United States and after that date the United States granted credits of over £1,400 million to the Allies, of which some £740 million went to Britain. Britain, of course, disposed also of a great many of her American investments. This change in the American situation is clearly illustrated in the figures of the balance of payments showing the inter-

[1] Brebner, pp. 109-10.   [2] Hacker, p. 20.   [3] Brebner, p. 239.

national investment position of the United States between 1843 and 1935; the sums are in billions of dollars.[1]

Year	Net Position Creditor + Debtor –	Total U.S. Investments Abroad	Total Foreign Investments in the U.S.
1843	– 0·20	negligible	0·20
1869	– 1·46	0·08	1·54
1897	– 2·71	0·69	3·40
1908	– 3·90	2·50	6·40
1914 (30 June)	– 3·70	3·50	7·20
1919	+ 3·70	7·00	3·30
1924	+ 7·00	10·90	3·90
1930	+ 8·80	17·20	8·40
1931	+12·10	15·90	3·80
1935	+ 7·10	13·50	6·40

This demonstrates clearly the nature of the change in America's investment position which took place in the first war.

By the onset of the Great Depression she was an exporter of capital on an enormous scale; this indeed, as is well known, contributed much to the dizzy heights of the boom which preceded it. In 1914 Europe had been virtually the only creditor of the United States; in 1918 Europe was both her principal debtor and her principal creditor. In this interesting relationship Britain was prominent. In 1928 Europe (chiefly Germany, but also others, including Britain) owed the United States 53 per cent of her credits abroad, while of her long-term debts abroad in 1927, of which 79 per cent were owed to Europe, Britain still owned 34 per cent. Great Britain probably also owned more of America's short-term capital liabilities than any other power except France. In 1914 British investments in the United States made up 20 per cent of her total foreign investments, as compared with 47 per cent in the British Empire; in 1935 the American constituted only 5·4 per cent, whereas the Imperial had risen to 58·7 per cent. On the other hand, in 1935 Britain still owned 19·9 per cent of the total foreign investment in the United States. The years of the depression saw a decline in American investment abroad and a relative increase in the figures of foreign capital moving to the United States; during the thirties, once the financial crisis of 1931 was over for Britain, her dependence upon

[1] *Historical Statistics of the United States, 1789-1945* (United States Department of Commerce, 1949), Series M, Columns 1, 4 and 9, p. 242.

the United States was not direct or obvious, as it had been in World War I.

But the second war and the years which followed it heavily emphasized that dependence once again. During the "cash and carry" period Britain pledged or actually sold her American holdings with alarming swiftness, and Lend-Lease, as we shall later see, came only just in time to save her, much as American loans in World War I had also done. The figures of Lend-Lease alone are eloquent testimony to the economic relationship in the war years. The United States between March 11, 1941, and September 30, 1946, disbursed $50,692,109,000 in Lend-Lease aid, and received only $7,819,322,000 in return, in the form of Reverse Lend-Lease; of the aid, no less than $31,392,361,000, or well over half, went to the British Empire, the United Kingdom getting by far the largest share. This dependence continued on into the years of peace. In 1946 the United States lent Britain $3¾ billion, plus a credit for outstanding Lend-Lease of 650 million; following the economic crisit of 1947, she had received, by the time she was able to suspend Marshall Aid, at the close of the better year 1950, a further $1,822,000,000; and the necessity for rearmament produced a further crisis in 1951, which was met by substantial American subsidies for military purposes. These transactions, though primarily economic in character, took place on the political level, thus contrasting with Britain's loans of a century before, for in the twentieth century governments had come to play a much greater part in the lives of nations. America, it is true, retained much of the spirit of free enterprise, even under the Democratic Administration, but individual Americans could not be easily induced to invest in European economies which were liable to socialization at any moment, and this forced governments to intervene to fill the $8 billion gap, which existed in 1948 between what the United States imported and what she exported. This gap in Britain's case a hundred years earlier had been largely filled by such private investment.

The persistence of the so-called dollar gap was partly due to the fact that the United States did not adopt after 1919 the international economic role played in the past by Britain. At the turn of the century Brooks Adams had warned that the focus of energy and wealth was shifting westward, and that "the United States must shortly bear the burden England has borne, must assume the responsibilities and perform the tasks which have within human memory fallen to the share of England, and must be equipped accordingly."[1] In the administrative

[1] B. Adams, *America's Economic Supremacy*, pp. 143-4.

sphere, she was not so equipped, for "Every progressive nation is superior to us in organization, since every such nation has been reorganized since we began."[1] As Brebner graphically puts it, "On grounds of analogy the United States might have been expected to take over a good many of Great Britain's traditional attributes after 1918."[2] She was now the world's greatest industrial producer and she possessed a unique 35 per cent of the world's visible gold supply; after 1815 Great Britain in similar circumstances had, by free trade and a free gold market, led the world, but the United States could not make so abrupt a break with her past. Even the ailing President Wilson saw the error of this when he said of the tariff of 1921: "If there ever was a time when America had anything to fear from foreign competition, that time has passed. If we wish to have Europe settle her debts . . . we must be prepared to buy from her".[3]

Whatever the differences, however, the analogy between Britain's financial dependence on America in mid-twentieth century and that of the United States upon the United Kingdom in mid-nineteenth, is too impressive and too important to be missed, and it would be well to examine it a little more closely. Upon the second we do not need to dwell any longer, for it is in the very air we breathe. But, though such contrasts are dangerous and unreliable, it could probably be maintained that the contribution made by British capital to American development then was relatively more important than the American contribution to Britain's survival now. Certainly it was on a lavish scale, for America offered much better conditions for investment than any other area in the world; British North America might offer more security but it offered much less opportunity for handsome returns, although it, too, had the same language and a kindred legal system. Investment suffered, however, severe setbacks as a result of the great American repudiations of debts accompanying the financial collapse of 1837 and the stoppage of interest payments on their debts in 1841-2 by a number of states. These defalcations aroused bitterness in the breasts of men like Charles Dickens and Sydney Smith, and Englishmen failed to understand the niceties of division of responsibility between the state and federal governments; even as late as the first decade of the twentieth century they were mystified by the effect on their investments of the Anti-Trust activities of Theodore Roosevelt. But the overwhelming pressures of

[1] Ibid, p. 48.   [2] Brebner, p. 275.
[3] President Wilson (1921): q. Brebner, p. 275.

commerce and finance bore down all such obstacles and overrode any such misgivings.

The commerce of the first half of the nineteenth century between the two countries was dominated by British wealth to such a degree that Talleyrand once declared: *"C'est donc réellement l'Angleterre qui fait le commerce de consommation de l'Amérique."*[1] In Buck's picture of its organization at this period Anglo-American trade is seen to be honeycombed with British credit. In the earlier post-war decades almost all goods were exported from Britain at the risk and on the account of the British merchant or manufacturer; nearly all American merchants operated on credit, and so keen was the competition between the British capitalists that it could be obtained for an average period of a year and often for as long as eighteen months. Anglo-American financial houses did not confine these arrangements to the direct trade, but served Americans engaged in commerce with other parts of the world, such as the Far East, where credit facilities of this kind replaced the old habit of shipping specie. A number of great English houses, such as Baring Brothers and Company, specialized in American business;[*] often they had American partners, such as Joshua Bates, or close connexions with the United States, such as those of Alexander Baring, Lord Ashburton, through his American wife. Another example of this type of connexion was the setting up, in 1860 by J. Pierpont Morgan, of a New York house, acting as agent for the London firm of Peabody and Company, of which his father was a partner. Nor were the activities of these houses confined to direct commercial operations of this kind; British trade came in fact to be partly supported by the willingness of British investors to buy American securities. "British exports settled the balances against the United States wherever they arose throughout the world; and to cover the large overdrafts which the luxurious tastes of Uncle Sam were continually running up, the merchant bankers took his stocks. Thus the bulk of the foreign trade of the United States came to depend

[1] Q. N. S. Buck, p. 113.

[*] The Barings dominated Anglo-American trade in its heyday, and between 1843 and 1867 were the sole financial agents of the Federal Government in London. From 1815 to 1828 they turned their main attention to the American scene, and by the latter date were the leading Anglo-American house; they retained their leadership till the middle of the century, for the crisis of 1837 strengthened rather than weakened their position. But in 1842, and even more in the fifties, they began shifting their principal activities to the Empire and Europe. By 1857 the American was no longer their predominant interest. This development was characteristic of that of the whole of Anglo-American economic relations. [R. W. Hidy, *The House of Baring in American Trade and Finance* (Harvard, 1949).]

upon a system of banking kept in motion by an increasing willingness of Englishmen to buy American securities."[1] Thin partitions, indeed, divide the bounds of commerce and long-term capital investment, and the export of capital from Britain to America took manifold forms. By far the largest proportion, however, went into the purchase of securities floated in the United States by state and municipal authorities and by private concerns, and nothing demonstrates more clearly than the history of these investments the dependence of the United States upon Britain at this period.

Some doubt is, indeed, expressed as to the exact importance of this outpouring of British capital; the author of *The International Financial Position of the United States,* for instance, points out that "not more than 5 per cent of the money value of the nation's economic wealth was ever represented by securities and other property titles held abroad".[2] While this is no doubt broadly true, it may be misleading, because what was needed for rapid American development was liquid capital and ready money. The importance of British investment was great because it was marginal, and the whole history of the debtor frontier, with its demand for specie, for paper currency and for inflationary monetary policies, from Shays to Bryan, witnesses to the extreme significance of British capital in American history. One has only to glance at the purposes for which it was employed to confirm this fact; though it had many and various uses, the large preponderance of it was employed in the swift opening up of the West. It went to finance a number of the states of the Middle West in the period of their greatest need for swift economic development, where it constructed or improved rivers and canals, roads and harbours, bridges and lighthouses, at a time when the Federal Government would care for none of these things; it went on a vast scale into the construction of railroads, such as the Baltimore and Ohio and the Illinois Central, which was actually controlled from abroad through its foreign stockholders; it went, finally, into private American enterprises of all kinds.

President Jackson estimated European holdings of State and corporation stocks and bonds in 1839 at $200 million, mostly British. The Erie Canal was financed by New York State bonds; between 1807 and 1825 over $7 million were raised, almost all of which passed at once into English hands. Before 1836 over $90 million had been invested

[1] L. H. Jenks, *The Migration of British Capital to 1875* (New York and London, 1927), p. 70.

[2] R. A. Young, *The International Financial Position of the United States* (Ph.D. Thesis, University of Pennsylvania, 1929), p. 29.

in Northern transportation facilities, most of it coming from Britain. In 1829 Barings made an issue of Louisiana securities to finance the Planter's Bank, one of the many which supported the development of the slave and plantation system in the South. Between 1860 and 1876, issues of private companies operating abroad made in London totalled £232 million, of which £70½ million were in American railways, while only about £19 million were in those of South America. There was much investment of an indirect kind, through State Banks, in the industrial revolution of the United States, as well as much of a direct nature. In 1800 no American securities were quoted on the London Stock Exchange; by 1825 nine issues of United States bonds, United States Bank shares and a number of city and State bonds were quoted. In 1869 Williamson estimates that the foreign indebtedness of the United States was $1,000 million, of which $243 million were payable in London to facilitate English investment; and by 1908 $9,000 million of American securities were quoted on the Stock Exchange. By the time that the American national debt was paid off in 1835, the categories of State and municipal bonds had enormously increased in number, and it is indicative of contemporaries' feeling of their financial dependence upon Britain that there was a widespread fear before it happened that the paying off of the debt would sweep away all specie, and that many states introduced legislation to enforce the holding of a majority of the stock in American banks by residents in the state.

But the best evidence of the strength of the economic bonds is still the sheer magnitude of the investments. The end of the Napoleonic Wars and government borrowing freed the abundant capital of the only great industrial power for export, and it went principally to Western Europe and the United States. Of perhaps £100 million raised in Britain in the years 1816-25 on account of foreign nations, about £9 million was for the United States.[1] With the development of the joint stock principle in Britain this process was facilitated, and in 1854 Jenks estimates that British overseas investments totalled between £195 million and £230 million, of which £50-60 million were in the United States. There followed in the third quarter of the century the greatest period of British export of capital, and between 1870 and 1880 the total market value of British overseas investments in Government bonds was approximately £458 million, of which £160 million were American, and in railway securities £175 million, of which £40 million were American. But already the amount flowing to the United States had been checked, first by the Civil War, after which there was a resurgence; then by the

[1] C. K. Hobson, *The Export of Capital* (London, 1914), p. 105.

crash of 1873, in which many railways defaulted; and then by the bimetallic controversy; above all, however, Britain was beginning to meet severe competition from America herself. The investments of the past half-century and more had had their effect, and the growing maturity of the American economy began to result in increasing domestic funds available for investment. She even began to export capital to Britain and the building of some of the London tube railways was partly financed with American capital. As a result more and more British capital began to flow to other parts of the world. In 1914, whereas 20 per cent of Britain's overseas investments were in the United States, approximately 47 per cent were in the British Empire. Nevertheless, in 1899 it is estimated that out of $3,100 million of European holdings in the United States, $2,500 million were British—more than ten times the holdings of the Dutch, the next greatest investors.

But the intimacy can best be felt, as opposed to seen, through the heated personal relationships which lay behind these financial transactions. Commerce is made for man, not man for commerce, and these close economic contacts between two peoples who had, not more than two generations before, violently severed their political connexion, were of a character to bring home at once that combination of intimacy and bitterness, of attraction and repulsion which we have seen to be peculiar and important to the Anglo-American relationship. The effect on government of the fact that the bulk of America's foreign debt had accumulated in British hands was considerable; as a contemporary declared at the height of one Anglo-American crisis in mid-century: "Railways, steamers, telegraphs and free trade are fast creating a diplomacy which will supersede notes and protocols. The ablest note of Lord Clarendon speaks with feeble force compared with a Stock Exchange List or Price Current, which tells people of a civilized country by breakfast time next morning that their property is depreciated 10 per cent because their Government has committed a folly overnight."[1] Economic incidents, however, did not always serve to promote goodwill by restraining the follies of governments; they could do the very reverse. Though the financial crises of the first half of the nineteenth century did not provoke serious Anglo-American disputes on the government level, they aroused the strongest private feelings, and these unquestionably kept alive the tradition of Anglo-American bitterness much beyond its normal term. (Such crises today, it may be observed, tend always to involve governments directly, which is far from an unmixed blessing.)

[1] Samuel Laing, *The Times*, 20 October, 1856: q. Jenks, p. 286.

British investment in American securities, particularly American state issues, reached a dizzy height in the boom of 1836; it was estimated that in one trip in the late spring of that year Samuel Jaudon of the United States Bank carried $20 million of securities to London. When the crash came in 1837, Nicholas Biddle of the same bank was able to start a revival, owing to his intimate connexions with "the most eminent Bankers of London", all of whom were "inspired with the same confidence"[1] in him, but the British crop failure of 1838 brought nemesis, for Britain would no longer buy securities or cotton. In the end the United States Bank itself disappeared in the wreck. American finance could not support the structure of Anglo-American credit: not until the British Cabinet in 1931 waited to see if their economic measures would gain the approval of New York financiers was such another drama to be enacted. The results in Anglo-American relations were not happy. "Angered at the folly with which they had incurred indebtedness, American Commonwealths sought to vent their rage upon the obliging creditors. And . . . there arose a debacle of American credit as complete as the confidence which it had formerly elicited had been unquestioning. The tide of revulsion flowed anew in England against the foreign borrower. . . . What caused American stocks to join those of Portugal and Mexico and Greece in the ghettoes of finance was the failure of nine sovereign commonwealths to pay the interest upon their debts." That it was beyond the power of some of the states to pay; that in Louisiana a tax of $3 on every man, woman and child in the state would have been necessary to pay it, a tax which, if levied, would have resulted in a popular move to Mississippi; and that gullible investors in a free enterprise society must pay the price of their gullibility—these things did not affect the fact that for a decade after 1838 there was a virtual cessation of British lending to America. The circumstances gave Englishmen ample scope for that type of superior condemnation which above all other things Americans hated from them. Sydney Smith put it in its classical form in his *Humble Petition to the House of Congress at Washington,* which, of course—no doubt to its great delight—had no jurisdiction in the matter:

Your petitioner lent to the State of Pennsylvania a sum of money for the purpose of some public improvements. . . . If their refusal to pay (from which a very large number of English families are suffering) had been the result of war . . . if it had arisen from civil discord . . . if it were the act of a poor State struggling against the barrenness of nature, every

[1] Jenks, p. 95.

friend of America would have been contented to wait for better times; but the fraud is committed in profound peace, by Pennsylvania, the richest State in the Union. . . . It is an act of bad faith which (all its circumstances considered) has no parallel and no excuse. . . . The Americans who boast to have improved the institutions of the Old World have at least equalled its crimes. A great nation, after trampling under-foot all earthly tyranny, has been guilty of a fraud as enormous as ever disgraced the worst king of the most degraded nation of Europe."[1]

But human economic need, or even human cupidity, overcomes the most serious apprehensions, and before long the banker merchant, and in due course the ordinary investor, began to pour into American rail-roads money as abundant as had once flooded into State securities. The panics of 1857, 1866 and 1873 administered further checks to the foreign loan mania in Britain, but by then her real work in America had been done.

This work had been to expedite American development. That development would have gone on in any case, but it would not have gone on nearly so fast; it owed most, of course, to American resources and to the genius of the American people and their economic system of free enterprise, but it owed much to British capital. Though the United States gained political independence by 1783 and economic emancipa-tion by 1816, she did not cease to rely upon parental assistance—albeit profitable to the parent, too—until the fourth quarter of the century, no matter how much she disliked to admit it. The wheel had indeed come full circle when Britain held out her hands—though in an appeal as much political as commercial—for American aid in 1945 and 1947. Certainly the mutual economic dependence of the two throughout their history is plain in their financial dealings, and the political dangers which may arise from this peculiar economic relationship hardly less so. If that economic intimacy is to be maintained as between equals, it is clear that the British Commonwealth as a whole must be associated in it, and from the political point of view no consummation could be more devoutly to be wished.*

[1] Ibid, pp. 98-9, 104-5.

* Since 1952, when this chapter was originally written, the economic position of Britain vis-à-vis America has substantially improved. Six years of Republican rule have not resulted in any drastic changes for the worse in American tariff policy or foreign aid programmes, while British economic strength has increased. Her drive for dollar trade has been especially successful, and the percentage of her exports which go to the United States has markedly increased, as has the stability of sterling.

CHAPTER FOUR

SOCIAL AND POLITICAL CONTACTS

I

THOUGH there may be statistical difficulty in establishing the details of Anglo-American economic relations, there can be no doubt of their general pattern; but the interplay of certain social and political factors is considerably more nebulous, and more difficult to discern and trace with accuracy. There is, nevertheless, one important aspect of the relationship between the two peoples which is susceptible of a rudimentary quantitative assessment—the intermingling of the two national stocks, or what might be described as their racial relationship. The degree to which the two peoples have common origins is obviously of the first importance in the development of Anglo-American relations; among other things it accounts in part for the mutual sense of the peculiarity and uniqueness of those relations. This remains true despite the cloud under which the whole idea of 'race' has passed in the last twenty years. Because scientists cannot produce precise and all-embracing definitions of race, because racial edges are increasingly blurred by intermarriage, and because, in common political fact, races and nations are not capable of exact delineation, there has been an inclination to adopt an overall attitude of philosophic doubt on the matter. But biological inheritance of racial characteristics is plainly a fact, and there seems no clear proof that it does not also operate in the sphere of national character and even psychology. The fact of common Anglo-American racial origins has been of immense importance in their relationship. It has given them their greatest bond, the common language, which carries insensibly with it a hundred other ties, derived from common patterns of thought, and, though the direct importance of the common tongue is primarily cultural, it has also indirect effects.

And it is not only in public life that the persistence of national habits is important; it is far more so within the bosom of the family, where the main features of men's behaviour have in the past been developed. America has relied upon public opinion and a public educational system to Americanize her legions of newcomers, but these things did not by any means completely destroy the basic, powerful and subtle influence of family life. In childhood the habits of generations past in different lands were insensibly renewed; it was indeed by processes such as this that, combined with wider cultural assimilations, America's membership of Western civilization has been assured. Samuel Lubell's whole book, *The Future of American Politics,* is in a sense evidence for the importance of the national origins of the American immigrants. He questions whether the "influence of ethnic and religious background on voting" can "ever really disappear", and asserts that one of the important factors responsible for American isolationism is "anti-British ethnic prejudices".[1] Because Frederick Jackson Turner said that the frontier took the European and made him into an American, it does not follow that his European origins were no longer of consequence; indeed, Turner stated his case so strongly partly because his immediate predecessors had greatly exaggerated the importance of American overseas origins. He was part of a reaction against the excessive emphasis on race which was characteristic of much thought in both Britain and America in the last years of the nineteenth century. Those years saw the luxuriant growth of the Anglo-Saxon legend, which burgeoned after 1880 and had a spectacular efflorescence in 1898. The legend had some substance in it, for as Rosebery said: "But whether you call it British or Anglo-Saxon, or whatever you call it, the fact is that the race is there and the sympathy of the race is there."[2] Senator Beveridge of Indiana put the same point with a boisterousness characteristic of the American plains: "God has not been preparing the English-speaking and Teutonic peoples for a thousand years for nothing. . . . No! He has made us master organizers of the world to establish system where chaos reigns."[3] In view of the phenomenon of 'Anglo-Saxonism' alone, the extent of the Anglo-American racial relationship demands some attention.

The study of that relationship rapidly resolves itself into a consideration of British emigration to the United States, for the vast bulk of the traffic was one way, east to west; indeed, in the nineteenth century the very ships which carried American goods to Britain carried emigrants back again to America. The total amount of immigration into Britain from all parts of the world has obviously been minute compared with that of immigration into the United States; between 1861 and 1931, for

[1] S. Lubell, *The Future of American Politics* (London, 1952), p. 132.

[2] Q. Heindel, p. 128.

[3] Q. M. Curti, *The Growth of American Thought* (New York, 1943), p. 675.

example, no decennial census in Great Britain showed a total of aliens and naturalized British subjects exceeding ·82 per cent of the whole population, the figure for 1911.[1] For vivid contrast it is only necessary to recollect that in 1910, 1920 and 1930 there were more than 13 million foreign-born in the United States, a figure of over 10 per cent of the whole population in the last year and very much more than that in the earlier ones. Indeed, from the middle of the nineteenth century onwards, and probably for a long time before that, Britain lost more migrants than she gained, despite the fact that a number of aliens in transit, particularly to the United States, in fact settled permanently in Britain.

American immigration into Britain, including, be it noted, returning emigrants, was on a very small scale. The rough figures for certain years before and after World War I are as follows; though they are not to be relied on as precisely accurate, they do give some idea of how limited it was compared with that in the reverse direction.

| 1913—16,619 | 1921—13,925 | 1925—8,045 |
| 1920—17,084 | 1923— 7,042 | 1927—6,765 |

In the thirties the numbers swelled markedly, in all probability owing to the increase in the number of emigrants forced to return home by the conditions created in America through the depression, but the number of native Americans emigrating to Britain was very small. This was even more true, no doubt, during the nineteenth century, but it is important to note that ever since the Revolution there has been a trickle of them, and that this trickle has had an influence out of proportion to its numbers, because it has contained a very high ratio of able and wealthy men. The main bulk of Britain's emigrants to the United States have been working people; many American expatriates to Britain have been of the leisured or professional classes. Some names, like those in literature of Henry James and T. S. Eliot, spring to mind, but there were many others, beginning with a number of prominent Loyalists immediately after the Revolution. One and all were castigated by Theodore Roosevelt as "that most undesirable class of citizens, the educated émigré."[2] Nevertheless, no degree of quality could outweigh the quantity of British emigration to America, and Whelpley is correct when he writes: "British influence upon American life is really far greater than that of American influence upon British life, but it does not lie so much in the obvious."[3] Only the statistics bring it home.

---

[1] *Chambers Encyclopedia* (New Edition, 1950), XI, pp. 81-7.
[2] Q. Whelpley, p. 204.   [3] Ibid, p. 192.

Conclusive evidence is provided by the fact that in 1851 the number of persons in the United States who were from the United Kingdom, excluding Ireland, was approximately six times as great as the total number of foreigners from all countries in Great Britain, which was then not far from equal in population to the United States. Though this proportion was to shrink and America's population to augment far more rapidly than Britain's, up to World War I there were never less than three times the number of British-born in America than there were foreign-born from all countries in Britain.

The statistics of British emigration to America are very impressive, but we must be cautious about them none the less. In the first place, the American figures prior to 1850 are not exact, since immigrants were not enumerated by country of origin, and prior to 1820 are little more than estimates, while the British figures of emigration did not distinguish before 1880 between British emigrants and emigrant foreigners shipping from Britain, though it is true that the former greatly exceeded the latter in the years prior to that date, as far as can be judged.

In the second place, it is very important to bear in mind the general background of American immigration. Beginning as a stream of some 250,000 persons in the whole period between 1776 and 1820, it swelled throughout the nineteenth century until it became a seething flood in the first years of the twentieth. Whereas in 1850 there were 2,244,602 foreign-born in the United States, in 1880 there were 6,679,943 and in 1910 13,515,886; in 1930 there were 14,204,149 and even as late as 1940 there were still 11,594,896. 1907 was the peak year of immigration with the fabulous total of 1,284,349 immigrants. One of the results of this phenomenon was the growth of anti-foreign or Nativist feeling in the United States; it sometimes took extreme forms, like Know-Nothingism or the Ku-Klux-Klan, but gradually, from 1850 onwards, increasingly tight checks were imposed upon immigration; first of undesirables, whether morally, physically or racially, and then, much later, by the quota system, of all immigrants by nationalities.

Amidst the isolationism of the nineteen-twenties Acts were passed in 1921, 1924 and 1927, which laid down that the total of persons to be admitted was "to be distributed among the various foreign countries in the same proportion that persons of the corresponding national origin were found in the general population of the United States. . . ."[1] But in fact the quota system operated—and deliberately so—in a very in-

---

[1] H. P. Fairchild, *Immigration, A World Movement and its American Significance* (New York, 1928), p. 461.

equitable manner, for the assessment of racial origins involved calculations of racial stocks at the time of the birth of the republic, and these gave a singular advantage to the British. They discriminated heavily against the "new immigrants" of the late nineteenth and early twentieth century, who were chiefly from southern and eastern Europe, such as Slavs and Italians, and in favour of the old immigrants of earlier years, chiefly British, German and Scandinavian. Thus the quota for Great Britain and Ireland in 1938 was 83,754, but only 3,347, or less than 5 per cent of that number, actually came; during the seven years ending in 1938 only a quarter of the immigrants allowed actually entered, and even the German quota, despite Hitler, was not filled, whereas the quotas of the "new immigrant" countries were filled to overflowing. It does not seem likely that the quota system will be substantially altered in the future; it was liberalized to some degree after World War II, but not fundamentally, and not without very strong opposition. A permanent restriction of this severity would seem to have riveted the fundamental British racial predominance into the American system, for it is difficult to conceive of circumstances in which it could now be destroyed.

But the third, and final, proviso we must make is best put in the form of a question: what figures give the fairest indication of the strength and importance of the racial bond in Anglo-American relations?* The figures of United Kingdom emigration might be the most straightforward, but they involve two difficulties. The first is that from the point of view of establishing Anglo-American bonds, they are not adequate, since they did not include the very substantial immigration to the United States from British North America which had nearly, if not quite, the same effect as that direct from the mother country. Thus it has been estimated that roughly 9 million people went to the United States from the British Isles between 1820 and 1919, but another 2 million or more from Canada and it is important that, as Brebner points out, people moved back and forth across the Canadian-American border, particularly in the first half of the nineteenth century, with remarkable freedom either from interference or from national self-

---

* That this question, because of its extreme complexity and its emotional implications, bristles with difficulties, is shown by A. B. Faust's *The German Element in the United States* (New York, 1909). He considered the German immigrants up to that period to have outnumbered those of any other group, but he not only separates Irish, and even Canadians, from British, but also (under the influence of the Nordic racial theory) includes both Swiss and Dutch in his German figures; furthermore, he takes little account of the serious political and religious divisions between Germans in the years prior to 1870.

consciousness. It might, therefore, serve our purpose much better to take the figures of English-speaking immigrants, were it not for the very serious problem of the Irish, who constituted more than half the total emigration from the British Isles between 1820 and 1945, and who exceeded somewhat the total of immigrants to the United States from British North America in the same period. To what extent can the Irish-Americans, who were thus so numerous, be reckoned an agent of co-operation between Britain and America? Not in the very least, it would seem at first sight, but rather the reverse. It may, however, be found on closer examination that they have constituted a kind of bond, like that which binds together relatives whose temperaments are plainly incompatible.

The Irish have always played a very influential part in American history. Though the number of "Scotch-Irish" in America in the eighteenth century has sometimes been exaggerated, we must bear in mind that there is a strain, albeit a highly recessive one, of orange in the green of the Irishmen of America; William Jennings Bryan, for example, at one time favoured special treatment of Ulster because of its staunch Protestantism. This remains true despite the immense influence of the Irish in the Catholic Church in America, a tribute to the importance of the common tongue as well as to Irish organizing experience. It must also be remembered that Irishmen in America often felt, or appeared to feel, even more strongly about British activities in Ireland than did Irishmen who remained there; Abel and Klingberg can write of Daniel O'Connell, the great Irish leader, that his "hatred of America was so intense because of what he regarded as her gross hypocrisy"[1] on the slavery question. It can be maintained that the solution of the Irish problem was made considerably more difficult by Irish-American interference. For all in all, American Irishry was vociferously anti-British, and had an influence quite proportionate to its numbers, which were very great. Irish historians, according to one of them,[2] have claimed that one-third of the population of the thirteen colonies was Irish and that fifty per cent of Washington's soldiers were Irish; though both are gross distortions, the latter may be more nearly true than the former. At least Washington accepted membership of the Friendly Sons of St. Patrick as "a Society distinguished for the firm adherence of its members to the glorious cause in which we are embarked."[3] Nevertheless, in early days, the incoming Irish often "had

[1] A. H. Abel and F. J. Klingberg, *A Side-Light on Anglo-American Relations, 1839-1858* (Lancaster, Pa., 1927), p. 31.

[2] E. F. Roberts, *Ireland in America* (London, 1931).   [3] Q. Ibid, p. 30.

to face the fact that public opinion in their new home invariably was shaped and directed by men who had inherited many of the prejudices and antipathies of their English oppressors."

They made their mark, however, from the beginning, in walks of life as diverse as those of Andrew Jackson and Robert Fulton, and during the years after 1828 began to become indissolubly associated with the Democratic party, particularly in the big cities whose political machines owed much to "the peculiar genius of the Irish for political organization",[1] particularly covert organization, and this they had certainly learned at the hands of the English. This skill, like their language, they carried with them, and it was a sort of bond with Britain whether they liked it or not. They had captured Boston, Philadelphia, and New York City, including Tammany, by 1820, and in 1899 John Hay wrote to Henry White in London that all the State conventions of the Democrats "put the anti-English plank in their platform to curry favour with the Irish (whom they want to keep) and the Germans (whom they want to seduce). It is too disgusting to have to deal with such sordid liars."[2] It is probable that the Irish group had more influence upon American foreign policy than any other body of opinion, and that influence was usually anti-British; its effect was frequently specific, whereas the anti-Irish feeling which kept it in check—its power was shown in the defeat of Al Smith in 1928—was more generalized and thus less efficacious in practice. It is significant that journalism was a favourite Irish profession (something which once again they owed to the common tongue) and also that they were as prominent in the organization of the trades unions as they had been in the political machines, which was yet another thing they owed to their British experience. The persistence of the Irish problem in the British Isles kept American anti-British feeling alive, and it was not until after the settlement following World War I that it began to die away.

This curious dichotomy made the Irish free of the British tradition, but at the same time made them hate it; gave them the invaluable asset of the English language and British experience, and thus made them England's most formidable critics; and made them unwilling instruments of the perpetuation of some forms of British influence in the United States. It is very nicely illustrated in one of the sayings of Mr. Dooley. Of the remarkably similar waves of imperialist feeling, which swept Britain and America in the last years of the nineteenth century, he said, in a curiously mixed vein of irony and reluctant understanding:

[1] Ibid, pp. 76, 124.

[2] Q. R. B. Mowat, *The American Entente* (London, 1939), p. 131.

101

"I tell ye, Hinnissy, ye can't do th' English-speakin' people. . . . Th' Anglo-Saxon race meetin's now goin' on in th' Ph'lippeens an' South Africa ought to convince annywan that, give us a fair start an' we can bate th' wurruld to a tillygraft office." He went on to comment on the volte-face of the hitherto anti-British Senator "Hinnery Cabin Lodge", who relied so much on the Boston Irish vote: "Now where's Hinnery? Where's the bould Fenian? . . . Faith, he's changed his chune, an' 'tis 'Sthrangers wanst, but brothers now,' with him, an' 'Hands acrost th' sea an' into some wan's pocket'." Very soon, Mr. Dooley predicted, the time might come when "th' subjick races" would rebel against the Sahibs "beloved iv Gawd an' Kipling".[1] Mr. Dooley and his countrymen can hardly be accounted agents for the promotion of Anglo-American goodwill, but neither can they be disregarded altogether as carriers of the germs of British culture and institutions. We must therefore give the figures, as far as possible, of Irish emigration, but must distinguish them whenever we can from the rest. With these things in mind we can turn to a brief examination of British emigration to America.

Brebner estimates that, of those who left Britain between 1815 and 1940 for English-speaking societies, "about 58 per cent went to the United States, and 18 per cent to Canada, about 10·5 per cent to Australasia, about 6 per cent to South Africa, and about 7 per cent to all other regions."[2] Between 1841 and 1900 some seven-tenths of all British emigrants went to the United States; before 1840 more had gone to British North America than to the United States, but after that the balance altered decisively. The scale of this movement was very remarkable, and it was largely a free movement unassisted by the public authorities. It was true that there were inducements to emigration to America; plenty of land, freedom from taxes and tithes, lack of actual want, social and political equality, and good prospects for the children. But there were also serious deterrents; fear of the Indians, lack of employment for mechanics, extremes of climate, fierce competition in everything but subsistence farming, lack of comforts and pleasures, and the deep human fear of the unknown. But the stream bore down all obstacles in its path.

British emigration to North America rose to three peaks, one between 1846 and 1854, one between 1869 and 1873, and one in the years before World War I.[3] It was much affected by conditions both

[1] Q. Brebner, p. 252.   [2] Ibid, p. 109, note.

[3] S. C. Johnson, *Emigration from the U.K. to North America, 1760-1912* (London, 1913), passim.

at home and in the new continent; thus in the Hungry Forties men were pressed out of the British Isles, and after 1849 were attracted by the California Gold Rush; they were encouraged to emigrate by British unemployment in the nineteen-twenties, and repelled by the even worse conditions in America in the thirties. The following table gives figures which clearly show the relative importance of emigration from Britain to the United States and to other parts of the British Commonwealth during the pre-World War I period.[1]

Date	Emigrants to British North America	Emigrants to the United States	Emigrants to Australia and New Zealand
1821–30	139,269	99,801	8,935
1831–40	322,485	308,247	67,882
1841–50	429,044	1,094,556	127,124
1851-60	235,285	1,495,243	506,802
1861–70	195,250	1,424,466	270,499
1871–80	232,213	1,531,851	311,946
1881–90	395,160	2,546,018	383,729
1891–1900	328,411	1,814,293	131,629
1901–10	1,142,550	2,714,188	235,852
	3,419,667	13,028,663	2,044,398

Nearly four times as many British emigrants went to the United States as went to British North America in these years, and six times as many as went to Australasia.

After World War I the numbers fell off substantially, particularly in the thirties, a process which continued after World War II. In 1947 there were 18,555 emigrants from Britain to the United States, 22,960 to British North America, 13,012 to Australia, and 5,918 to New Zealand.[2] Although in the pre-1914 figures the Irish are, of course, included, and although it has been estimated that a very large number of nineteenth-century emigrants to America returned home, the scale of emigration is obviously such as to constitute a very powerful bond between the two societies.

This is borne out by the figures at the receiving end, although they are considerably more complicated to evaluate. A comprehensive table is perhaps the clearest way of doing so, but reliable figures do not exist prior to 1820, and precisely accurate ones not till 1850. Official esti-

[1] Ibid, Appendix I, Tables 1 and 2.
[2] *The Statesman's Year Book, 1949*, p. 57.

mates have been made, however, of the racial composition of the American population at the end of the colonial period, which prove some sort of guide, if not a close one; they show 82·1 per cent English, 7 per cent Scotch, 1·9 per cent Irish, a total of 91 per cent. In the next forty years most of the immigrants came from Britain and Germany, and the figures take up the tale more lucidly from 1820 onwards. They show that between 1820 and 1945 English-speaking immigration into the United States accounted for just under one-third of the total from all countries, and English-speaking minus Irish for just under one-fifth of the whole. In more detail, they show that between 1820 and 1849 the English-speaking was well over one-half of all immigration, and English-speaking less Irish over one-sixth; that between 1850 and 1879 the proportions were over one-half and just over one-quarter; that between 1880 and 1909 they had sunk to just over one-fifth and just over one-eighth, owing to the rush of the new immigrants; and that from 1910 to 1945, under the influence of the wars and the quota system, they rose to just over and just under one-quarter. These are all, even those for 1880-1909, very substantial ratios.

A closer examination demonstrates that the English-speaking contribution to the American population was by far the biggest of all the national and racial groups. The next largest groups after the British are Germany, Italy and Russia; their figures are as follows.

Period	Germany	Italy	U.S.S.R. and Baltic States
1820-49	515,913	4,131	886
1850-79	2,451,575	64,792	37,270
1880-1909	2,352,975	2,801,896	2,134,100
1910-45	708,324	1,849,939	1,206,849
	6,028,787	4,720,158	3,379,105

Thus the lead of the English-speaking group is proportionately greatest in the earliest years, so that, given the high rate of natural American increase, the number of Americans of British stock has always exceeded all other groups; this lead has never been lost, and, with the coming of the quota system, is unlikely ever to be lost.* This remains broadly true, though to a less degree, of the English-speaking group without the Irish. It is, of course, somewhat misleading to talk of this

* Faust estimated that in 1900, 20,400,000 Americans were of English stock, 13,900,000 of Scots and Irish stock, and 18,400,000 of German stock. The total white population of the United States in 1900 was 66,990,000.

TOTALS OF IMMIGRATION INTO THE UNITED STATES[1]

Period	All Countries	Great Britain excluding Ireland	Ireland	Canada and Newfoundland*	Australia and New Zealand	Total English Speaking Immigrants, less the Irish	Total English Speaking Immigrants
1820-49	2,094,220	319,258	878,434	48,457		367,715	1,246,149
1850-79	7,637,952	1,556,725	1,879,169	506,459	8,969	2,072,153	3,951,322
1880-1909	17,145,250	1,609,177	1,424,711	619,030	21,687	2,249,894	3,674,605
1910-45	11,583,973	783,885	410,853	1,885,288	26,512	2,695,685	3,106,538
Total	38,461,395	4,269,045	4,593,167	3,059,234	57,168	7,385,447	11,978,614

[1] Based on *Historical Statistics of the U.S.*, pp. 33-4.

* Canadian figures subject to reservations in that they include some Irish and French Canadians, as well as other foreign strains.

group as a group at all; as the years passed the stock became more and more native and Americanized and would increasingly have resented any suggestion that it was British. On the other hand, they were very frequently—witness such areas as the South—very proud of their British ancestry and by no means uninfluenced by the fact in their political judgments, let alone their private habits. It is probably no coincidence that every American President, except Van Buren, Eisenhower, and the Roosevelts, has been of almost entirely British stock.

Thus in every year before about 1892 except 1854 (when the Germans were more numerous) the British immigrants, from all sources, outnumbered the largest other single group, but by the end of the century they were regularly outnumbered in the "new immigration." After 1921, with the operation of the quota system, the British group becomes again the largest, and remains so, except for 1939 and 1940, when it was exceeded by the German. This supremacy is partly due to the fact that there are three great internal waves of predominance within the British group. Between 1820 and 1879 the Irish form the largest element; in the later of these years they do so, if at all, by slight margins. From 1880 to 1909 the element from the rest of Great Britain takes the lead, again by a narrow margin. After that date the Canadians and Newfoundlanders take a very substantial lead, with the Irish still running somewhat behind the rest from the British Isles. But it is unnecessary to labour further the strength of the racial bond between the British and the American peoples. One might echo the words of Emerson, exaggerated though they are, that "the American is only the continuation of the English genius into new conditions".[1]

One further point should perhaps be made. It was pointed out of American expatriates to Britain that their strength was in their quality, while that of the British emigrants to America was in their numbers. This would be misleading if it gave the impression that the British immigrants were relatively of poor quality; in fact nothing could be farther from the truth when they are compared with the immigrants coming from other lands. Despite the fact that in 1825 the inquiries of a committee into British emigration to America revealed that the main argument in its favour from the labouring classes was good wages and good food, "three meat meals a day",[2] and despite the fact that the

[1] Q. Mowat, *Americans in England*, p. 133.
[2] E. D. Adams, *Great Britain and the American Civil War* (London, 1925), I, p. 24.

106

steerage fare from England to the United States was still only about six pounds just before 1914, Henry B. Fearon, sent to America to prospect for English emigrants, wrote correctly in 1817: "It was no longer merely the poor, the idle, the profligate, or the worldly speculative, who were proposing to quit their native country; but men also of capital, of industry, of sober habits and regular pursuits".[1]

This conclusion is decisively borne out by the analysis of immigrants by occupations made by John R. Commons in his *Races and Immigrants in America*, which is based on the year 1906. In that year there were 1,100,735 immigrants, of whom 285,460 declared that they had "no occupation", these being chiefly women and children. The table speaks for itself:

People	Total (100%)	Occupation (Per Cent)			
		Professional	Commercial	Skilled	Unskilled
English	28,249	10·8	13·5	51·3	24·4
Irish	35,387	1·7	2·9	15·1	80·3
Scotch	11,207	5·7	9·9	62·8	21·6
Welsh	1,639	4·9	6·7	62·4	26·0
Polish	77,437	0·2	0·2	7·7	91·9
Scandinavian	47,352	1·8	1·6	23·5	73·1
German	55,095	4·3	6·7	29·7	59·3
Magyar	34,559	0·6	0·5	9·3	89·6
Total (for all countries	815,275	1·8	3·1	21·7	73·4

Thus, with the exception of the Irish, who were inferior in this respect to all the nations cited save the Magyars and the Poles, the British very easily led all others in the quality of their immigrants; they sent a far higher proportion of professional, commercial and skilled workers than any other country, and a far smaller proportion of unskilled workers. This fact augmented the already greatly superior strength and influence in the United States of those of British origin. That influence has often been underestimated because the group was far less homogeneous than some, but it is a paradoxical fact that there has never been a "British" vote or "English" lobby, except the Irish one, largely because the ethnic group has been too large to function as a whole and has been so readily absorbed. But it is, none the less, of great residual strength and of corresponding importance in the history of Anglo-American relations.

[1] A. Nevins, *American Social History as Recorded by British Travellers* (New York, 1923), p. 77.

It remains only to note that these facts throw considerable light on our major theses. Though it was virtually one way, except for a substantial number of returned emigrants to Britain (placed at 207,683 between 1908 to 1937), this racial intercourse helps notably to explain the progress of Anglo-American cordiality. In the early years the shock of the breach was great, but by 1814 the emancipation of the United States from British political tutelage was complete. During approximately the next quarter century the British contribution of well over half America's immigrants was predominantly Irish; far more than two-thirds of them, in fact. Driven out by poverty and economic oppression, they carried with them much hatred of England, but some knowledge of her political methods. This has unquestionably much to do with that curious and paradoxical mixture of intimacy and dislike which is characteristic of Anglo-American feelings in the middle years of the century; it illuminates the fact which we have noted—which also applies in this realm of immigration—that economic bonds were strongest when affection was weakest. In the third quarter of the century those of British stock still constituted more than a half of total American immigration, but Ireland provided only a few more than the remainder of the United Kingdom; and it was a period in the political arena when old habits persisted but were losing their strength. By the years between 1880 and 1909 Ireland's portion of total British immigration had sunk somewhat, and she sent less than the remainder of the United Kingdom, while between 1910 and 1945, with the vast inflow of Canadians, her contribution was less than one-sixth of the whole, and she sent little more than half the number who came from the United Kingdom. It is true that between 1880-1909 the British flow was swamped by the flood of new immigrants, but it regained its impetus between the wars, and in any case its work had already been done. As to the Irish, the new preponderance of the rest of the British, in the years at the turn of the century, began to drown out their persistent brogue, and must have contributed much to the fact that, as we shall see, these were the crucial years in the rise of Anglo-American friendship. Developments after World War I did nothing but strengthen this trend. Less changeable than the channels of commerce, where America's growth is spreading her influence farther and farther afield from the exclusive Anglo-America waterway, the course of America's racial history, particularly in view of the quota system, seems predetermined; it should remain a constant factor in Anglo-American amity.

II

WE have seen that the racial intermingling was, broadly speaking, one way only; more casual social contacts were certainly not. In 1922 approximately 20,000 Americans were resident in Great Britain. The number of Americans who visited Britain between 1910 and 1914, excluding those who came from Europe, was nearly 320,000, while American tourist expenditure in Britain pre-1914 averaged between 15 and 20 million dollars annually; in 1927 the figure was 40 million dollars and in 1933 18 million dollars. Nor is it true that the only British arrivals in America were emigrants. Between 1898 and 1914, for example, over one million British nationals entered the United Kingdom after embarking from the United States; between 1900 and 1903 approximately 22,500 non-immigrant aliens arrived in America from England, Scotland and Wales, and between 1921 and 1936 about 250,000 Britons went to the United States. But the balance of this non-immigrant traffic is increasingly in American favour, for whereas in 1920 over 200,000 Americans came to England, only 50,000 Britons went to the United States. The obvious fact is that, with the coming of steam and other increasingly rapid and efficient means of communication by the middle of the nineteenth century, the extent of Anglo-American social intercourse entered a period of swift expansion which has not ended today. Manifold further examples of this could be quoted. One might note at hazard that Henry Irving became the first great Anglo-American stage figure after his visit to the United States in 1883; and that in 1908 the cheap Anglo-American postal rate was introduced, and inaugurated a persistent growth in postal traffic. Nor was intercourse unsupported by deliberate encouragement, for the Rhodes Scholarships, which began early in the century, were reciprocated in 1925 by the Commonwealth Fund Fellowships, also for student residence across the Atlantic, and these were but the outstanding organizations of the kind. The increase in intimacy was perhaps first symbolized by the visit of the Prince of Wales, later Edward VII, to America in 1860, and it is characteristic of its continued development that that of his grandson eighty years later should have been an equal success, and of its consistent character that it should have actually followed very much the same geographical route.

These other forms of social contact—and one can do no more than scratch the surface of this subject by quoting a random miscellany of examples—which began to blossom so swiftly from the latter years of the nineteenth century onwards are a conclusive illustration of the shift of the balance of Anglo-American power across the Atlantic, which we have seen so distinctly in the economic sphere. As Brooks Adams forecast between 1898 and 1900, in Britain's heyday, "In inventions, in industries, in political institutions, in scientific theories, even in social fashions, all Europe has taken her as a model. Americans, in particular, have relied on her to police the globe and keep distant markets open, allowing them to sit at home and reap the advantage without cost and without danger. . . . All signs now point to the approaching supremacy of the United States. . . ."[1] Britain's domination over American life in the colonial period was near to absolute; it was weakened but by no means destroyed by the Revolution; and it remained important throughout the nineteenth century. As America grew stronger, however, she began to turn the tables, and by the last years of the century she was, as in so many other things, beginning to take the lead in social influence. Though these historical processes are seldom, if ever, abrupt, the American people seemed to move into a position of power, socially as well as politically, with dramatic suddenness in these years of the closing of the frontier. It was as if the rest of the world, like she herself, became suddenly conscious of the strength of this new giant in its midst. From this time forward the pressure of the American society upon the British is progressively heavier than its counterpart. Upon this phenomenon of shifting power we can only dwell momentarily, and it is unnecessary in any case for us to do more, since it has been vividly depicted by R. H. Heindel in a book with the pregnant title, *America's Impact on Great Britain 1898-1914*. To quote but a few of his facts will amply demonstrate our contention.

American influence upon the British Press was very marked, ranging between the introduction of *The Times'* Supplements by Robert P. Porter after his American experience, and Northcliffe's sensationalism in the *Daily Mail,* for which he hired Pomeroy Burton of Hearst's *Evening Journal.* Though British coverage of America remained markedly inferior to American coverage of Britain till after World War II (in 1939 there were eighty-five American pressmen from daily newspapers in Britain and only about ten British journalists in America), and though this was a constant cause of complaint by Americans, Lodge saying once to Balfour, "Until very lately your newspapers gave us less space than to Belgium and Holland",[2] it did improve gradually; Northcliffe's interest in America, for instance, was reflected in his good American coverage. American magazines like *Harper's*, which started

---

[1] *America's Economic Supremacy*, pp. 190-2.   [2] Q. Heindel, p. 15.

an English edition in 1880, began to circulate and have a great influence. *Country Life* was made possible by American developments in fine printing, and American companies began to push linotype in England about 1889. Even British trade journals became notably more breezy under American competition. Similarly, the American influence on English education was considerable, particularly in the technical sphere; America's economic progress was increasingly ascribed to her concentration in education on practical preparation for life rather than on culture. The development of research degrees, as well as of co-education, owed much to American experience, and her example became more widely appreciated with the growth of the study of American history and institutions led by men like James Bryce and G. O. Trevelyan.

The same growing impact can be seen in many aspects of British social life. Intermarriage increased apace, sometimes in the form of alliances between British gentility and American wealth, and sometimes for more romantic reasons, a phenomenon which provoked a spate of British novels on the subject. By 1903 over seventy Americans had married titled Englishmen, by 1914 over a hundred and thirty; among famous American matches were those of Joseph Chamberlain, Rudyard Kipling and Lord Randolph Churchill. In 1901, for the first time, the volume of letters sent from the United States to Great Britain exceeded that in the other direction; between 1894 and 1920 the volume of American letters to Britain doubled; and—for those who like fantastic statistics—the letters and postcards which passed from the United States to Britain between 1920 and 1936 would make a pile 276 miles high. American charitable endowments, like those of Peabody and Carnegie, became very lavish. American religious influence became significant in the case of new religions like Christian Science and Mormonism, and very important in the case of Nonconformity and Revivalism, through media such as Moody and Sankey, and later, exotics like Aimée Semple MacPherson. As W. T. Stead wrote, "To those who have been brought up in the sectarian seclusion of the Anglican cult, it is difficult to realize the extent to which American books, American preachers, American hymnody, mould the lives of the Free Churchmen of this country."[1] *Per contra,* America was responsible for a certain loosening of social conventions and an increasing emphasis on domestic comfort and labour-saving devices; light kitchen utensils and the ice habit (even including iced champagne) came from America, as did the chapter of Dr. Charles Knowlton's *Fruits of*

[1] Q. Heindel, p. 364.

Philosophy on birth control, which was reprinted in 1876 by Charles Bradlaugh and Annie Besant, who were prosecuted for the action, as a result of which the publication ran through 200,000 copies in a week. The impact of American science was illustrated by the increase after 1889 of "foreign" American members of the Royal Society. American dentistry long led the way to British, and (with its bad as well as good results) American capacity to sell proprietary and patent medicines. There was much British admiration for American surgery and for medical schools like Johns Hopkins, while many influential improvements came from America in spheres like hospital planning, sanitation and such aspects of public health as milk control.

But it was, as perhaps befitted a democracy, in the pleasures and pursuits of the people that the American influence was probably most radical. Americans began to gain sporting triumphs in such fields as golf and athletics; they won Olympic victories in 1908 and 1912. On the stage *The Belle of New York* inaugurated a formidable rival to the English music hall, even though it appealed to somewhat different audiences, and by 1902 Americans controlled eight London theatres. "Nigger minstrels" had long been a popular item, and Buffalo Bill and Western plays prepared the way, as it were, for the coming of the films. In popular music the arrival of rag-time and modern dance steps was immensely important; by 1912 250,000 copies of "Alexander's Rag Time Band" had been sold in England, and between 1919 and 1933 eleven of the sixteen most popular songs in England were of American origin. As with the Press, radio was slowly beginning to transmit more programmes eastward across the Atlantic, but the demand was not notable till after World War II; in 1930 there were a hundred westward to two eastward broadcasts, in 1936 a hundred to thirty-one—British provincialism and conservatism was hard to break down in some spheres. But the cinema was not one of them, and it is here that the most spectacular American impression was made. An investigation in 1936 showed that for British children aged 13-16 the cinema was the most important source of ideas about America, and six times as important as the next source, the Press. Between 1908 and 1914 it is estimated that 60 to 75 per cent of the films shown in Britain were American, and in 1917, with British loss of production in the war, 90 per cent, while the weekly English cinema audience in 1914 was already about seven million. With the coming of the talkies the influence increased, because it became aural as well as visual, and in 1933, 330 out of 476 important films shown in Britain were American.

Such was the sort of impact which America had upon Britain during this crucial period in the shift of the balance of power. Naturally it did not go unobserved or unopposed. There was strong criticism of many of its aspects. Englishmen deplored the excessive commercialism of Americans and their lack of social and aesthetic taste; they disliked the high American divorce rate; they pointed to such social scandals as those depicted in *The Jungle* of Upton Sinclair; they never missed a lynching; above all, they still displayed a Dickensian mistrust of what they regarded as the extreme American worship of the Golden Calf. Though some of these criticisms were perhaps justified, Englishmen, because of their likenesses to their American cousins, were in a poor position to cast the first stone. But whatever their feelings—and, sometimes insensibly, sometimes reluctantly, sometimes approvingly, they accepted, as the new century wore on, a vast number of American innovations—the American social pressure was continuous and increasingly strong, and it would remain so into the foreseeable future. The destiny of America had indeed been fulfilled since there landed on the Virginia shore in 1607,

> "...on the twenty-sixth day of April,
> Just over four months from London,
>
> .   .   .   .
>
> A handful of men in hot, heavy, English gear,
> With clumsy muskets, sweating but light at heart".[1]

III

IN THE political, or, perhaps one might describe it as constitutional, sphere, there is at once apparent the same drawing together as in social life, and it is much more sustained in later years than the economic intimacy. It reflects—indeed, is partly responsible for—the gradual affiliation which is the keynote of the diplomatic history. Its great theme is the development of democratic government, which is the supreme contribution of the English-speaking peoples to the civilization of mankind, that combination, as Mahan said, common to both peoples, of individual freedom with subjection to law. Webster had put it more fully in 1843: "I find at work everywhere, on both sides of the Atlantic ... the great principle of *the freedom of human thought, and the respectability of individual character*. I find, everywhere, an elevation ... of the individual as a component part of society. I find

---

[1] S. V. Benet, *Western Star* (New York, 1943), pp. 49-50.

everywhere a rebuke of the idea, that . . . government is anything but an *agency* of mankind."[1] When the Anglo-American *rapprochement* was nearing completion in World War II, Churchill was able more succinctly to convey the same idea in the phrase "the English-speaking democracies." After it Lord Halifax declared, "that 'life, liberty and the pursuit of happiness' is our common aim; and that from it flows the sap which determines and invigorates our policy . . . [I]t is this kinship of thought and purpose that will weight the scales . . . [F]orces are at work stronger than any event or any human opinion; forces invisible but irresistible, holding the two peoples together. . . ."[2]

With this immense subject we cannot grapple here, but no study of Anglo-American relations could be right which did not lay great emphasis upon it, as one of the integral factors in the maturing of Anglo-American friendship. Broadly speaking, the story can be understood in terms of the development of British democracy, for one of the main difficulties in the way of co-operation and understanding in early days was the persistence of that aristocratic tradition in Britain which was so suspect to Americans; for a century the difficulty was a serious one, but its effects have not, even yet, ceased to ruffle the surface of the relationship, notably in the social sphere. Yet this generalization must be accepted with reserve; no idea of a United States, democratic since 1783, dragging a reluctant Britain into the democratic fold can be substantiated. American democracy has been of enormous importance as a pioneer in whose footsteps other nations could follow, and with the huge growth in her power during the nineteenth century her influence upon Britain greatly increased; the Civil War was in a sense, as Lincoln claimed, a war to test whether any nation conceived in liberty and dedicated to the proposition that all men are created equal, could long endure, and its vindication of democracy was instrumental in the advancement of the cause in Britain. Some historians have, as we shall see, exaggerated the importance of this, since the seeds of democratic development were latent in the whole of British political development; indeed, it was to their English forebears that the Americans in the American Revolution looked for inspiration, and Emerson wrote in 1847-8: "The tendency in England towards social and political institutions like those of America, is inevitable".[3] More than that, any idea that the United States in 1789 was a fully democratic country would

[1] Q. J. R. Dos Passos, *The Anglo-Saxon Century* (New York, 1903), pp. 63-4.

[2] Lord Halifax, *Anglo-American Relations* (Fifth Montague Burton Lecture on International Relations, Leeds University, 1947), p. 12.

[3] *The Works of Ralph Waldo Emerson* (London, 1888), p. 116.

be mistaken; a glance at the electoral laws of, for instance, South Carolina, will effectively dispose of it. America was more democratic than Britain, but then Britain was much more democratic than almost all the other powers in Europe. It was not until Jeffersonian and Jacksonian Democracy had done their work that the United States really began to be a democracy in the full sense of the word. At the other end of the scale, Britain in the years of Liberal rule before 1914 and in the Labour years 1945-50 was, if the word democracy be not interpreted in a strictly and exclusively political, as opposed to economic, sense, far ahead of the United States. This fact was succinctly expressed by H. W. Nevinson in his farewell to America in 1922: "Goodbye to the land where Liberals are thought dangerous and Radicals show red! Where Mr. Gompers is called a Socialist, and Mr. Asquith would seem advanced."[1] Later, Harry Hopkins noted that even Conservatives in Britain were far ahead of America in such matters as social security and public housing; in fact, "the British statute book was raided on a wholesale scale" by the New Deal.[2]

But, with such reservations as these, one can accept the picture of the years 1783-1952 as ones of common progress towards democratic government and popular economic policies; the United States attains political democracy so much more swiftly than Britain that the latter's slowness is for a period a formidable obstacle to understanding, while in movement towards the welfare state Britain later went much faster than did America. But this growing and persistent similarity of object and methods, of ends and means, has been of inestimable importance in the development of fraternity, and particularly so in the twentieth century when, amidst a world of conflicting and often anti-democratic ideologies, the Anglo-American political affinity has become ever more marked and significant. It is perhaps the most powerful evidence for one of our main theses, that the likenesses of America and Britain are at bottom greater than their contrasts.

This, of course, is only relatively so, and there are many instances to the contrary. The constitutional systems of the two countries broadly illustrate both similarities and differences. The American constitution has undergone less apparent change than the British since 1789, but it is possible that the alterations made, by convention rather than law and indirectly rather than directly, are not much less important than the revolutionary ones made in the British system of government. But, though both have endured radical changes, they have retained their

[1] Q. Nevins, p. 554.　　[2] Brebner, p. 307.

basic structure from the eighteenth century to the present day; the American constitution, after all, was closely modelled on what its makers thought the then British constitution ought to be. About a hundred years later Gladstone was able to say that, "as the British constitution is the most subtle organism which has proceeded from progressive history, so the American constitution is the most wonderful work ever struck off at a given time by the brain and purpose of man."[1]

Nor did the only important contrasts between the constitutions lie in the methods of their birth; the separation of the powers in the American, and legislative sovereignty in the British, the fissure between President and Congress in the one and the Cabinet's indissoluble bonds with the House of Commons in the other, have been significant motifs from the beginning. In Anglo-American relations this difference has taken awkward shape in the Senate's treaty-making powers, which have tended on occasion to produce diplomatic crises. As early as 1824, when the Senate altered a convention between the two countries in the course of ratification, Canning wrote to the American Minister:

> The knowledge that the Constitution of the United States renders all their diplomatic compacts liable to this sort of revision undoubtedly precludes the possibility of taking exception at any particular instance in which that revision is exercised; but the repetition of such instances does not serve to reconcile to the practice the feelings of the other contracting party whose solemn ratification is thus rendered of no avail, and whose concessions in negotiation having been made . . . conditionally, are thus accepted as positive and absolute, while what may have been the stipulated price of those concessions is withdrawn.[2]

But, as John Quincy Adams, who was quite a match for Canning, replied, other powers were not under any obligation to ratify before they heard of the actions of the Senate, while they were quite willing to refuse to ratify treaties themselves when their agents exceeded their instructions, a particularly effective dig at Canning. But until the study of American institutions became more popular towards the end of the century, Englishmen tended to share the bewilderment of the Prince Regent related by Adams: "He seemed not to comprehend how it was possible to manage a Government where the members of the executive Government could not sit as members of the Legislature".[3]

[1] Q. Dos Passos, p. 133.

[2] *American State Papers, Foreign Relations, 1818-1826,* V. p. 365.

[3] Beckles Willson, *America's Ambassadors to England,* 1785-1928 (London, 1928), p. 137.

(Initially Americans, with their experience and historical knowledge of British political life, were at an advantage in knowledge of one another's institutions, though later the advantage was lost, since far more was written about the American than about the British constitution.) American officials, like Secretary of State Hay, were long to bemoan the actions, though not always the powers, of the Senate, and even to envy, like Secretary of Defence Forrestal, the Canadian system of unified government control, but no radical alteration was likely in a nation which genuinely looked to public opinion for support and even guidance of executive policies.

The constitutional problem could, however, usually be evaded by tact and goodwill, of which Canning had so much less in diplomacy than Castlereagh, who had advised Canning's cousin when he went to Washington as Minister in 1819: "The first precept which I will recommend is to transact your business with *the American Government as far as possible by personal intercourse with the Secretary of State rather than by writing notes,* thereby avoiding diplomatic controversy. The tendency of the American Government is rather to contentious discussion. Their official notes are generally seasoned to the temper of their people, being more frequently communicated to their Legislative bodies than the papers of other States usually are."[1] This tendency to greater publicity in American foreign policy was to persist; it took formal shape after a century in Wilson's demands for open covenants openly arrived at, but later American diplomats, like George F. Kennan, spoke up in criticism of a system which tended to place policy at the mercy of every gust of popular passion. The truth is that, though British public opinion had by the end of the nineteenth century fully asserted its control over the Government's policy, the long tradition of governmental leadership, and the power of custom in an ancient and compact community, made it less immediately effective; this gave a stability to British policies which, at first sight paradoxically, was lacking in the apparently more rigid American system.

The institutional contrast is very interestingly elaborated by Max Beloff in his article, *Is there an Anglo-American Political Tradition?*[2] He emphasizes the differences more than the similarities, but it would appear that these only stand out in the mind of the student if the Anglo-American relationship is considered *in vacuo;* if it is compared with that between other powers, the likenesses become instantly predominant. Nor, perhaps, is sufficient account taken of the democratiza-

[1] Beckles Willson, *Friendly Relations* (London, 1934), pp. 109-10.

[2] History, XXXVI, 1951, pp. 73-91.

tion of Britain or the growth of political and economic centralism in the United States. This contrast between British authoritarian habits and American egalitarian instincts was at first very marked; in the preamble to Jay's Treaty there is a notable antithesis in the references to "His Majesty" on the one hand, and the "people" of the United States on the other. It was to become less marked as time went on—indeed in the twentieth century the power of judicial review often came to seem highly undemocratic to Englishmen—but it never died away entirely. John G. Winant, after his Ambassadorship in London in World War II, wrote: "With us there is a tacit assumption that sovereignty is lodged in the people. . . . This is quite a different plan of government from the British. . . . The Acts of Parliament . . . are not subject to judicial review. . . . In Great Britain loyalty is owed to the Crown; with us it is an idea symbolized by the flag." He records that the refusal of Churchill to hold press conferences for American journalists in Britain caused some heart-burning, since it was not appreciated that Parliament was the Prime Minister's principal forum. But once more tact was able to do much to smooth out such difficulties.

Nor can one say that one method of government is better than the other. To Englishmen the separation of the powers seems inefficient, while to Americans there seems something morally wrong about anything which prevents an extension of popular control over government. The British system of centralized control often seemed to the American to produce delay and inefficiency in war; as Winant wrote, "The clear authority delegated under the constitution . . . to the Executive, which included war powers, allowed wide discretion of action within the administrative field. . . . This . . . often gave us a time advantage in dealing with the British Ministers. . . . It is outside usual British practice to delegate political authority to the military."[1] By contrast, it seems dangerous to Britons that Congress alone can declare war, a fact which can only with difficulty be reconciled with explicit military alliances. But the pragmatic character of the two peoples has made the necessary compromises possible. Thus, when there was much criticism in Britain at one period of World War II of Churchill's dual role as Defence and Prime Minister, it was to some extent undermined by the American Ambassador's public reminder that it greatly facilitated his dealings with the President, who is also Commander-in-Chief.

In general, though the offices of President and Prime Minister are

[1] J. G. Winant, *A Letter from Grosvenor Square* (London, 1947), pp. 70-1, 78-9.

118

clearly distinguished by the fact that the former is a Head of State, their responsibilities in the field of foreign affairs are very similar; in the case of strong personalities they tend to assert control, but in other circumstances they leave more in the hands of the Secretary of State and the Secretary of State for Foreign Affairs. These two officials have almost exactly analogous functions, and preside over departments which are very, and always have been quite, alike. The office of Foreign Secretary as we know it was established in 1782, only seven years before the State Department was created; it then threw off the encumbrance of domestic duties, a few of which the Secretary of State fulfilled until well into the nineteenth century. Neither Foreign Office nor State Department was adequately staffed or very efficient; the Foreign Office, an Under-Secretary recorded in 1789, kept no note or index of the despatches from foreign governments, so that it was necessary to rummage over a whole year's accumulation to find a particular one, and in its early years the State Department had sometimes to send original papers to the Senate for want of copyists. Neither was assisted by the fact that there tended to be a sharp distinction between what in England was called the Diplomatic Service, and the members of the Ministry or Department at home. In America, it is true, there was a very efficient period of foreign representation in the first years of the Republic, but in the eighteen-twenties, with the Democratic inauguration of the spoils system, there began a long, and on the whole baneful, tradition of political appointments, which was matched in a milder form in Britain by the appointment of members of the Diplomatic Service through family influence.

Nevertheless, broadly parallel reforms were gradually instituted in both countries. In the eighteen thirties the State Department was reorganized, and in 1856 Britain took the first step in the direction of appointment to the Foreign Service by merit, with Clarendon's establishment of qualifying examinations; a Congressional reform of a similar nature in 1855, however, proved ineffective, and it was not until the re-emergence of the United States upon the international scene at the turn of the century that the merit system began to make serious headway in Washington. In 1870 the State Department was organized for the first time on a basis of geographical sections, which example was followed by the Foreign Office in 1881. As a result of the sudden strain placed upon the inadequate American machinery in World War I—the average output of letters multiplied tenfold almost overnight—an Act of Congress in 1924 reorganized the whole of it, combining the diplomatic and consular services in one Foreign Service, selection for which was by competitive examination. The examination system had now prevailed for a considerable time in Whitehall, but during World War II the British Foreign Service was unified in a similar manner, so that the two Foreign Services are now on much the same basis. This provides an interesting example, if not of political interaction, at least of similar reactions to similar circumstances on the part of the two societies.

IV

It is indeed a problem throughout their history to determine whether common or analogous courses of action in the two countries are due to direct influence of the one upon the other, or to similar responses to similar stimuli. There are certainly many examples of both. Because of the common language and increasing intercourse, men moved freely from one land to the other, preaching the causes they had at heart; because of their remarkably similar political reactions and of the many problems they had in common, the same arguments often tended to convince. Upon the diverse manifestations of this political interplay, we have no time to dwell; some have been investigated by historians, many more have not. But even to the casual glance there are broad parallels in the two histories which cannot possibly be ascribed merely to coincidence. The surging tide of Jeffersonian Democracy in the first years of the nineteenth century had a counterpart in the New Whiggism of Charles James Fox, but this was stunted in its growth by the over-whelming reaction of British middle-class opinion against the Jacobin menace; in the end, however, it was to save English democracy by leading the movement which passed the Great Reform Bill of 1832. The Federalist reaction in America was but an echo of the Tory voices in England led by Burke, because France was far away and because Tom Paine's arguments appealed more to Americans than to Englishmen, but it spoke the same language; the conservative elements in American society had done their great work in 1787 and 1788 when, as Brogan has pointed out, they ensured, by the formation of the Federal Constitution, that the American Revolution stopped where they intended it to stop. Truly they were fitting descendants of the Englishmen of 1688.

The long French wars distorted English history for a period, and there was no American counterpart to Peterloo and the Six Acts, but once the broad highroad of the nineteenth century had opened up before the two peoples, it began to become apparent that they were both moving towards very much the same goal. In this way, though they naturally differed in character and in immediate objectives, the reform movement, which sprang spectacularly to life in Britain around 1830, and Jacksonian Democracy, with its sudden-seeming triumph in 1828, were plainly comparable. They inaugurated, too, the final stage in the movement of both peoples towards democracy. Full American democracy came much quicker than that of Britain (which grew more steadily) and, partly perhaps as a result, suffered certain setbacks after the Civil War through the materialism of the Gilded Age, but the contacts between the reforming movements in the two countries were, as Brebner writes, "close and persistent. The visit in 1833 of Garrison, the Abolitionist, to Wilberforce, the dying Eman-cipator, was typical of the transatlantic to-and-fro of practising Utopians like the Owens, or the close communion between Emerson and Carlyle."[1] He goes on to point out the parallel between the move-ments against the established Churches in the two countries (the free Churches, old and new, Methodism and the Salvation Army, were always a powerful bond), between the secularizing tendencies in educa-tion which produced the University of London and the Universities of North Carolina and Michigan, and between the outburst of mechanics' institutes, libraries and lecture programmes on both sides of the water. A direct link was the enthusiastic American adoption of the English Young Men's Christian Association of 1844, and there were parallel temperance movements among the two peoples, the United Kingdom Alliance of 1853 being partly inspired by the Maine Liquor Laws. In the years 1837-70 nearly a hundred thousand Britons were converted to Mormonism, and over thirty thousand of the converts emigrated to the United States.[2] Rowland Hill inspired the American movement for cheap postal services, and even in the establishment of the popular press America owed much to British mass production of print. Frances Wright, the bold champion of feminism, was a Scotswoman who took up residence in America in 1824, and Chartist emissaries crossed the Atlantic from London. Brebner writes:

> The transatlantic interplay stands out again in the beginnings of trade unionism. The same British statute . . . in 1824 and 1825 . . . legalized trade unions and permitted the export of British machinery. The two crossed the Atlantic together, for the factory system which grew up in New England and the Middle States was never out of touch with the

[1] Brebner, p. 136.

[2] M. Hamlin Cannon, "Migration of English Mormons to America" (*Am.H.R.*, LII, 1947).

121

parent system in Great Britain. Thus the famous mill girls of Lowell . . . reflect Owen's New Lanark in Scotland; and the Workingmen's Association which was founded in 1828 at Philadelphia was the counterpart of the new British unions.[1]

So important an Englishman as Jeremy Bentham could go so far as to describe himself to Andrew Jackson as more of a United States man than an Englishman.

A specific example of co-operation was the development of British and American peace movements, which were strong at this period. It is interesting that, as in other spheres, Britain's leadership was vigorous; Phelps writes that London was the "radiating centre" for philanthropic enterprises.[2] There was a great similarity between the London Peace Society, founded in 1815, and the American Peace Society of 1828, while their officials made great efforts to keep in close touch; not only was there a good deal of personal contact and much correspondence, but also a mutual exchange of publications. They co-operated in what proved—interestingly enough from our point of view—the very uphill work of promoting Continental peace societies. Nor was their work merely academic; in the Anglo-American crisis of 1837-41 both societies were very active in endeavouring to assuage the war fever in the two countries. It is illuminating that in such cases the Americans relied chiefly on appeals to the public, the British on petitions to the government. The chief British names were Joseph Sturge and Henry Richard; the American, William Ladd and Elihu Burritt, of whom it was written that he "not only attended" but "actually organized on European soil, popular congresses for the promotion of humanitarian crusades."[3]

But the most fascinating and best documented of the common humanitarian movements is that of the anti-slavery agitators. Once again the importance of the British impulse is recognized; Abel and Klingberg write: "In the forward movements of the nineteenth century, British humanitarianism was one of the strongest forces . . . [W]hile the scope of the American was limited, that of the British covered a wider field". "If a religious or a benevolent society originated in the United Kingdom, its counterpart soon appeared in the United States."[4] The parallel between the two is striking: "And, across the Atlantic, en-

---

[1] Brebner, pp. 137-8.

[2] C. Phelps, *The Anglo-American Peace Movement in the Mid-Nineteenth-Century* (New York, 1930), p. 26.

[3] Curti, p. 400.   [4] Abel and Klingberg, pp. 1, 11.

thusiasts like the Tappan brothers and Jay and Leavitt and Goodall were to America what Clarkson, Wilberforce, Buxton and many another were or had been to England."[1] The British and Foreign Anti-Slavery Society was formed in 1839, and in 1840 the first World Anti-Slavery Convention was held in London and attended by a strong American delegation. In 1841 active co-operation began with the mission of Joseph Sturge and John Candler to the United States, and was followed up by a second Convention in 1843 and a further mission. There can be no doubt that "the English anti-slavery contest gave a powerful stimulus to that of the United States. Some Englishmen came to this country to propagate their views but much more important was the vast outpouring of British anti-slavery literature into America. . . . Such leaders as Garrison, Sumner and Mrs. Stowe drew inspiration from the success of the English effort. Brougham repeatedly stated the 'higher law' doctrine before it was taken up by Americans."[2] Abel and Klingberg go so far as to write that "the British of those years, at least the philanthropists, manifested an interest in and knowledge of American life and politics such as has . . . if equalled, assuredly never been surpassed."[3] *Uncle Tom's Cabin,* for instance, which was supposed to have been read three times by Palmerston, ran to a sale of 150,000 copies in its first year in America and over a million in Britain,[4] while Mrs. Stowe made triumphal tours of Great Britain in 1853, 1856 and 1859.[5] But the main traffic was in the other direction, so that in correspondence there "appears an amazing dependence upon British help and sympathy and an almost abnormal sensitiveness to British opinion."[6] Not only did a certain amount of money pass from Britain, but an immense mass of letters; apart from the Tappan and Leavitt letters which abound in political detail, one group of English philanthropists corresponded regularly with the Society of Friends, another with the American Colonization Society, and yet another with Garrison's rival American Anti-Slavery Society. George Thompson, during his visit to the United States in 1834-5, collected 2,400 publications on American slavery. Perhaps one of the best tributes to the extent of the British influence on American opinion over the slavery question comes from one not very well disposed towards it; Buchanan said to Clarendon in 1853: "Congress had no . . . power to . . . abolish

---

[1] Ibid, p. 10.

[2] F. J. Klingberg, *The Anti-Slavery Movement in England* (London, 1926), pp. 305-6.   [3] Abel and Klingberg, p. 24.   [4] Klingberg, p. 306.

[5] F. J. Klingberg, "Harriet Beecher Stowe and Social Reform in England", (*Am.H.R.,* XLIII, 1938), p. 547.   [6] Abel and Klingberg, p. 369.

... slavery ... yet ever since the establishment of the British Anti-Slavery Society and their associated societies in America they had kept up an incessant war on this subject. These fanatics ought to know that they were defeating their own ends".[1]

But it was going to need more than the protests of "Old Buck" to check the spate of Anglo-American political intercourse, just as it needed more than his words to stop the avalanche of Civil War. With the coming of that war and the triumph of the Northern cause, a pronounced fillip was given to the cause of democracy in Britain; the Reform Bill of 1867 owed much to American influence. In the late nineteenth and early twentieth centuries the general parallel between British and American political developments becomes very marked indeed. Britain's tendency to isolationism chimed in well with the familiar notes of American withdrawal behind the screen of the Monroe Doctrine. Their irruption once more upon the international scene came under the impulse of an imperialism which they both experienced and which was very remarkable in the case of the United States. In the second quarter of the nineteenth century British imperialism had been greatly weakened; the salutary lesson of the American Revolution had sunk deep home, and Englishmen tended to believe that their colonies would drop off the parent tree like ripe fruit when they came to maturity, a political doctrine which did not seem economically alarming in the heyday of free trade and British industrial supremacy. This was a tribute to American influence, and the United States was at the same time demonstrating, under her much more rigid constitutional system, how new territories could be equitably absorbed in the body politic; as Mahan pointed out, Britain had learned from her American mistakes: "Since she lost what is now the United States, Great Britain has become benevolent and beneficent to her colonies."[2] Now there came a revival of British imperialism, but it was only partly owing to the economic causes which have caught the eye of historians; these operated very little in America, but she felt the same impulse. It was to some extent inspired by racial ideas, which began to assume lunatic shape in the writings of Houston Stewart Chamberlain, but which, in a milder version, emphasized the superiority of the Anglo-Saxon race over "lesser breeds without the law," and its consequent responsibilities. This was the era of the *cri du*

[1] Q. W.A.A.E., p. 280.

[2] A. T. Mahan, *Lessons of War with Spain, and other Articles* (London, 1900), p. 243.

coeur for unity between the two great Anglo-Saxon peoples, when Britons took to their hearts, as the typical American, "Teddy" Roosevelt, the advocate of *The Strenuous Life*.

This aspect of America did not, of course, appeal to all of them, any more than did their own Empire to the pro-Boers and Little Englanders, and almost more remarkable than the correspondence between British and American Imperialism is that between the reactions which followed in both countries. There were many contacts, such as the influence of Bellamy on the English Socialists and of Henry George on the Fabians, but the main comparison between Wilsonian Democracy and Asquithian Liberalism is so inescapable as hardly to need elaboration; and it went to the roots of popular feeling, for, as no less a person than Joseph Chamberlain chided the Webbs, who were inclined to be anti-American, "Cultured persons complain that the society there is vulgar. . . . But it is infinitely preferable to the ordinary worker."[1] Though men in Britain deplored the corruption of American politics, the American democratic example was quoted constantly in the great struggles over Home Rule and the powers of the Lords. If more specific indications of the similarity are needed, they can be found in full measure in Colonel House's remarks to Asquith on the Democrats and Liberals in 1914: "I felt very much at home in London now, for the reason that his Government was being abused in exactly the same terms and by the same sort of people as were abusing the Wilson Administration in the United States. This amused him. I thought the purposes of the Liberal Government and of the Democratic Party were quite similar; that we were striving for the same end. . . . He agreed to this."[2]

World War I saw the two peoples to a great degree united in the objectives for which they fought their first war in alliance; Wilson became the supreme spokesman for many British radicals and the *bête noir* of many British Conservatives, so that he split British opinion almost as sharply as he did that of his own country. The day was not far distant now when Winston Churchill could address himself without offence or ambiguity to both peoples at once, but before it came there was a period of drifting apart in the twenties. In the thirties it was gradually reversed, partly because of the ultimate internationalism of Roosevelt and the Democrats, and partly because the New Deal tended to look back with approbation to some early British social and economic legislation; as Morison and Commager write, "Indeed, much that seemed revolutionary to Americans in the nineteen thirties had

---

[1] Q. Heindel, p. 242.

[2] *The Intimate Papers of Colonel House* (London, 1926), I, p. 275.

been accepted by conservative Englishmen . . . for a generation."[1] With the advent of the Labour Government in Britain in 1945 she moved once more farther and faster than America was prepared to go, even under the Fair Deal, but the two governments were certainly still facing in the same direction. With a moderate Toryism in control in Britain in 1952 and a liberal Republican Administration coming to power in 1953, it was possible to hope that the ideological sympathy of the two governments would still to some extent be maintained.

Whether it would ever be more than an ideological union, whether it would ever be less than two governments, is merely a question for conjecture. Ever since the closing years of the nineteenth century men have talked of Anglo-American unity. Nearly all have agreed with Whelpley that, "It is the logical destiny of the British Empire and the United States to draw ever closer together in the discharge of their international activities and responsibilities."[2] In 1890 Mahan had written: "In conclusion, while Great Britain is undoubtedly the most formidable of our possible enemies . . . it must be added that a cordial understanding with that country is one of the first of our external interests. . . . Formal alliance between the two is out of the question, but a cordial recognition of the similarity of character and ideas will give birth to sympathy, which in turn will facilitate a co-operation beneficial to both; for if sentimentality is weak, sentiment is strong."[3] In 1894 he felt able to write an article entitled *Possibilities of an Anglo-American Reunion,* and in 1898 Joseph Chamberlain made his famous plea for an alliance of the Stars and Stripes and the Union Jack. In 1897 Professor A. V. Dicey had, in an article warmly commended by Bryce, proposed, "That England and the United States should, by concurrent and appropriate legislation, create . . . a common citizenship, or, to put the matter in a more concrete and therefore in a more intelligible form, that an act of the Imperial Parliament should make every citizen of the United States, during the continuance of peace between England and America, a British subject, and that simultaneously an Act of Congress should make every British subject, during the continuance of such peace, a citizen of the United States." He was careful to point out that "Common citizenship . . . has no necessary connexion whatever with national or political unity", and added that

---

[1] S. E. Morison and H. S. Commager, *The Growth of the American Republic* (New York, 1942), II, p. 591.

[2] Whelpley, p. 327.

[3] *The Interest of America in Sea Power,* p. 27.

"It would be not only an absurdity, but almost an act of lunacy, to devise or defend a scheme for turning England and America into one state."[1] Despite his caution Dicey's suggestion fell absolutely flat, but the coming of the Spanish-American War in the very next year kindled the issue—and even more startling ones—into flames which have never quite died down.

In 1903 John R. Dos Passos could write a book proposing an Anglo-American union; he envisaged Canada entering the United States, a common British citizenship, free trade within the union, interchangeable coinage of the same value, and an arbitration tribunal to decide all questions in dispute. Others gave voice to similar hopes and projects. Andrew Carnegie, as became the great steel master, was splendidly confident: "Let men say what they will, I say that as surely as the sun in the heavens once shone upon Britain and America united, so surely it is one morning to rise, shine upon, and greet again the Reunited States—the British-American Union."[2] Such high flights of fancy lost their touch with reality, and such projects struck no roots. Despite the co-operation of World War I, the United States rejected even the League of Nations; perhaps one should not use the word "even", for it is possible that by demanding all, Wilson lost the opportunity to get anything, that a limited alliance might have proved more acceptable to the Senate than the "all or nothing" of the League. But the ideas sown at the turn of the century still fermented in the minds of men, and, under the pressure of events before and during World War II, they reappeared in new but kindred forms. Clarence K. Streit in *Union Now* struck a note reminiscent of the schemes of Dos Passos and many others. No less a person than Winston Churchill espoused the cause of a common Anglo-American citizenship, and the unprecedented intimacy of the Anglo-American relationship opened up rosy vistas of Anglo-American co-operation.

These were not, in the cool days of peace, fully realized, nor would the sober observer expect otherwise, but much was achieved; not only did America become a founder member of the United Nations, but, under pressure of the Russian menace, the North Atlantic Treaty Organization came into existence. Here were bonds of a positive kind, going beyond those of the purely conventional type of alliance by their establishment of a permanent organization headed by the North Atlantic Council and a Supreme Military Commander. Furthermore, the Berlin airlift, the stationing of American atom bombers in Britain,

[1] Q. Dos Passos, p. 212.
[2] *The Autobiography of Andrew Carnegie* (London, 1920), p. 282.

127

and the Korean War showed that the unique Anglo-American relationship was capable of swift revival when needed for special purposes. And there were new and exciting, strange and almost unheard of, intrusions of the ideal into the real world under the penetrating rays of Russian activity; at urgent American behest men actually began to try and put into effect the vision of European unity. It seemed unlikely that Britain would willingly play an integral part in this movement, and probable that her desire would be for closer relations within the whole North Atlantic basin; there were, indeed, those in Britain, and even in America, who desired above all else closer and more institutionalized relations between the British Commonwealth and the United States. There were grave practical obstacles in the way of such an achievement, but in a world where France and Germany were being forced in the direction of military union, little seemed impossible. It was, after all, a much farther cry to the days of Charlemagne than to those of Chatham. Certainly in the year 1952 it was by no means beyond the range of possibility that the deed of 1776 might in some sense be undone.

CHAPTER FIVE

THE CULTURAL TIE

I

THE cultural has probably been the most important of all the ties binding Great Britain to the United States, although its strength is very difficult to assess in any practical manner. Since the proportion of a people which can travel abroad must, even in this age, remain small, it is through the vehicle of culture that knowledge of one nation by another must be acquired. And that mutual knowledge is the only sure way to tolerance: an increase of international knowledge is an essential element in any increase in international understanding. In Anglo-American relations—it is another cliché of profound importance—the common language has made the process of reciprocal comprehension very much easier. We forget all too often how effective a barrier politically lack of a common tongue may be; nations can, like Switzerland, be solidly constructed without a single shared language, but the task is immensely more difficult, because language is the most cohesive national force. It is true that the English language may seem at first, as G. B. Shaw—that addict of the paradox—put it, to separate and not unite the two great peoples; that little of the savour of mutual comment is lost in crossing the Atlantic; and that superficially this makes always for dispute and has in the past made for immense Anglo-American bitterness. More subtly, it may, as Max Beloff has recently pointed out, lead to assumptions that there is an understanding more precise and complete than actually exists. But these are better than the deepest ignorance, and relatively—which is the only valid basis of comparison—the two peoples understand one another much better than peoples which do not possess a common tongue. Unless one takes a deeply gloomy view of human nature, one must believe that in the end he that increaseth knowledge does not increase sorrow; that, in most human relationships, beyond initial mistrust there lies understanding. Certainly the history of Anglo-American relations, with their persistent development of warmth and cordiality as reciprocal information multiplied, appear to be a triumphant vindication of this idea. The instruments of that swelling transmission of knowledge have necessarily been cultural.

Yet a realistic evaluation of the cultural tie is exceedingly hard. Any discussion of "culture"—the very word is suspect—must be conducted with infinite caution, even if it is not primarily concerned with cultural values. There can be no doubt, however, that the culture of the two peoples has, until quite recently, been dominated by England; it is indeed the sphere where the predominance of the British in earlier years was most overwhelming and where it was longest sustained. The air of the United States in the first half of the nineteenth century was filled with lamentations that Americans were

> intellectually the slaves of Britain. The longing for English praise, the submission to English literary judgment, the fear of English censure, and the base humility with which it was received, was dwelt on incessantly in magazines, in newspapers, in addresses, in recollections of distinguished men, and in the prefaces to books. . . . When we examine an American literary production, said the reviewer of a wretched book written in imitation of English models, the first thing we do is to determine whether the author has or has not adopted an English fashionable model. . . . The inevitable consequence . . . is a state of colonization of intellect, of subserviency to the critical opinion of the once mother country.[1]

This dominance was, of course, partly the result of historical events. Though the United States proclaimed her political independence in 1776, she could not assert her cultural independence at once, for the weight of the English tradition was too great and the American lack of it too absolute. Because in 1776 she had in effect no cultural history, America made the previous centuries of English culture her own, as indeed they already were, and with the voices of Chaucer, Shakespeare, Milton and the rest speaking from over the sea, it is small wonder that America long remained culturally subservient to Britain.

This she would doubtless have been in any case, but it was made doubly sure by the facts of her life. She was in 1783, and was to remain for many years, a frontier society; with prospects of immense riches before them, and only wealthy in the present through the sweat of their brows, Americans were more heavily engaged in pioneering in the wilderness than in the field of letters. When Gouverneur Morris said in 1787 that "The busy haunts of men, not the remote wilderness, was the

[1] J. B. McMaster, *A History of the People of the United States, from the Revolution to the Civil War* (New York, 1903), V, p. 287.

proper school of political talents",[1] he was on dangerous ground, but if he had applied his aphorism to culture, he would not have been. There is unquestionably, however difficult it may be to define precisely, a relationship between wealth and culture in society; culture can perhaps only bloom fully after a large economic surplus is attained. As Jefferson said in 1813: "We have no distinct class of literati in this country. Every man is engaged in some industrious pursuit".[2] Not, of course, as the very remark of Morris implies, that America was exclusively a frontier society or that she produced no literature or art. Within half a century of independence a genuine American literature had begun to make its appearance, and Melville, Hawthorne, Emerson and Longfellow could be matched against much that England could show. But their voices were not the voices of America; indeed to some extent they were voices crying not so much in as to the wilderness, for the function of New England in American life was largely educative. In a curious way she was to the rest of the United States, and particularly the Great West, what England was to her: just as her schoolmarms spread enlightenment towards the frontier, so "The true Bostonian always knelt in self-abasement before the majesty of English standards; far from concealing it as a weakness, he was proud of it as his strength."[3] But in due time, America's wealth and cultural confidence developed, and the cultural ascendancy of Britain tended to diminish.

But it was considerably slower to disappear than any of her other ascendancies, such as those in commerce and in political power, which we have already seen to be over and done with before World War I. In fact, it may be open to question whether it has yet disappeared entirely. Certainly if educated Englishmen are asked to point to any aspect of life where they are not yet outweighted by their American rivals and friends, they would be inclined to point to literature, and possibly music and the arts; equally certainly this is a claim which would be bitterly rebutted by many Americans. It is one which it is obviously peculiarly difficult for an Englishman to evaluate justly, while, partisanship apart, questions of this kind have an intrinsic complexity and nebulosity, which make generalization highly dangerous. It does seem possible that cultural bloom tends to follow rather than to precede, or even to accompany, economic maturity—though each of these terms in succession defies exact analysis—and that American native springs of talent have

---

[1] S. E. Morison, *Sources and Documents Illustrating the American Revolution, 1764-1788* (Oxford, 1923), p. 270.

[2] Q. Mencken, *The American Language*, p. 17.

[3] *Education of Henry Adams*, p. 19.

yet to develop their full strength. Indications that English culture can still hold up its head in the presence of American, that it still equals if it no longer surpasses it, are not entirely lacking. Admittedly, the hey-day of the American intellectual emigré is over; there will be few more Jameses and Eliots, at least until Britain's economic position becomes a good deal better than it is, and there were, after all, Huxleys moving in the reverse direction, even when England was still, in the nineteen-thirties, quite well off. There are, naturally, many more now. But England can still produce practitioners in the arts to rival any nurtured by America, and it is not without significance that in 1951 Britain, with only a third of the population, produced eighteen thousand book titles to America's ten thousand. She is still in some degree a cultural Mecca, not merely to the English-speaking peoples of the Commonwealth, but to Americans also.

If this is so, how is it to be explained? It is at least arguable that it is owing to Britain's aristocratic tradition; that it is not only because of the existence of the American frontier, but also of the democracy which it helped to foster. There are some grounds for believing that, in the initial stages of a society's growth, democracy is not the most fertile of soils for the seeds of culture; indeed it remains to be distinctly proven that democracy is ever positively good for the arts. This is obviously a question that bristles with difficulties, and in which it is more than doubtful if proof can ever be forthcoming, but it is a suggestive basis for the analysis of the Anglo-American cultural connexion. No one who has seen Mount Vernon, or Monticello, or even Lee's home at Arlington, can doubt the cultural value of early America's contribution. But those years were in many senses aristocratic years; after them there came, with the triumph of the North in the Civil War, the decadence of the Gilded Age. But a similar decadence can be seen in the architecture, and some of the associated arts, of the Victorian era in the Old World. (Notice in passing as evidence of the strength of the cultural connexion the common American use of the term Victorian.) And this Old World vulgarity may also be due to the strength of a new social class, if, indeed, it is not simply a product of industrialism. But the effects of this revolution were perhaps less marked in Britain, where tradition dies hard; taste depends in a high degree upon the acceptance of social and artistic authority, and this came more naturally to Britain than the United States. What K. B. Smellie writes of the development of the English Civil Service may be very aptly applied to the realm of taste: "It may be said that it was the very slowness with which in

132

England democratic government was substituted for aristocratic privilege that made possible the success of our Civil Service. It was rescued from private patronage without becoming public spoils."[1]

It may be that this persistence of aristocratic traditions in social life accounts for a division among the English in their reception of American culture, which has been more readily accepted by the common people, and more frequently rejected by the upper classes. It is through the media of mass culture that the power of America has been chiefly exercised, such as the press, popular music, and the cinema. English influence on America remains greatest in the more esoteric cultural realms, for, as Tocqueville would have it, the "permanent inequality" of Europe led men to "the arrogant and sterile researches of abstract truths, whilst the social conditions and institutions of democracy prepare them to seek immediate and useful practical results of the sciences."[2] Pessimistic observers see in this fact a gloomy fulfilment of the destiny of the West hinted at by Toynbee, in which, because the springs of culture remain pure and vigorous and undefiled only in the immediate area of its central wells, the massive powers on the peripheries of civilizations inevitably experience the debasement of culture at the hands of a powerful proletariat. It is from this point of view that criticisms of American materialism become most to the point and most alarming.

For such criticisms reasonable grounds can be found, but they can also be found with nearly equal reason for similar criticisms of the developing pattern of British life. If American culture has points of inferiority to English, they are merely matters of degree; if the Americans are, as Oliver Wendell Holmes said in 1858, "the Romans of the modern world—the great assimilating people",[3] the English are only to an exceedingly limited degree its Greeks. They are tarred too much with the same brush, of pragmatism, democracy, industrialism and materialism, for deep cleavage. Even America is not wholly democratic culturally; there are remarkable enclaves of aristocratic culture in the cosmopolitan and tradition-bound society of the eastern seaboard, whose members look east towards Europe far more than they look west towards the heartland of Americanism. If any doubts are still felt on the score of America's cultural vigour, a glance at Soviet Russia, whose whole life, including its culture, is in the iron grip of an inflexible materialist dogma, will rapidly dispel them; for the present situation of all her arts, save those most remote from politics, show clearly the effect of the dead hand of Communism.

[1] Q. Brebner, p. 139.   [2] Q. Curti, p. 338.   [3] Q. ibid, p. 233.

But judgments of American culture are more dangerous than even these things suggest, because they are essentially judgments of value. Who shall dare to weigh quality against quantity with infallible certainty? English university teachers are well aware of the fact that the average academic standard of the American student of university age is below that of his English counterpart, and this fact is often loudly proclaimed as a general criticism of the American educational system. The criticism has some validity, but the English superiority is gained at a price; how many of the critics are aware of the *magnitude* of the American educational effort compared with the British? Average American schoolchildren are educated considerably longer than their British counterparts, and a far higher proportion of them (almost certainly much more than twice as many) go to a college than proceed in Britain to university or technical college or their equivalent. There are some qualitative advantages in Britain to offset these facts, but a great deal of English quality is needed to make up for this tremendous American superiority in quantity. Particularly is this so when one of the primary reasons for the economic failure of Britain today is the lack of that abundance of skilled technicians which American universities do so much to produce. Critical Britons might well be reminded that those who live in such a precarious and draughty glass-house are singularly ill-equipped to cast the first-stone at the super-heated dwellings of their American friends.

II

IF WE turn to examine the common language as an index of the extent of Anglo-American cultural intercourse, we are, although not immune from the infection of value judgments, in a much healthier atmosphere, for it provides a fascinating and relatively concrete guide. To explore it fully the reader has only to turn to H. L. Mencken's monumental but absorbing work, *The American Language*. In the first place, however, one must consider to what extent one can truly talk of the common language. It seems that one can more justifiably do so in mid-twentieth century than one could do at any time in the preceding two hundred years, for very soon after the formation of the colonies, the new environment began to produce swift changes in the language of the inhabitants; though, as in other spheres, they were not able to throw off the domination of the mother tongue till after the War of 1812, they did so then with a vengeance. During the succeeding years the flow of language eastward increased steadily in volume until, despite a sustained British resistance up to World War I, it had virtually conquered by the middle of the twentieth century. This history provides a remarkable illustration of the course of the whole Anglo-American relationship. It not only shows the gradual but insistent restoration of an intimacy unmatched since 1776, despite the ill-feeling of the early nineteenth century, but also the assumption by America of the dominant role in the partnership; the main difference is that America's insensible effort to dominate the language began much earlier than her efforts in other spheres, for the tide of language had begun to turn by the second quarter of the nineteenth century. This swift reaction was due primarily to the stimulating effect of a new environment—the settlers simply had to invent new words to describe new things—and to the tremendous racial admixtures in the new state, but there can be no doubting also the American genius for improvisation, in this as in other branches of human activity, and its swift growth in the climate of freedom, and liberation from tradition, which America offered.

American innovations had begun as early as 1621, with such words as *maize* and *canoe*, and they increased steadily in number. They were derived not only from the Indian, as with *caribou, hickory* and *warpath*, but also direct from the Spanish, as well as from Spanish adaptations of the Indian, as in the case of *tobacco, tomato* and *hammock*; some came from the French, such as *portage* and *bogus*; and yet others from the Dutch, such as *dope* and *waffle*. As well as making new words out of old English material, as with *stumped, locate* and *oppose*, they altered the meaning of old ones, such as to *squat*, and revived English archaisms, such as the *fall, cross purposes, din* and *offal*. Above all they invented new terms, such as those of politics, to *endorse, affiliate, let slide, high falutin, filibuster* and *lobbying*.

According to Sir William Craigie, writing in 1927, the tide began to turn about 1820, in the surge of nationalism after the War of 1812, which finally severed America's English moorings. "For some two centuries . . . the passage of new words or senses across the Atlantic was regularly westward; practically the only exceptions were terms which denoted articles or products peculiar to the new country. With the nineteenth century, however, the contrary current begins to set in. . . ."[1] Then, indeed, the swelling flood begins. John Pickering's *Vocabulary or Collection of Words and Phrases which have been supposed to be peculiar to the United States of America*, published in 1816, contained some five hundred terms; a similar glossary by John

[1] *The American Language*, Supplement One, p. 440.

135

Russell Bartlett in 1848 contained 412 pages, and another edition of the same work, in 1877, 813 pages. Richard Harwood Thornton's *American Glossary* of 1912 listed 3,700 terms; the University of Chicago's *Dictionary of American English on Historical Principles* of 1944, edited by Sir William Craigie, contained 2,552 large double-columned pages and listed 26,000 terms. Indeed, as one picks at random in this mighty cataract, one is amazed at the words which are in fact Americanisms; *reliable, influential, lengthy, to phone, editorial, filing cabinet, worth-while, make good, fall for, stand for, placate, antagonize, donate, presidential*—the list could be indefinitely extended. As Alastair Cooke said in 1935: "Every Englishman listening to me now uses thirty or forty Americanisms a day."[1]

Some had a longer struggle for acceptance than others, such as *caucus* and *bunkum* (until it was instantly received as *bunk*); others had a special send-off, such as the *"Indian Summer" of a Forsyte* by Galsworthy, and *shyster* in R. L. Stevenson's *The Wrecker*; but mostly they came flooding in, not silently but often unnoticed. Noah Webster was certainly wise when he said in 1827: "[I]t is quite impossible to stop the progress of language—it is like the course of the Mississippi, the motion of which, at times, is scarcely perceptible; yet even then it possesses a momentum quite irresistible."[2] In the twentieth century, with the coming of such instruments of culture for the masses as the cinema, the flood got almost beyond measurement, as the succession of new editions of Mencken's work nicely illustrates, for it was primarily, as Tocqueville had seen a century earlier, in the spoken word that the American impact was felt.

The growth of American power in later years is glaringly illustrated by the paucity of the westward flow of language, for though a few terms like *browned off, good show* and possibly *char*, may make a very precarious lodgement in the spoken vocabulary of some Americans, most English expressions, such as *shop, maid, nursing home, rotter,* which are for the most part "society" terms, undoubtedly have for Americans—and it is perhaps significant—"a somewhat pansy cast."[3] It is not surprising that the influence of America is so overpowering; as Brogan pointed out in 1943, "If American could influence English a century ago, when the predominance of the Mother Country . . . was secure, and when most educated Americans were reverentially colonial in their attitude to English Culture, how can it be prevented from influencing English to-day . . . ? . . .Of the 200 million people speaking

[1] Q. Mencken, p. 232.   [2] Q. Nevins, p. 156.
[3] J. M. Cain: q. Mencken, p. 264.

English, nearly seven-tenths live in the United States. . . . As an international language, it is American that the world increasingly learns. . . ."[1] Certainly it is not artifacts like Basic English, which, as Roosevelt once pointed out, could do no better "with five famous words" than "blood, work, eye water and face water".[2] As an Englishman wrote as early as 1926, "It is chiefly in America—let us frankly recognize the fact—that the evolution of our language will now proceed."[3]

This frank recognition has been but reluctantly extorted. Ever since in 1735 Francis Moore set the tone of English criticism with the words "the bank of the River (which they in barbarous English call a bluff)",[4] the English have fought a strong delaying action, sometimes, as in the case of John Witherspoon, who invented the term Americanism in 1781, and Richard Grant White after the Civil War, aided and abetted by culture-conscious Americans. The reactions of the main body of the American people have been very different. A committee of Congress as early as 1778 set the tone by talking of "the language of the United States"; but it was Noah Webster, with his *"American" Dictionary of the English Language* of 1828, who was perhaps the most important single opponent of subservience to Britain's fiat, declaring that "As an independent nation, our honor requires us to have a system of our own, in language as well as government."[5] During the period of the great literary battles of the nineteenth century, which were exacerbated by the comments of British travellers and the waspishness of certain English periodicals, a ferocious struggle ensued over language; it caused particular bitterness because it took the form which has always infuriated Americans most, lofty and contemptuous British denunciation. The English assumption of superiority which it implied was resented all the more because it seemed to extend far beyond the cultural sphere and to involve a denigration of democracy; this attack upon the ark of the American covenant still further added to American political rancour against Britain, and fortified the American belief in the fundamental iniquity of the Old World habits and aristocratic institutions of the mother country.

In 1787 a London review of Jefferson's *Notes on the State of Virginia* read: "*Belittle!* What an expression! . . . For shame, Mr. Jefferson!

[1] Ibid, Supp. One, pp. 75-6.

[2] Elliott Roosevelt (Editor), *F. D. R., His Personal Letters* (New York, 1950), II, p. 1514.

[3] Q. Mencken, p. 611.   [4] Q. ibid, p. 3.   [5] Q. ibid, pp. 4, 9-10.

Why, after trampling upon the honour of our Country, and representing it as a little better than a land of barbarism—why, we say, perpetually trample also upon the very grammar of our language, and make that appear as Gothic as, from your description, our manners are rude?" Even more difficult for Americans to take than this forthright sort of attack was the process of damning with faint praise, and assenting with civil leer, which is to be found in such comments as those in 1804 on John Quincy Adams's *Letters on Silesia*: "The style of Mr. Adams is in general very tolerable English, which, for an American composition, is no moderate praise."[1] The apogee of English sarcasm was reached in the works of the—from this point of view—terrible twins, Charles Dickens and Mrs. Trollope. It is necessary only to quote the former's comments on the American use of the word *fix*:

> I asked Mr. Q . . . if breakfast be nearly ready, and he tells me . . . the steward was *fixing* the tables. . . . When we have been writing and I beg him . . . to collect our papers, he answers that he'll *fix* 'em presently. So when a man's dressing he's *fixing* himself, and when you put yourself under a doctor he *fixes* you in no time. T'other night . . . when I had ordered a bottle of mulled claret . . . the landlord . . . fear'd it wasn't properly *fixed*. And here, on Saturday morning, a Western man . . . at breakfast inquired if he wouldn't take some of "these *fixings*" with his meat.[2]

Henry James was later, it is not surprising to note, to agree with his predecessor, for when his niece said to him: "Uncle Henry, if you will tell me how you like your tea, I will *fix* it for you", he replied, "Pray, my dear young lady, what will you *fix* it with and what will you *fix* it to?"

But if British resentment began to subside in the closing years of the nineteenth century, American counter-resentment did not; indeed it rose to new heights as American power and confidence grew, and only finally died with the passing of the English contempt for Americanisms which had given it birth. Edward Everett carried the battle to the enemy by declaring that "there is no part of America in which the corruption of language has gone so far as in the heart of the English counties", and Walt Whitman proclaimed his wonted faith in the future of America with the words: "The Americans are going to be the most fluent and melodious voiced people in the world—and the most perfect users of words."[3] As the Middle West was the home of isolation-

[1] Q. ibid, p. 14. [2] Q. ibid. p. 26. [3] Q. ibid, pp. 67, 68, 73.

ism, so it "has always been the chief centre of linguistic chauvinism",[1] and it was there that, in the era of Mayor Thompson of Chicago, a bill was moved in the Illinois Legislature—and passed in a modified form in 1923—in these terms: "*Whereas,* since the creation of the American Republic there have been certain Tory elements in our country who have never become reconciled to our republican institutions and have ever clung to the tradition of King and Empire . . . the . . . official language of the State of Illinois shall be known hereafter as the 'American' language, and not as the 'English' language."[2] Perhaps the official issue to British and American soldiers twenty years later of what were, in fact, little Anglo-American dictionaries, may be deemed to have closed this chapter of Anglo-American history.

For, however loud the British protests, they were steadily drowned out. Take the word *talented* as an instance. In 1832 Coleridge called it "that vile and barbarous vocable"; in 1842 Macaulay designated it a word which it is "proper to avoid",[3] but in that same year Pusey used it without comment; and fifteen years later it received the imprimatur of Gladstone. The American humorists, such as Petroleum V. Nasby and Artemus Ward, who actually moved to London at the end of his life, did much to break down the barrier, and in 1899, perhaps for the first time, a decided English voice, that of William Archer, was raised in favour of the American influence: "Let the purists who sneer at 'Americanisms' think for one moment how much poorer the English language would be today if North America had become a French or Spanish instead of an English Continent."[4] Soon others were heard, such as Robert Bridges, Wyndham Lewis and Edward Shanks; and Virginia Woolf wrote: "The Americans are doing what the Elizabethans did—they are coining new words. . . . In England, save for the impetus given by the war, the word-coining power has lapsed. . . . All the expressive, ugly, vigorous slang which creeps into use among us first in talk, later in writing, comes from across the Atlantic."[5] So, as the years passed, the clamour died, until *The Times* could write in 1943: "There is urgent need for surmounting what someone has called the almost insuperable barrier of a common language. It would never do for Great Britain and America to think they understand, yet miss, the point of each other's remarks just now. Both versions of the common language must be correctly understood by both peoples."[6] In fact that great journal was, after a fashion not unknown to it, pontifically shutting the stable door after the horse had escaped, for, broadly

[1] Ibid, p. 81   [2] Q. ibid, pp. 82-3.   [3] Q. ibid, p. 223.
[4] Q. Nevins, p. 446.   [5] Q. Mencken, p. 47.   [6] Q. ibid, Supp. One, p. 76.

speaking, the common people had then been talking American prose all their lives without being aware of it. As Mencken claims, amongst the younger generation the languages are almost approaching assimilation. There are still many traps, differences and obstacles; as Churchill points out, for example, the phrase "tabling a motion" has exactly opposite meanings in the political life of the two countries. But there is a greater linguistic intimacy, something nearer to a truly common language, than there has been since early colonial days.

III

IN THE wider cultural sphere America was very much slower to make her influence upon the mother country felt. There is no need to emphasize the "unique legacy of the English-speaking Colonial Americans"[1] to the culture of the United States; they were in 1776 even more dominant in letters, the law, political ideas, scientific knowledge, economic theories and social practices than they were in race. What requires, perhaps, more attention is the continued English ascendancy in culture after the attainment of political independence. It is true that other influences began to play a part; French influence, in the democratic movement led by Jefferson, who, although he revered the England of the seventeenth century, despised what he considered its eighteenth century decadence; German influence, particularly in education; and even Italian, Spanish and South American influence, as a reaction from dependence on Britain. It is true also that America began to try hard to stand on her own feet, and that the popularization of knowledge began to develop apace, spurred on by the mistrust of what were believed to be the Anglophile tendencies of the patrician leaders of culture. Thus already Americans were displaying the tendency to spread what knowledge they had much more widely than the British, and by 1815 the United States produced annually three million more copies of newspapers than did Britain, which had a very much larger population, while American popular education was very much more advanced. But the most important factor in American culture was still the English supremacy, and nothing shows it so clearly as American resentment of the fact. An American wrote in 1816: "Dependence, whether literary or political, is a state of degradation, fraught with disgrace; and to be dependent on a foreign mind, for what we can ourselves produce, is to add to the crime of indolence, the weakness of

[1] Curti, p. 3.

stupidity."[1] As Henry Cabot Lodge remarked at the end of the century, "The first step of an American entering upon a literary career was to pretend to be an Englishman in order that he might win the approval, not of Englishmen, but of his own countrymen."[2] This habit of looking up to England as the fountain head of fashion in every aspect of social life was not entirely due to lack of American models or natural subserviency, for, as McMaster writes, "Their preference was not subserviency, but sound literary judgment. Never in the course of two centuries had Great Britain produced at one time such a goodly company of men of letters."[3] But the subserviency remained real none the less.

Partly it did so for purely practical reasons, arising from a natural course of events, closely analogous to those producing the dependence which we have observed in the economic sphere:

> Much the same condition prevailed, another critic remarked, in the literary as in the industrial world. In the manufacture of coarse fabrics we distanced Great Britain. In the manufacture of fine goods we could not approach her. The great literary staple of our country was the newspaper, on which the very best talent was spent and wasted. Next must be placed pamphlets, magazines, and periodicals, which, with a few books of travel and some popular histories, generally succeeded and were widely read.[4]

At the time of the Revolution colonial printing presses had been very poor; the first foundry for casting type had been established only in 1772. Such presses as did exist were occupied chiefly with the journals, so that most books were imported from Britain; 80 per cent of the total still in 1820, and 70 per cent in 1830.

Partly it was that colonial pride in the glories of English letters died very hard—indeed did not really die at all—in the years after the Revolution; a great deal of space was still given to English *belles lettres* in American newspapers. There was a persistent flow of teachers and intellectual leaders, including men like Longfellow, Legaré, Ticknor and Cogswell, to Europe and back again. An institution like the University of Virginia drew liberally for its staff upon British universities. American artists had a pronounced tendency to become expatriates; in these early years they included J. S. Copley, Benjamin West and John Turnbull, who set the example for Abbey, Sargent and Whistler later.

---

[1] Q. Curti, p. 233.   [2] Q. Mencken, pp. 20-21.
[3] McMaster, V., p. 290.   [4] Ibid, p. 287.

Partly it was that the conservative reaction of the Federalists against the Enlightenment drew greatly upon Britain for its inspiration; against the figure of Jefferson must be matched that of Hamilton, to whom it seemed that "To create in America an English system of finance, and an English system of industrialism"[1] was the surest way to achieve the kind of American society he desired. Nor was his admiration of Britain confined to the economic sphere, for Jefferson reported him as saying of the English political system: "purge it of its corruption" and "give to its popular branch equality of representation, and it would become an *impracticable* government; as it stands at present, with all its supposed defects, it is the most perfect government which ever existed."[2] Nor could this Federalist warmth towards Britain, which was enhanced during the French Revolution, be regarded as Tory and pro-British in the old sense, and thus expelled or eradicated, for, though Hamilton, who was born in the West Indies, might be suspect, no one could seriously regard George Washington or John Adams as traitors to the American Revolution. This conservative force, despite the triumph of Jefferson in 1800, had gained an important victory by the establishment of the Federal Constitution.

The English influence varied very much in intensity from section to section. It was always far weakest in the West, where the European most rapidly became American. It was strongest in the East, except for the Middle States, largely because of the cosmopolitanism of parts of Pennsylvania and New York. Yet even here one finds Washington Irving, perhaps the most Anglicized of early American writers, and James Fenimore Cooper, of whom Parrington writes not only that he was "an English squire of the old school turned republican, who did not quite like the company he found himself in", but also that "No other American was so unsettled by contact with European civilization", whose "dignified and generous culture . . . was a challenge to his Americanism."[3] The English influence upon the Mind of the South is indisputable, for since the mid-eighteenth century, when, as Wertenbaker points out, the seventeenth-century Virginia merchant-class gave way to one which modelled itself upon the Cavaliers, the South had aspired "to realize the ideal of the English country gentleman."[4] When the English Romantic movement reached the plantations in the eighteen-twenties, the Southern social system was transmuted into a legendary ideal, which was petrified in golden colours by its passing,

[1] V. L. Parrington, *Main Currents in American Thought* (New York, 1927), I, p. 396.

[2] Q. ibid, p. 302.   [3] Ibid, II, pp. 223, 226.   [4] Curti, p. 28.

in the War between the States. Yet the English squirearchy which Southerners admired was one which they supposed to have existed in an earlier age, and, as Owsley points out, the South was in fact more influenced by the England of the eighteenth century than of the nineteenth. The English romanticism which they made their own was pre-eminently that of Scott, rather than of Shelley. There were, of course, more recent contacts, such as the familiarity of Legaré and Grayson with Bentham and J. S. Mill, but the flavour was pre-dominantly "old world." Nevertheless, of the strength of the English influence upon the South there can be no question. Legaré wrote of Charleston: "We are decidedly more English than any other city of the United States",[1] and Robert Toombs "quite frankly preferred the English system to the American."[2]

But it was in New England that direct admiration for contemporary Britain was most pronounced. Producing the best of American native literature, New Englanders were steeped in English culture, past and present. The Transcendentalists had many sources of inspiration, but important among them was Coleridge and "the English intuitionalists".[3] "All through life", wrote Henry Adams, "one had seen the American on his literary knees to the European",[4] and what he said of Charles Sumner was true of most of the Boston Brahmins: "He, too, adored English standards. . . . He was rarely without a pocketful of letters from duchesses or noblemen in England".[5] Lothrop Motley early said to Adams that "the London dinner and the English country house were the perfection of human society." By the time that Adams himself left London after the Civil War, it "had become his vice . . . he had become English is the extent of sharing their petty social divisions . . . he took England no longer with the awe of American youth, but with the habit of an old and rather worn suit of English clothes."[6] Imitation is, indeed, the sincerest form of flattery, and it is significant that Parrington can write of that New Englander of New Englanders, Daniel Webster: "No Englishman was ever more English than he"; with his estate, his farm, and his good living, he was "an English country squire". He was equally English in his political views, for "He was of the distinguished line of political realists, from Harrington through Locke and Burke, to Hamilton, Madison and John Adams".[7] Emerson said of him, "In Massachusetts, in 1776, he would, beyond all question, have been a refugee."[8] The fact that New England was the first American area to

[1] Q. Parrington, II, p. 109.   [2] Q. ibid, p. 86.   [3] Curti, pp. 303-4.
[4] *Education of Henry Adams*, pp. 319-20.
[5] Ibid, p. 30.   [6] Ibid, pp. 200, 236.   [7] Parrington, II, p. 304.   [8] Ibid, p. 315

follow in the industrial footsteps of Old England—almost exactly in them what is more—constituted another powerful contemporary bond. As Henry Adams remarked: "The Paris of Louis Philippe, Guizot and De Tocqueville, as well as the London of Robert Peel, Macaulay, and John Stuart Mill, were but varieties of the same upper-class bourgeoisie that felt instinctive cousinship with the Boston of Ticknor, Prescott and Motley. . . . England's middle-class government was the ideal of human progress."[1]

In the first half of the nineteenth century, the cultural domination of America by Britain still seemed complete. This resulted in one of the most interesting phenomena in the whole history of Anglo-American relations, the outburst of mutual criticism and ill will which centred around the so-called Battle of the Quarterlies. The two torrents of abuse, flowing at the literary, or at least the literate, level, were certainly unequalled at any other period, except perhaps that of the American Revolution itself, and the interesting thing is that they suddenly burst into flood in the years after the War of 1812. Before that event they had flowed in the same way but with nothing like the strength they acquired later, and one is more and more driven to the conclusion that that disastrous episode set back by half a century the cause of Anglo-American friendship. After 1783 British interest in American thought and writing had been considerable, and "The great majority of English readers were disposed to be fair, though they were unable to restrain the expression of their own feeling of superiority, and were likely to adopt a paternal, if not a patronizing manner."[2] The English periodicals began to align themselves on the American issue, for and against, but "In general . . . British utterances regarding the intellectual state of America show a strange combination of bewildered curiosity, ignorance of exact conditions, prejudice, and more or less condescending goodwill."[3] The feverishness with which the early American writers worked is evidence of their extreme sensitivity to the charge that America had no literature, but the impression with which we are left before 1812 is of two nations of the same race and language, "both sore as a result of a bitter war, watching each other rather better satisfied to be offended than to be pleased, yet both honest enough in the determination to be true to the best in literature wherever they saw it."[4] But, after the second, and in some ways more

[1] *Education of Henry Adams*, p. 33.
[2] W. B. Cairns, *British Criticisms of American Writings, 1783-1833* (Madison, 1918), Part I, p. 93.   [3] Ibid, p. 37.   [4] Ibid, p. 62.

galling, war, much of this honest determination was blown to the winds.

Some of it had, indeed, been lost in the difficult years of embargo and Non-Intercourse; as commercial rivalry grew, so did American resentment of her cultural, as well as her economic, dependence upon Britain. *Niles's Weekly Register* in 1812 contained the accusation, later to become familiar: "It cannot for a moment be doubted that such men as Smyth and Moore, Ashe and Parkinson, have been well paid by the ministry for their tours and travels through the United States. A government under whose benign influence all are happy, all are equal, must be an eternal reproach to the tyrants of Europe."[1] For this accusation of conspiracy, which took detailed shape in charges that the British attacks were for motives of revenge, or to stave off parliamentary reform, or to check emigration, or to protect British markets against American enterprise, there was no vestige of evidence, but there is no doubt that the attacks on American life and culture in English publications increased sharply in volume and bitterness. The attacks were based, as Nevins has shown, not only on American literary productions, but on the published accounts of the increasing number of English travellers in the New World searching for new experiences and fresh literary material. When their comments on American life were published, names like those of Captain Marryatt, Basil Hall, Mrs. Trollope and Charles Dickens made headlines in both countries, but for purposes chiefly of execration in the United States. We shall see the effect of their utterances upon broader national feelings in the next chapter, but they added, because some of them were considerable literary figures, highly combustible fuel to the flames of the literary battle. The struggle had already been rendered more confusing, but no less embittered, by the peculiar effect of the war, which was, in the words of Cairns, "almost unique in the fact that so many citizens of both contending countries opposed it. Even during the period of hostilities the American cause was warmly supported in British periodicals. At the same time, no real Briton could have escaped a feeling of satisfaction when his nation won a victory, or a feeling of chagrin when she suffered a naval defeat. This conflict between intellectual judgment and patriotic emotions continued after the war."[2]

British periodicals fell into three main groups; the *Quarterly Review*, the *Edinburgh Review*, and the *Literary Gazette* were strongly anti-American; *Blackwood's* and the *Athenaeum* were mildly patronizing, though not notably hostile; and—a very much longer list—the *Monthly*

[1] Q. McMaster, V, p. 308.   [2] Cairns, Part II, p. 295.

Review, the *Gentleman's Magazine,* the *Eclectic Review,* the *West-minster Review,* the *London Magazine* and the *Literary Chronicle and Weekly Review* were sympathetic. But the first group's accusations, abetted by books and pamphlets, accusing the Americans (apart from slave-flogging, moral grossness, political corruption, and demagogism) of lack of true religious feeling, materialism, bad taste, vulgarity, bigotry, ignorance and vanity, were the ones most frequently apprehended on the other side of the Atlantic; Americans were, naturally enough, primarily conscious that a number of Englishmen despised them, as, in the words of McMaster, "[A] whittling, spitting, guessing, reckoning, gambling, slave-beating, dram drinking people".[1]

The worst outburst of trouble began with a highly critical article about the Americans, which was in the form of a book review, in the *Quarterly Review* of January, 1814, rumoured to have been written by the Poet Laureate, Southey. Timothy Dwight and James Kirke Paulding took up arms in defence of their countrymen, the former beginning, however, by expressing his great "regret that two peoples which ought to be firm friends were rapidly becoming implacable enemies";[2] they not only rebutted each charge against America by pointing to similar British failings, but attacked such characteristic English vices as exploitation of the people by the decadent remnants of a feudal aristocracy. But the anti-American periodicals in Britain were now in full cry, with such characteristic criticisms as: "The North American Republicans are the most vain, egotistical, insolent, rodomontade sort of people that are anywhere to be found", and "The greater number of States declare it to be unconstitutional to refer to the providence of God in any of their public acts."[3] Men, like Robert Walsh Jr., Alexander H. Everett, Christopher Gore, and Joshua E. White, and periodicals, like the *North American Review,* now counter-attacked violently; White, a Southerner, denounced the blot of the British factory system, and Walsh, in a comprehensive onslaught, attacked British mercantilism, the English origins of the slave trade, Britain's treatment of Catholics, paupers and imprisoned persons, her brutal love of prize and cock fighting, and the corruption of her courts and legislature. He also emphasized the proper American defence against charges of lack of civilization, that the hands of the American people were all too full for cultural activities, in their conquest of the wilderness, which was a task of whose magnitude and difficulty Englishmen had no conception.

[1] McMaster, V, pp. 313-14.   [2] Ibid, p. 313.
[3] *Quarterly Review:* Q. ibid, pp. 315-6

It was when the battle was at its height that, at the hands of Sydney Smith, the chorus of denunciation enjoyed its only moments of artistic immortality. In the *Edinburgh Review* for the quarter beginning December, 1818, he had reviewed four books of travel in America—the usual source of misunderstanding, be it noted—and had begun with genuine praise for America's achievements of expansion and democratization. He had proceeded, however, to point out that, apart from a few small pieces, "Native literature the Americans have none. It is all imported. . . . But why should the Americans write books when a six weeks' passage brings them in their own tongue our sense, science and genius in bales and hogsheads? Prairies, steamboats, grist-mills, are their natural objects for centuries to come. By and by, when they have got to the Pacific Ocean, they may have epic poems, plays, pleasures of memory, and all the elegant gratifications proper to an ancient people who have tamed the wild earth and sat down to amuse themselves."[1] This, McMaster writes, was "galling enough": why was it so? It had an appearance of truth, and was couched in characteristic Sydney Smith terms, but it grossly under-emphasized the speed of America's conquest of the continent (although it was early days yet), and it emphasized to an uncomfortable degree the truth of America's cultural dependence upon the erstwhile mother country. Possibly these things might have been forgiven, but the attack on slavery which followed was not. "What is freedom where all are not free? . . . Let the world judge which is the more liable to censure, we who in the midst of our rottenness, have torn off the manacles of the slaves all over the world, or they who, with their idle purity and useless perfection, have remained mute and careless while groans echoed and whips cracked around the very walls of their spotless Congress". This cut a great deal too near the bone not to damage American self-esteem seriously, and it seemed to his readers in the United States that Smith was guilty of an extreme complacency, considering that slavery was not abolished in the British Colonies until 1833.

But the portly cleric—who was not only a wit but accounted a liberal in his own land—had not yet hurled his last shaft. In the first quarter of 1820 appeared the most famous of his attacks upon America. Beginning with a résumé of the material and political achievements of the United States, he declared:

Such is the land of Jonathan, and thus has it been governed. In his honest endeavours to better his condition and in his manly purpose of

[1] Q. McMaster, V, p. 318.

147

resisting injury and insult we most cordially sympathize. Thus far we are friends and admirers of Jonathan. But he must not grow vain and ambitious, or allow himself to be dazzled by that galaxy of epithets by which his orators and newspaper scribblers endeavour to persuade their supporters that they are the greatest, the most refined, the most enlightened, and the most moral people upon earth. The effect of this is unspeakably ludicrous on this side of the Atlantic. . . . During the thirty or forty years of their independence they have done absolutely nothing for the sciences, for the arts, for literature, or even for the statesmanlike studies of politics or political economy. . . . In the four quarters of the globe, who reads an American book? or goes to an American play? or looks at an American picture or statue? What does the world yet owe to American physicians or surgeons? What new substances have their chemists discovered, or what old ones have they analysed? What new constellations have been discovered by the telescopes of Americans? What have they done in the mathematics? Who drinks out of American glasses? or eats from American plates? or wears American coats or gowns? or sleeps in American blankets? Finally, under which of the old tyrannical governments of Europe is every sixth man a slave whom his fellow-creatures may buy and sell and torture?[1]

One American might write in 1819: "We attach too much consequence to these attacks. They cannot do us any essential injury. . . . We have but to live on, and every day we live a whole volume of refutation",[2] but one can sympathize with the bitter resentment of the majority of his countrymen. Even when the English were being restrained, according to their own standards, they could not avoid the appearance of lofty condescension which Americans detested even more than outright abuse. Thus later numbers of the *Edinburgh Review* tried to smooth things down, but did so in such a patronizing manner as merely to add to the offence. Characteristic of this softer, yet no less irritating, approach was an article in *The New Monthly Magazine and Literary Journal* of February, 1821, which was obviously intended to be friendly:

Now, the generality of Englishmen know of their own knowledge that in this country America is not the object of hatred and contempt. On the contrary, we take a very anxious interest in all that relates to her. We feel the endearing influence of consanguinity in all its force. . . . Many generations must pass away and great changes in our common sentiments and relations mark the close of each before a contest between America and Great Britain can be anything else than what the late one was—an

[1] Q. McMaster, V, pp. 328-30.
[2] Q. J. L. Mesick, *The English Traveller in America* (New York, 1922), p. 285.

unnatural civil war. We cannot but feel that the character of the principles and institutions that most attach us to our own country is vitally connected with the moral and political destiny of the United States; that, in spite of the violent separations . . . the Americans of future times will be regarded by the world as a race either of improved or degenerate Englishmen.

Thus there came a sting in the tail, but that was not the end of it.

"Other nations boast of what they are or have been, but the true citizen of the United States exalts his head to the skies in the contemplation of what the grandeur of his country is going to be." Though Americans are not prone to understatement of their own virtues (or of anything) what else should they do? "Others appeal to history; an American appeals to prophecy"—and very accurate the prophecy in many respects—"and with Malthus in one hand and a map of the back country in the other he boldly defies us to a comparison with America as she is to be and chuckles in delight over the splendors the geometrical ratio is to shed over her story. . . . If an English traveller complains of their inns and hints his dislike to sleeping four in a bed he is first denounced as a calumniator and then told to wait a hundred years and see the superiority of American inns to the British." And very superior they are in 1952. "If Shakespeare, Milton, Newton, are named, he is again told to 'wait till we have cleared our land, till we have idle time to attend to other things; wait till 1900, and then see how much nobler our poets and profounder our astronomers and longer our telescopes than any that decrepit old hemisphere of yours will produce'." It is true that T. S. Eliot moved to England, but there remains Palomar. "The American propensity to look forward with confidence to the future greatness of their country may be natural and laudable. But when they go further and refer to the wished-for period as one in which the glory of England shall be extinguished forever, their hopes become absurdities. . . . Let us suppose the time arrived when American fleets shall cover every sea and ride in every harbor for purposes of commerce, of chastisement, or protection; when the land shall be the seat of freedom, learning, taste, morals, all that is most admirable in the eyes of man, and when England, sinking under the weight of years and the manifold casualties by which the pride of empires is levelled in the dust, shall have fallen from her high estate." An uncomfortably true vision, albeit a distorted one, of the mid-twentieth century reality. "In that day of her extremity . . . might an Englishman . . . not truly say: America has reason to be proud; but let her not forget whence came the original stock of glory she has laid out to such good account. . . . America can achieve no glory in which England has not a share."[1]

Here indeed was the rub. Independent though the two nations now were politically, they were indissolubly joined by their common history, traditions and culture; as members of the same family the common effects of their childhood could never be eradicated, and constituted a peculiar and powerful bond between them. These were the fundamental facts. To them was added the English vexation, albeit concealed to some extent, at the original loss of the United States and at their surprising subsequent successes; this was increased by the exaggerated American claims to cultural equality, and fanned by the mischief-making reports of many of Britain's travellers. The British attitude was, therefore, a mixture of reluctant admiration, some envy of America's future, and an unwise emphasis on Britain's power over the lives even of independent Americans. These things rubbed the people of the United States on the raw. Conscious also of the common bonds, they were highly sensitive to their extreme cultural and economic dependence upon a mother country from whom it was their greatest pride to be politically independent. Knowing deep in their bones the tremendous future that was in their grasp and believing that Englishmen, in their ignorance, hugely underestimated their achievements, Americans resented their cultural subservience, while at the same time forced in honesty to continue it till they produced work as good. Psychologically men always tend to resent dependence, particularly when the person depended upon is not slow to point out its existence. Into this explosive atmosphere came the spark of war in 1812, the most inconclusive and one of the least bloody of wars; the national passions were not, happily, purged by victory or defeat or exhaustion, and when the peace came they found vent in the storm of ill-feeling which we have described.

In time the storm died down. America began to stand on her own feet and to obtain recognition of the fact in Britain. The works of Irving and Cooper appeared, and were successful on both sides of the Atlantic; Emerson gained the respect of other Britons besides Carlyle; the full flowering of New England literature began. In other spheres, such as political economy, America, with the beginning of protectionism, began to show its intellectual independence; in the works of men like Henry Carey, for instance, whose "inherited dislike of England led him to fear its industrial pre-eminence".[2] Symptomatic was the fact that in 1816 Congress actually imposed a tariff on foreign books. Between

[1] Q. McMaster, V, pp. 332-4.   [2] Parrington, III, p. 106.

1841 and 1846 at least 386 American books were reprinted in England, although many of them were for export to the United States. From this time forward the predominant factor in the betterment of feeling between English and American men of letters was the growth of America's contribution to the common culture.

But the improvement was very slow. The warning of the *North American Review* in 1824, that if the campaign of abuse went on it would "turn into bitterness the last drops of good-will toward England that exist in the United States,"[1] had been heeded none too soon. The literary travellers kept the skies dark, at least, according to Nevins, until 1845, and their task was made easier by the American financial crisis of the second quarter of the century. Nor did the vexed question of copyright improve English literary tempers, for pirated editions of English novels made their appearance in their cheap thousands within a matter of hours of the arrival of the first editions in America; this situation became so intolerable that in 1836 fifty-six English authors vainly petitioned Congress for copyright legislation. This financial loss, combined with that from repudiated investments, proved too much for Dickens, whose *American Notes* of his visit in 1842 gave free rein to his opinions of America, which also found expression in *Martin Chuzzlewit*. Though his reputation across the Atlantic was eventually restored before his last visit, the copyright question was not settled till after his death, by a Congressional law of 1891. The lack of it before that date was, as G. S. Gordon points out,[2] not only maddening to English authors, but highly detrimental to Americans who had to compete with English works sold at cut-throat prices. As an Englishman said to Emerson: "As long as you do not grant us Copyright we shall have the teaching of you."[3]

By the thirties, however, "England seemed settling into the attitude of distrust and slight disdain which characterized her views of America for so much of the nineteenth century. . . . Most reviewers gave to American writings all the praise they deserved, but they so mixed with this a modicum of censure that the flavor of the whole mass was tainted."[4] This legacy of the great literary battle has only ceased to be of importance, if indeed it has ceased to be so, after the passage of fully a century. That it was such an unconscionable long time a-dying was partly due to the facts of the situation, to the relatively high quality and quantity of British output, to the continued slowness of American

---

[1] Q. Mencken, p. 23.
[2] *Anglo-American Literary Relations* (Oxford, 1942), pp. 82-98.
[3] Works, II, p. 16.   [4] Cairns, Part II, p. 57.

cultural development, and to her continued sense of British cultural leadership—and partly to an obstinate British determination to cling to almost the only form of pre-eminence left to her in the face of American competition.

But steadily the ill will did abate, and the puffs and squalls of anger and resentment became fewer and weaker. America's intellectual maturity approached; Walt Whitman and Mark Twain were fully and truly American, the latter in particular, with "everything European fallen away, the last shred of feudal culture gone, local and western yet continental."[1] But not all the dependence upon Europe, and Britain especially, disappeared; this was very true of the East, for there were two reactions among intellectuals to the Gilded Age, one to demand reform, the other to revive the tradition of deference to the Old World. Henry Cabot Lodge wrote: "Our literary standards, our standards of statesmanship, our modes of thought . . . were as English as the trivial customs of the dinner table and the ballroom",[2] and in some American intellectuals, notably Henry James, the reaction took the form of a desire to escape, which was naturally resented by many of their countrymen. William Archer could write as late as 1900: "I am much mistaken if there is a single club in London where American periodicals are so well represented on the reading-room table as are English periodicals in every club in New York."[3] But English influence came to be less irritating in proportion as America was able to reciprocate. Men like E. L. Godkin, who went to America in 1856 at the age of 25, might be equipped, as he was, with the complete social philosophy of J. S. Mill, but they remained in the United States to make their life, which was balm to Americans' wounded pride. Equally satisfying was the work of such a man as James Bryce, with the publication in 1888 of his great and friendly masterpiece, *The American Commonwealth*. But most satisfying of all, as the century closed, was the knowledge of a growing galaxy of American stars whose light shines too in Britain, like John Dewey, William James, Oliver Wendell Holmes, Thorstein Veblen, Frederick Jackson Turner, William Dean Howells and Marion Crawford. This was reflected in the fact that by 1903 at least ten firms of English publishers were importing American books on a substantial and ever-increasing scale. From this time forward there was a steadily growing intimacy between the two peoples in art and letters. As H. W. Nevinson declaimed in 1922, "Goodbye Americans! I am going to a land very much like yours. I am going to your spiritual home."[4]

[1] Parrington, III, p. 86.   [2] Curti, p. 522.
[3] Q. Heindel, pp. 22-3.   [4] Q. Nevins, p. 555.

CHAPTER SIX

EMOTIONAL BONDS

Hard as certain of the other aspects of Anglo-American relations are to assess with accuracy, the emotional is much the most difficult to describe and to evaluate. Not only must the predilections of the writer hinder balanced judgment, but there are immense obstacles in the way of accurate generalizations about human emotions, even in the case of individuals, let alone of whole nations. This is true of a nation like Great Britain, which is homogeneous and unified in a high degree, but it is doubly so of one which, like the United States, is bewildering in the variety of its origins, surroundings and circumstances. J. F. Muirhead in his *Land of Contrasts,* published in 1898, wisely wrote that the object of his book would be "achieved, if it convinces a few Britons of the futility of generalizing on the complex organism of American society from inductions that would not justify an opinion about the habits of a piece of protoplasm."[1] From time to time glaring examples of the disregard of this salutary advice thrust themselves upon the attention; Geoffrey Gorer's *The Americans* is a supreme instance of the nemesis which overtakes even observant and perspicuous men who rush into complex social problems and emerge hastily with simple "scientific" solutions. The many notes of interest which he strikes are utterly vitiated by the fact that he raises upon the precarious pinpoint apex of a neo-Freudian theory of universal American "father rejection" a vast inverted pyramid of unsubstantiated conclusions. The writer may, therefore, be pardoned if he approaches such questions with the utmost caution.

Yet approached they must be, for human actions are very frequently emotional; this is true of national as well as of individual decisions— no one who witnessed the career of Adolf Hitler can have any doubt of that—and we must therefore hazard some generalizations about national emotions, for in international affairs we have, to some extent, to live by such conclusions. It is peculiarly necessary to do so in the case of peoples who have advanced to democracy for, as Mahan pointed out in the germinating years of Anglo-American friendship, in nations

[1] Q. Nevins, p. 531.

153

"of more complex organization . . . the wills of the citizens have to be brought not to submission merely, but to accord."[1] It has been a commonplace, at least since 1820 when Castlereagh spoke the words, that "there are no two states whose friendly relations are of more practical value to each other and whose hostility so inevitably and so immediately entails upon both the most serious mischiefs [than] . . . the British and American nations".[2] With the development of full-blown democracy and the re-entry of America into world affairs, the feelings of the two peoples towards one another have become of crucial importance to the destiny of mankind, and it behoves us to venture some discussion of them. Nor is the way unlighted nor all the precedents discouraging; whatever the obstacles, men like Bryce and Brogan have brilliantly overcome them, and may help us to do so. But we cannot hope in the space of a brief chapter even to hint at all the important facts in a subject which has filled many books and could fill many more. We shall try merely to indicate in what ways the predominant cast of Anglo-American feeling has altered since 1783, and to show how complex, unstable, and often transient, are the movements lying behind these general changes.

I

THE writer is emboldened to generalization by the undoubted fact of common national reactions to the phenomena of other lands. Shortly after returning from his first visit to the United States in 1946, he read J. B. Priestley's *Midnight on the Desert,* and was powerfully struck by the identical impressions made upon him and upon Priestley by a multitude of things American both great and small, despite the passage, since the book was published, of a decade which altered much in life on both sides of the Atlantic. These impressions were not merely of things physical—the contrast, for instance, between the overwhelming antiquity of the western deserts and the neoterism of humanity; or the fabulous nature of the Grand Canyon. Nor yet only of the works of men—the ubiquity of the advertisement in American life, the shoddy untidiness of much of the countryside, the superb magnificence of Boulder Dam, or "that long dissonant, mournful cry of American trains, that sound which seems to light up for a second the immense

---

[1] Q. Forrest Davis, *The Atlantic System* (New York, 1941), p. 27.

[2] W.F.R., title page.

distances and loneliness of that country."[1] They were impressions also of the American people themselves—the combination of individual kindness and mass heartlessness in American life, the lack of a feeling of security, the sense of harsh realities not far beneath the surface of things, the emphasis on individualism and yet the lack of individuality, the extent of anti-Semitism in America, or the bizarre culture of Southern California, where a neon sign "Psychologist," recalled by Priestley, matched one recalled by the writer, "Jesus Saves." Some changes were visible even in ten years—a growth in appreciation of art and music, for example, and a diversification of the economy of Southern California—but a surprising amount remained the same.

Similarly, one can take courage from the correspondence of so many American views of Britain; a multitude of Americans have been impressed by the sort of things that are recorded, for instance, by Margaret Halsey in *With Malice Toward Some,* published in 1938. The smallness of English trains and the diminutive scale of the patchwork countryside (Robert Benchley once said that the British "take pleasure in such tiny, tiny things"[2]); the splendour of English flowers; the Stygian gloom of the English Sunday; the waitress who, when asked by adults for a glass of milk, shakes her head and says, "You Americans!" (the writer once blurted out that Englishmen never drink milk after they have "grown up"); the English "blend of shabbiness and imperturbable good nature"[3] (Emerson noted a century earlier that the English were "good-natured",[4] and that an English lord "dresses a little worse than a commoner"[5]); the wonder constituted by polite English children; the courtesy of English railway porters, and the horror of English railway stations (an appalled American of the writer's acquaintance habitually referred to Euston as the Hall of Death); the rural English refusal to recognize the existence of English industrialism; the constant English criticism and jealousy of America: "They have just one big blanket indictment of America. It isn't England"; the masculine dominion in English society; the lack of high pressure salesmanship in British stores; and the placidity of English life compared with American, where there is so much more violence, "a good deal in England makes the blood boil, but there is not nearly so much occasion as there is in America for blood to run cold."[6] Here again, the war has wrought

[1] J. B. Priestley, *Midnight on the Desert* (London, 1937), p. 2.

[2] Q. Alistair Cooke, *Letters from America* (London, 1951), p. 113.

[3] Margaret Halsey, *With Malice Toward Some* (London, 1938), p. 53.

[4] Mowat, *Americans in England,* p. 134.

[5] Works, II, p. 57.   [6] Halsey, pp. 201, 239.

changes—the courtesy of porters is not now so marked and placidity has almost degenerated into inertia—but much remains unaltered.

Nor are such generalizations as these altogether invalid over longer stretches of time. Some English comments upon America run like a recurrent theme through almost the whole history of the two peoples. The wooden houses of Americans have been remarked upon by travellers from Cobbett to the present day; their rocking chairs and their abundant use of ice for almost as long a period; the wonders of the New England fall make a universal impression ("Lord Bryce, not a reticent man about American vices, couldn't trust his English reserve to speak properly about its virtues. Lloyd George confessed after his only trip to America that no matter how inconclusive his political mission he would at least go home remembering the overwhelming experience of the fall. A hundred years ago, Mrs. Trollope, who liked very little about these United States, broke down and wrote that at this season of the year 'the whole country goes to glory'."); the lack of privacy which was bemoaned by Basil Hall on the river steamboats is regretted by J. F. Muirhead in railroad sleeping-cars; the power of the Press and the persistence of its reporters is noted from Dickens to Priestley; the heat of the houses is constantly the subject of comment by Englishmen, so that even Henry James installed central heating in his English home, and could report, "my poor little house is now really warm—even hot"[2]; their headlong hurry is almost universally decried from the earliest times, even before Thackeray wrote: "There is some electric influence in the air and sun here which we don't experience on our side of the globe; people can't sit still, people can't ruminate over their dinners, dawdle in their studies, they must keep moving"[3]; there is even more universal praise for their "crushing hospitality"; the allegedly high rate of dyspepsia among them frequently calls forth amateur diagnoses and no doubt equally erroneous suggestions for cure; but the one persistent trait for which there is never any sympathy is the chewing and spitting habits of the land dubbed by Rupert Brooke, "El Cuspidorado".[4]

There are also constant strains in the comments of Americans about England during the last century and three-quarters. Gouverneur Morris commented on the stiffness of English manners, and Fenimore Cooper on their proneness to silence, but both found friendship beneath the somewhat forbidding exterior; Morris lamented English cooking, and

[1] Cooke, p. 151.   [2] Q. Mowat, p. 225.
[3] *The Virginians* (London, 1899), p. xvii.
[4] Rupert Brooke, *Letters from America* (London, 1916), p. 4.

more than a century later that great Anglophile W. H. Page wrote, "they have only three vegetables and two of them are cabbages"; Cooper's complaints about the English weather found a similar echo in Page: "In this aquarium in which we live . . . it rains every day"[1]; the London fog comes in for almost as much condemnation as the English rain, although G. H. Putnam spoke of the rush of reminiscence produced by "a whiff of that wonderful compound of soot, fog and roast mutton that go to the making of the atmosphere of London"[2]; Cooper experienced, upon seeing the White Cliffs of Dover for the first time, a common American feeling of being "home"; Hawthorne also struck a familiar, but more unpleasant, note, when he said: "These people think so loftily of themselves and so contemptuously of everybody else, that it requires more generosity than I possess to keep always in perfectly good humour with them"; he also found the deadweight of English rural tradition, where "Life is . . . fossilized in its greenest leaf", very distasteful, and declared that it was better to endure the ceaseless changes of the New World than this "monotony of sluggish ages"[3]; yet, as Emerson admired the orderliness of English life, so Hawthorne loved its scenery, which presented a "perfect balance between man and nature"[4]; almost as many Americans have commented adversely upon the dirt of English barbers' shops, as (from Emerson to Santayana) favourably upon the domesticity of the English; and there has been continuous and universal contempt for the "abject"[5] servility involved in the English social system.

II

SOME generalizations about the mutual feelings of the British and American peoples are, then, possible. In the formation of those feelings their attitude to one another's institutions and ideas is clearly of primary importance, and those attitudes have been conditioned by the quantity and quality of the information upon which they were based. Walter Page could still write during his ambassadorship, after many years of mutual indoctrination by such bodies as the Anglo-American Association (1871), the Anglo-American League (1898), and The Pilgrims (1901): "The longer I live here the more astonished I become at the fundamental ignorance of the British about us and at our funda-

---

[1] Q. Burton J. Hendrick, *The Life and Letters of Walter H. Page* (London, 1923), I, p. 158.   [2] Q. Mowat, p. 203.

[3] Q. ibid. pp. 162, 171.   [4] Q. ibid, p. 169.   [5] Page, p. 155.

mental ignorance about them."[1] The position has improved since then, but to one who has specialized to any extent in Anglo-American history new examples are repeatedly forthcoming. Another Anglo-American Ambassador, Lord Halifax, pointed to one deficiency as late as 1947: "The teaching of American history in British schools too often ends at Yorktown, as the teaching of American history in American schools too often begins with Bunker Hill. . . . It might be said . . . that Anglo-American history was for Englishmen to learn and for Americans to rewrite."[2] Nevertheless, it remains true that American knowledge of Britain has always far exceeded her knowledge of any other country, and that British knowledge of America has improved out of all recognition in this century, and is now, perhaps, with the advent of the mass media of information, approaching its counterpart in quantity.

There are two main sources of such knowledge; direct, through travel and reports thereof, and indirect, through culture. In the case of direct knowledge the two peoples have perhaps been on an equal footing; in the case of indirect, the Americans were at first at an unquestionable advantage, though in recent years the English have probably been able to reverse this situation and learn more about the United States. But in any case the common language has always made mutual knowledge far easier than it normally is between different nations. It was no isolated instance when Nathaniel Hawthorne, steeped in English literature, wrote: "Almost always, in visiting such scenes as I have been attempting to describe, I had a singular sense of having been there before"[3]; familiarity with England through the reading of English literature is a factor of the utmost importance in American understanding of Britain. Not that it is always without disadvantages; it often renders information out of date and misleading. To Henry Adams on his first visit to London, "Aristocracy was real. So was the England of Dickens. Oliver Twist and Little Nell lurked in every churchyard shadow. . . . In November, 1858, . . . it was the London of the eighteenth century that an American felt and hated."[4] Frequently, too, as we have seen, Americans reacted against this cultural bondage, as witness the oration of an American schoolboy heard by Captain Basil Hall in 1827-8: "Gratitude! Gratitude to England! What does America owe to her? . . . We owe her nothing! For eighteen hundred years the world had slumbered in ignorance of liberty. . . . At length, America arose in all her glory, to give the world the long-desired lesson."[5]

[1] Q. W.A.A.E., ix.   [2] *Anglo-American Relations*, pp. 6-7.
[3] Q. Mowat, pp. 159-160.
[4] *Education of Henry Adams*, pp. 72-3.   [5] Q. Nevins, p. 119.

But in the end the balance of true knowledge outweighed the distortions and the emotional rejections.

Perhaps the most reliable gauge of Anglo-American feeling is to be found among the travellers between the two lands, and here the historian of Anglo-American relations is fortunate enough to find two monographs on the subject ready to his hand. Allan Nevins in his excellent analysis and anthology, *America through British Eyes,* gives a most comprehensive account of American social history as seen by British travellers, which throws much light on the emotional relationship between the two peoples. He sees the subject as falling into five main periods, each in its turn broadly reflecting, with one exception, that ripening of friendship over the years, which we know to be one of the main features of Anglo-American relations. The first period, from 1783 to about 1825, he characterizes as one of utilitarian enquiry, which marked a distinct improvement after the hatred of the Revolutionary period; the tone of reports was on the whole factual and just. Men like Henry Wansey, interested in American woollen manufacture, Henry B. Fearon, investigating for the settlement of twenty English families, George Glover, who laid out a number of English settlements in Illinois, John Woods, one of those Illinois settlers, and William Cobbett, best known to American readers as *Peter Porcupine,* set the tone of commentary, and drowned out the ill-natured accounts of unreliables, like Thomas Ashe and Isaac Weld, and simpletons, like William Faux.

Unfortunately, in the second period, from about 1825 to 1845, the hyper-critical and malicious voices gained the mastery, and the result was a distinct deterioration in Anglo-American feeling. The outburst of mutual ill-will, which we have seen in the cultural sphere after the War of 1812, was both reflected and caused by the new type of traveller; "instead of seekers after a living, there came seekers after new sights and experiences."[1] Political passions also played their part, for men like Captain Marryat, Captain Thomas Hamilton and Godfrey T. Vigne, while admitting the necessity of democracy in America, bitterly opposed its extension to Britain; their criticisms were made more telling by the fact that, with the advent of Jacksonian Democracy, the tone of American political life had deteriorated in comparison with that of patrician days. Furthermore, the visitors tended to penetrate farther west, where conditions were worst; it was the western experiences of *Martin Chuzzlewit* that were the most unpleasant, and it was Dickens's description of them that Americans found it hardest to forgive, because,

[1] Nevins, p. 111.

159

although they contained much that was true to life, they were at once the most characteristically American and yet—however unpleasant—the most indispensable for the development of the country. Above all, because the new travellers included so many authors in search of literary material, American weaknesses were exposed with merciless and often consummate skill. Dickens was not mealy-mouthed at home, and, though his *American Notes* were not so very harsh, they seemed immensely so, because of his popularity in America, and because, with unerring instinct, he put his finger on the tenderest spots in American life, such as slavery. Dickens had, in fact, a number of very appreciative things to say, as did others like Hamilton, Marryat, Thackeray and Charles Augustus Murray, while Harriet Martineau, after careful and searching investigation, was full of praise for many aspects of American society. Unfortunately, men are prone to remember criticism and to forget praise, and Americans in particular, conscious of the newness of their nation, have always been acutely sensitive to criticism—much more so throughout their history than the smug British, long inured to abuse—and never more so than in these formative years of what Tocqueville called "irritable patriotism", when English criticism was most virulent and supercilious.

The tone of it was unhappily set by critics like Basil Hall, and above all, Mrs. Trollope, whom Nevins justly describes as a "censorious harridan."[1] Her son, who made amends for his mother's bitterness in his own account of America later, described her *Domestic Manners of the Americans* as "somewhat unjust . . . to our cousins over the water", and as one of those works which have "created laughter on one side of the Atlantic, and soreness on the other."[2] Her pen was veritably dipped in gall: "I do not like their principles, I do not like their manners, I do not like their opinions". Her supercilious assumption of English superiority struck Americans, as always, on the raw; religious "[p]ersecution exists [in America] to a degree unknown, I believe, in our well-ordered land since the days of Cromwell": it would be hard to pack more, calculated to pain Americans, into a single short sentence. Her absolute want of sympathy may be explained by her personal difficulties; it may even be pardoned to her for the gallant struggle she made to support and bring up her family, but it cannot be forgotten. Her ill-humoured comment on American lawlessness contrasts too painfully with the later good humour of, for example, G. K. Chesterton. She wrote: "In England the laws are acted upon, in America they are

[1] Nevins, pp. 3, 114.
[2] Evan John, *Atlantic Impact, 1861* (London, 1952), p. 12.

not"[1]; his words were: "The Americans may go mad when they make laws, but they recover their reason when they disobey them."[2]

But before the tolerance of Chesterton could replace the contumely of Mrs. Trollope a respite was needed. This was provided by the years from approximately 1845 to 1870, a period of narration and description, or what Nevins calls unbiased portraiture. Akin in tone to the first years of the relationship, its accounts are less practical in object and wider in scope, but the "incorrect and caricatured"[3] reports, as William E. Baxter called them, fall into disrepute. There are still some hostile voices, such as Edward Sullivan, Hugh Seymour Tremenheere, and Nassau William Senior, but they are once more drowned out by those of juster critics, such as Sir Charles Lyall, Lord Carlisle, Colonel Arthur Cunynghame, Lady Emmeline Stuart Wortley and Mrs. Houston. Most significant were the serious and encyclopedic works of James Silk Buckingham, and, above all, Alexander Mackay. Despite the differences of opinion in the Civil War between such men as W. H. Russell, who believed the Union could never be restored, and Edward Dicey, who was much more favourable to the North, nearly all Englishmen tended to be well disposed towards the United States as a whole. This was very true of such representatives of the British working class as James D. Burn in his book, *The Working Classes in the United States*. Without doubt this was to a considerable extent due to the growing English realization of the potential power of America. As Eliot Warburton wrote in 1846: "Most of the present generation among us have been brought up and lived in the idea that England is supreme in the Congress of Nations . . . but . . . this giant son will soon tread on his parent's heels."[4]

By 1870 Britain was almost overtaken, and there began the first period of serious and comprehensive analysis, of the quality as well as the scale of which the mere list of the leading names gives ample proof: Rudyard Kipling, James Bryce, H. G. Wells, Matthew Arnold, Herbert Spencer, E. A. Freeman, Frederic Harrison, Arnold Bennett, and G. K. Chesterton. In this era a second Mrs. Trollope, Sir Lepel Griffin, was a curious anomaly, whose name is lost to all but the specialist. Not that the British were no longer critical. Bryce himself, the greatest figure of them all in Anglo-American relations, made plain his dislike of corruption in politics. Arnold, as might be expected, found plenty of the same Philistinism that he denounced at home. Spencer and

[1] Q. Nevins, p. 116.
[2] *What I Saw in America* (New York, 1922), p. 254.
[3] Q. Nevins, p. 283.   [4] Q. Nevins, p. 290.

Kipling echo the criticism of political corruption. Wells spoke out against the extreme manifestations of capitalism which were equally his target in Britain. But the criticisms were based on sound information and were much more just and balanced as a result; what is more, almost all the signs of offensive superciliousness have disappeared, and an increasing warmth of appreciation pervades the whole. Bryce's massive work is instinct with admiration for the United States. Bennett's account was acute and friendly, and Chesterton's amiable despite the wildness of his paradoxes—"this land had really been an asylum; even if recent legislation . . . had made" some people "think it a lunatic asylum."[1] Wells paid tribute to the "enormous scale of this American destiny."[2] Some works by lesser figures were important because of their thoroughness, such as James F. Muirhead's *America the Land of Contrasts,* or their enthusiasm, such as William Archer's *America To-day* and W. T. Stead's *Americanization of the World,* all three published between 1898 and 1902. Even Kipling, who did not mince matters—he characterized the American spittoon as "of infinite capacity and generous gape"[3] and remarked of an American boom town: "The papers tell their readers in language fitted to their comprehension that the snarling together of telegraph wires, the heaving up of houses, and the making of money, is progress"[4]—declared:

> Let there be no misunderstanding about the matter. I love this People, and if any contemptuous criticism has to be done, I will do it myself . . . I admit everything. Their Government's provisional; their law's the notion of the moment . . . and most of their good luck lives in their woods and mines and rivers and not in their brains; but for all that, they be the biggest, finest, and best people on the surface of the globe! Just you wait a hundred years. . . . There is nothing known to man that he will not be, and his country will sway the world with one foot as a man tilts a see-saw plank![5]

To such criticism Americans did not find it too hard to reconcile themselves.

The fifth and final period continued this process of amelioration; from World War I onwards, and particularly during World War II, good feeling grew apace under the influence of the increasing likenesses between the two societies. There were still discordant cries, but a new

[1] *What I Saw in America,* p. 48.
[2] Nevins, p. 451.   [3] Q. ibid, p. 447.
[4] Kipling, *From Sea to Sea and Other Sketches* (London, 1900), II, p. 154.
[5] Ibid, pp. 130-1.

note of respect and admiration for many aspects of American life tends to be dominant. As Priestley, who was by no means unreserved in his praise, put it in 1936: "America is definitely in front. She hardly knows she is leading us, but she is. Russia can turn the old economic and political system upside down, but no sooner has she done so than she takes a long look at America. One country after another follows suit."[1] As the number of travellers increased, so did the flow of books, many of them ephemeral. But there was a residue of works of permanent value, pre-eminent among them *The American Political System* of D. W. Brogan, who worthily continued the work of Bryce. Others were those of J. A. Spender, who almost erred on the side of charity to the Americans in *The America of Today* (1928); of L. P. Jacks, *My American Friends* (1933), who displays that insight which is so characteristic of his other works; and of Graham Hutton, *Midwest at Noon* (1946), who depicts the Middle West in a fascinating period of change from isolationism to something nearer to an active will to participate in international affairs. Most English commentators were impressed by the fact that the New Deal brought the two countries into much closer accord, but the dominant impression, particularly after 1940, is of the growing strength and increasing warmth of Anglo-American friendship.

The picture painted by R. B. Mowat of American travellers' views of Britain, *Americans in England,* is much less comprehensive than that of Nevins. Nevertheless, it makes it obvious that the attitude of American travellers has changed very much less over the years. In the first place, because American travellers to Britain were of the wealthier classes, they tended to be sympathetic to the English for cultural reasons; indeed, "background" was what they were usually seeking. Because so much American business was in British hands, there were relatively few American business men in England in earlier days, and these might have constituted the most critical section of the well-to-do American public. This meant that there was never a very bad period in American opinion of Britain comparable with British opinion of America in the second quarter of the nineteenth century. The mere list of early American travellers, who left a mark, indicates their sympathetic attitude; Gouverneur Morris, the Federalist, who described the "madness" of war in 1812 as the work of men, "who for more than twenty years have lavished on Britain the bitterest vulgarity of Billingsgate because she impressed her seamen for self-defence"; the cosmo-

[1] *Midnight in the Desert,* p. 88.

politan and Anglophile Washington Irving, who painted so romantic a picture of English society; Fenimore Cooper, who, though less sympathetic, seemed to be won over despite himself to something like respect, and even wrote on one occasion that "the English gentleman stands at the head of his class in Christendom"; Emerson, who retained many close British friendships, such as that with Carlyle, for over forty years; and Nathaniel Hawthorne, who said: "I seldom came into personal relations with an Englishman without beginning to like him, and feeling my favourable impression wax stronger with the progress of the acquaintance. I never stood in an English crowd without being conscious of hereditary sympathies."[1] These men found many things in Britain to condemn, and did so freely, but they were altogether more restrained in their criticism or more sympathetic in their approach— showed, not to put too fine a point on it, better manners—than their opposite numbers. Though the correspondent of the *New York Observer* who wrote in 1831, "England to an American is not foreign", exaggerated, Henry Adams spoke for his countrymen who visited England when he wrote later: "Considering that I lose all patience with the English about fifteen times a day . . . I get on with them beautifully and love them well."[2] With the great development of friendly contacts which began in the last years of the century, the broadly sympathetic attitude of American travellers did not change materially, but simply fitted in better with the growing warmth of British views of America.

But it is a sign of the unreliability of the views of travellers as a complete guide to Anglo-American feelings, that the nineteenth century appears from them as a period of American goodwill to Britain, when in truth Anglophobia was at its height. The fact is that, though American travellers, who were few, tended to be sympathetic, the mass of the American people at home tended to be hostile; the factors which made for American hatred went deep into her history, and it was only exaggerated by her continued economic and cultural dependence on Britain. It had been born in the Revolutionary period, and had waxed under the impact of the War of 1812 and the literary battle which came afterwards; it remained a powerful influence until the middle years of the century, and a significant, though declining one, for nearly a hundred years more. Only after World War II did the slumbering animosity really seem to be sinking into the grave. There is no doubt that it had been kept alive and active by British abuse in the second quarter of the century, but that the advocacy of American travellers and Anglophiles generally had done much to hasten its demise. As

[1] Q. Mowat, pp. 70, 116, 161.   [2] Q. ibid, pp. 104, 223.

Mowat justly remarks: "[T]he American was more generous in his appreciation, and the Englishman less sensitive in his reaction."[1] Mencken puts it in a different way: "There is in the United States . . . a formidable sect of Anglomaniacs . . . but the corresponding sects of British Americophils is small and feeble though it shows a few respectable names."[2] Though this contains some truth—that Anglophiles in America were vigorous and outspoken, partly because of the challenge of widespread and violent Anglophobia—it is not correct to deny the importance of English Americophils, for one of the characteristics of Anglo-American history is that there has always been a group in each country strongly advocating the cause of co-operation with the other. Successors to the English Whigs and the American Tories of the Revolution have never been lacking, although for many decades they tended to be small minorities amongst their own people. The progress of Anglo-American friendship has in fact consisted in turning those minorities into majorities; majorities were achieved somewhere near the end of the nineteenth century, and by the middle of the twentieth, they had become overwhelming.

The course of this development was not the same in England as in America. The pro-American elements had, until the coming of democracy in the last half of the nineteenth century, been a radical and progressive minority, instead of, as in America, a conservative one. Though the American Anglophile group was predominantly wealthy, there were among the pro-American British radicals a number of great Whig aristocrats, like the first Lord Lansdowne, "full of love and kindness for America".[3] Nor was the mass of the British people ever anti-American, in the way that the mass of the American people was anti-British; truth to tell, the impact of America upon Britain was much less than that of Britain upon America until the last quarter of the century. Britons had other interests in plenty, and were never anything like as conscious of American shafts as were Americans of British barbs. The vast majority of Englishmen were indifferent to America until the close of the nineteenth century, all the more so because of their relative political ignorance and immaturity; in America where democracy and literacy were far ahead, the feeling against Britain was genuinely popular. It follows that the anti-American feeling of the British was largely confined to a dominant Tory minority, and that it owed its violence in considerable degree to their consciousness that the great threat to the aristocratic system they represented came from

[1] Ibid, p. 162.　[2] *The American Language*, p. 28.
[3] Gouverneur Morris: q. Mowat, p. 62.

the example of American democracy. In America it was a case of an Anglophile minority and an Anglophobe majority; in Britain of anti-American and pro-American minorities, and an indifferent majority. But as the cause of democracy triumphed, so did popular awareness of America and her increasing power grow, and so did the hold of the anti-American upper classes diminish. It was on the basis of a common democracy that Anglo-American friendship was finally built.

This much is clear. The hurricane of 1776 left the waters of Anglo-American relations vastly troubled; when it looked like blowing itself out, the turbulence was renewed by the storm of 1812 and its aftermath; after that had, by the middle of the century, died away, a calm began, slowly but steadily, to settle upon the rough waters; by 1914 only a surface swell remained, while by 1945 there was something approaching stillness; and in 1952, despite the drop in pressure in 1950, the barometer seemed to be set fair yet. But further than these generalities it is perilous to go. If we try to survey the unruly seas more closely and more accurately, the chart becomes so complex as to diminish rather than increase our understanding. The breezes and eddies, the winds and currents of Anglo-American emotions and attitudes are so disconcerting, variegated and uncertain, that they defy investigation in the short space at our disposal. To examine one only of the main cross currents of Anglo-American feeling is to become convinced that further elaboration of such a study merely adds confusion, but it is salutary to make the examination in order that we may become fully aware of how dangerous it is for Englishmen and Americans to sit in judgment upon one another.

III

LET us take, as our one example of the hazards of this subject, the familiar accusation, which buzzes insistently through Anglo-American history, of the "materialism" and "vulgarity" of the United States. The indictment was most fully drawn by Henry James: "There is but one word to use in regard to them—vulgar, vulgar, vulgar. Their ignorance—their stingy, defiant, grudging attitude towards everything European—their perpetual reference of all things to some American standard or precedent which exists only in their own unscrupulous wind-bags . . . these things glare at you hideously". But James is a just man, and, his predilections apart, sees the other point of view: "On the other hand we seem a people of *character*, we seem to have

166

energy, capacity and intellectual stuff in ample measure. What I have pointed at as our vices are the elements of the modern man with *culture* quite left out. It's the absolute and incredible lack of *culture* that strikes you in common travelling Americans."[1] Arnold Bennett, interestingly enough, gives him a lesson in tolerance of his countrymen: "But it ought to be remembered by us Europeans (and in sackcloth!) that the mass of us with money to spend on pleasure are utterly indifferent to history and art. . . . I imagine that the American horde 'hustling for culture' . . . will compare pretty favourably with the European horde in such spots as Lucerne."[2]

Nevertheless, James not only saw the other point of view, but the reason for it; in *The American* Newman says, "The fact is I have never had time to 'feel' things so very beautifully. I've had to *do* them, had to make myself felt."[3] More than that, standing as James did on the threshold of American greatness, he was aware of the part America would play, and anxious that it should be a worthy one. His apprehension comes out in the words of Mrs. Tristram to Newman: "You're the great Western Barbarian, stepping forth in his innocence and might, gazing a while at this poor corrupt old world and then swooping down on it."[4] The mutual feeling of discomfort in this period of cultural adjustment is epitomized in Newman's relationship with the Marquis, who "struck his guest as precautionary, as apprehensive; his manner seemed to indicate a fine nervous dread that something disagreeable might happen if the atmosphere were not kept clear of stray currents from windows opened at hazard. 'What under the sun is he afraid of?' Newman asked himself. 'Does he think I'm going to offer to swap jack-knives with him?' "[5] The lingering flavour of aristocracy, often sweet to Englishmen but unpalatable to Americans, is seldom absent from this question; as E. A. Freeman wrote, "the reading class . . . of those who . . . read enough and know enough to be worth talking to . . . form a larger proportion of mankind than they do in England. On the other hand, the class of those who read really deeply . . . is certainly much smaller."[6] James's predilections, however, would not be gainsayed; he became, as he said, a "cockney *convaincu*",[7] and, after moving finally to England in 1876, wrote to his brother William: "I . . . am turning English all over. I desire only to feed on English life and the contact of English minds. . . ."[8] He occasionally felt uneasy about this expatriate urge; as Roderick Hudson said: "It's a wretched

---

[1] *The Letters of Henry James*, I, pp. 22-3.   [2] Q. Nevins, p. 458.
[3] Henry James, *The American* (London), p. 37.   [4] Ibid, p. 38.
[5] Ibid, p. 185.   [6] Q. Nevins, p. 431.   [7] *Letters*, I, p. 74.   [8] Ibid, p. 54.

business . . . this virtual quarrel of ours with our own country, this ever-lasting impatience that so many of us feel to get out of it",[1] and it should be noted that Roderick succumbs to the temptations of the Old World, if in a less lurid way than Harry Warrington before him. But James was fundamentally unrepentant; in 1877 he wrote that he felt more at home now in London than anywhere else in the world, and his acceptance, at his life's end, of British citizenship at the height of World War I bore fitting witness to that fact.

But James was not alone in observing, and being fascinated by, this problem. Some saw it like him very much from the European point of view. Curiously, perhaps, Kipling was one of them, the Kipling of *Puck of Pook's Hill* and not the Kipling of *The Night Mail,* and in *An Habitation Enforced* the English countryman says : "Nah—there's no gentry in America, no matter how long you're there. It's against their law. There's only rich and poor allowed."[2] Others, like Mrs. Humphrey Ward in *Eleanor,* though seeing all round the subject, laid more emphasis on the contribution which a young, a fresh, even a naïve America might make to the progress of mankind. But even if it be accepted that some distinction of this kind exists between the two societies, to define the American attitude precisely bristles with new and complex difficulties. Supercilious Englishmen may talk of the Almighty Dollar, but the question is not as simple as that. As James makes Newman say, "If I cared for money-making, but I never cared so very terribly for the money. There was nothing else to do".[3] Chesterton pointed out that the Englishman's ideal was leisure not labour, the American's labour not dollars, and—acutely—that the American, quite apart from any love of money, has a great love of measurement. It might even be said that the snobbery of Americans is size, and the snobbery of Englishmen antiquity. The cast of mind is in some respects utterly different; as Henry Adams put it :

The English mind was one-sided, eccentric, systematically un-systematic, and logically illogical. . . . From the old-world point of view, the American had no mind; he had an economic thinking-machine which could work only on a fixed line. The American mind exasperated the European as a buzz-saw might exasperate a pine forest. . . . The American mind was . . . a mere cutting instrument, practical, economical, sharp and direct. . . . Americans needed and used their whole energy, and applied it with close economy; but English society was eccentric by law

[1] Henry James, *Roderick Hudson* (London), p. 30.
[2] Rudyard Kipling, *Actions and Reactions* (London, 1919), p. 37.
[3] *The American,* pp. 222-3.

and for the sake of the eccentricity itself. . . . Often this eccentricity bore all the marks of strength.[1]

This was not the kind of strength that America could afford: the great melting pot had to be strongly and rigidly constructed, and a ruthless pressure of public opinion—"a prairie fire"[2] Chesterton once called it— was needed to create a strong and patriotic American nation.

And the advantages were by no means all on the European side. Rowland might be able to say in *Roderick Hudson,* "But I have the misfortune to be rather an idle man, and in Europe both the burden and the obloquy of idleness are less heavy than here",[3] and reckon it in his heart of hearts a blessing for civilization that it was so; but Dickens saw another truth when he wrote: "By the way, whenever an Englishman would cry 'All right!' an American cries 'Go ahead!' which is somewhat expressive of the national character of the two countries."[4] If America owes much culturally to Britain, Britain's economic predicament at the present time can only be cured by a vigorous transfusion of the American spirit. America may be obsessed with technical progress, but technical progress is still highly necessary; as L. P. Jacks reminded his English readers as early as 1933, "standardization is a condition absolutely essential to all forms of human originality."[5] English lethargy and hidebound tradition are as suspect to Americans as American materialism is to Britons. As J. F. Muirhead wrote in 1898, "It is not easy for a European to the manner born to realize the sort of extravagant, nightmare effect that many of our social customs have in the eyes of our untutored American cousins. . . . The idea of an insignificant boy peer taking precedence of Mr. John Morley! [T]he necessity of backing out of the royal presence!"[6] And, as Henry James pointed out, the English did not take to satire against themselves quite as naturally as a duck to water: "It is an entirely new sensation for them . . . to be (at all delicately) *ironised* or satirised, from the American point of view, and they don't at all relish it. Their conception of the normal in such a relation is that the satire should be all on their side against the Americans".[7] Finally, be it noted, these differences are always rendered sharper by the fact of American overstatement and English understatement; Chesterton does not exaggerate when he writes, "But the

[1] *Education of Henry Adams,* pp. 180-1.

[2] *What I Saw in America,* p. 162.

[3] p. 66.   [4] Q. Nevins, p. 126.

[5] Q. Nevins, *America Through British Eyes* (Oxford, 1948), p. 414.

[6] Q. Nevins, *American Social History,* p. 440.   [7] *Letters,* I, p. 68.

real cross-purposes come from the contrary direction of the two exaggerations, the American making life more wild and impossible than it is, and the Englishman making it more flat and farcical than it is."[1]

Thus the complications, the reservations, the explanations, which are involved in such generalizations as this one concerning American materialism and English culture, become readily apparent. And this is not all. When such generalizations are extended in time, they become even more unreliable, and may prove simply untrue. It is not merely that in the eighteenth century an Englishman might appear overdressed in New York, and in the twentieth an American overdressed in London, nor that Fenimore Cooper in the eighteen-twenties found that his London comforts cost him a third of what they would have done in America, while Nathaniel Hawthorne in the fifties found living more expensive in London than at home. Nor is it only that, with the passage of time, the crude material basis of society becomes encrusted with the delicate evasions of civilization, so that Margaret Halsey could write with justice in 1938, "The English have refined upon our naïve American way of judging people by how much money they happen to have at the moment. The subtler English criterion is how much expensive, upper-class education they have been able to afford."[2] It is not these things alone: it may be that the whole national character has changed over the years. There are certainly, it is true, remarkable instances of continuity. It is quite fascinating, for example, to see Kipling in 1900 forestalling Aldous Huxley and Evelyn Waugh in his comments on the materialism of America's attitude to death. When he was talking to an American mortician on the subject of embalming, the undertaker said: "And I wish I could live a few generations just to see how my people keep. But I'm sure it's all right. Nothing can touch 'em after I've embalmed 'em". Kipling concludes, "Bury me cased in canvas . . . in the deep sea; burn me on a back-water of the Hughli . . . or whelm me in the sludge of a broken river dam; but may I never go down to the Pit grinning out of a plate-glass window, in a backless dress-coat, and the front half of a black stuff dressing-gown; not though I were 'held' against the ravage of the grave for ever and ever".[3] But, apart from the instances of continuity, there are also radical transformations. The America of 1929, the United States of H. L. Mencken and Sinclair Lewis, was in many ways unrecognizable to the visitor of 1946; the

[1] Q. Nevins, p. 461.   [2] *With Malice Toward Some*, p. 184.
[3] *From Sea to Sea*, II, p. 150.

development of the cultural maturity of the American people in the intervening years was phenomenal, for nothing chastens like a dose of adversity. There are many such instances, but there is in Anglo-American history one supreme example of this kind of change.

We have often had occasion to note the similarities between the two peoples, and, in particular, the way in which America has tended to assume the role played earlier by Britain. Before we accept generalizations about the materialism of the United States and our own high culture too freely, we should look at the impact made by Britain upon the rest of the world in the first half of the nineteenth century. It was not for their culture that the British were then primarily admired. George Santayana puts the matter well:

> Admiration for England, of a certain sort, was instilled into me in my youth. My father (who read the language with ease although he did not speak it) had a profound respect for British polity and British power. In this admiration there was no touch of sentiment nor even of sympathy; behind it lay something like an ulterior contempt, such as we feel for the strong exhibiting at a fair. The performance may be astonishing, but the achievement is mean. So in the middle of the nineteenth century an intelligent foreigner, the native of a country materially impoverished, could look to England for a model of that irresistible energy and public discipline which afterwards were even more conspicuous ... in the United States. It was admiration for material progress, for wealth, for the inimitable gift of success.[1]

Even more striking evidence of the dominance of materialism in the Britain of the Industrial Revolution is provided by the comments of Emerson during his visit to England in 1847-8. We have but to shut our inner eyes for a moment, as the remarks follow one after another, to be convinced in extraordinary fashion that they are spoken in judgment not of nineteenth-century England, but of America a century later. "The culture of the day, the thoughts and aims of men, are English thoughts and aims. A nation ... has ... obtained the ascendant, and stamped the knowledge, activity, and power of mankind with its impress. Those who resist it do not feel it or obey it less. The Russian in his snows is aiming to be English. The Turk and Chinese also are making awkward efforts to be English. The practical common-sense of modern society, the utilitarian direction which labour, laws, opinion, religion take, is the natural genius of the British mind." "Certain

[1] G. Santayana, *Soliloquies in England, and Later Soliloquies* (London, 1922), pp. 2-3.

circumstances of English life are not less effective; as, personal liberty, plenty of food; . . . open market, or good wages for every kind of labour; . . . readiness of combination among themselves for politics or for business strikes; and sense of superiority founded on habit of victory in labour and in war; and the appetite for superiority grows by feeding." "The bias of the nation is a passion for utility. . . . Now, their toys are steam and galvanism. They are heavy at the fine arts, but adroit at the coarse; . . . the best iron-masters, colliers, wool-combers, and tanners, in Europe." "Steam is almost an Englishman."[1] "Machinery has been applied to all work, and carried to such perfection, that little is left for the men but to mind the engines and feed the furnaces. But the machines require punctual service, and, as they never tire, they prove too much for their tenders." "What influence the English have is by brute force of wealth and power".[2]

Even in the broader effects of all this, in everything from the seeing of sights to the smoking of marijuana, the similarity is amazing. "The young men have a rude health which runs into peccant humours. They drink brandy like water. . . . They chew hasheesh . . . they saw a hole into the head of the 'winking Virgin', to know why she winks; . . . measure with an English footrule every cell of the Inquisition, . . . every Holy of holies. . . . There are multitudes of rude young English . . . who have made the English traveller a proverb for uncomfortable and offensive manners." "But the English stand for liberty. The conservative, money-loving English are yet liberty-loving; and so freedom is safe. . . . But the calm, sound . . . Briton shrinks from public life, as charlatanism." "There is no country in which so absolute a homage is paid to wealth. . . . An Englishman . . . labours three times as many hours in the course of a year, as any other European. . . . He works fast. Everything in England is at a quick pace. They have reinforced their own productivity by the creation of that marvellous machinery."[3] It is needless to pursue the analogy further. The counter to the present-day accusation of American materialism, that in the early nineteenth century England was equally materialist, can, of course, be modified by reference to the contemporary English cultural outburst and explained as the effect of a new and ill-understood industrialism upon a country where the aristocratic cultural tradition was yet able to survive. But we should have proceeded far enough to convince ourselves of the danger of further generalization: any effort here to make our outline chart of the ocean of Anglo-American emotions more detailed must be

[1] *Works*, II, pp. 15-16, 21, 37, 42.
[2] Ibid, pp. 46, 56.   [3] Ibid, pp. 59, 63, 68, 70.

doomed to failure. We must rest content with the conclusion that, apart from a distinct deterioration in the first half of the last century, there has been a persistent ripening of Anglo-American cordiality. It is indeed the most important theme of our story.

It justly gives ground for confidence in the future of Anglo-American friendship. There may be differences as to how best to promote that future. Many would agree with Hawthorne, that it would not "contribute in the least to our mutual advantage and comfort if we were to besmear one another all over with butter and honey."[1] Some would not, however, agree with Chesterton, that "the very worst way of helping Anglo-American friendship is to be an Anglo-American."[2] Most would agree with Lord Halifax, that the friendship which now exists between the two peoples "often demands more . . . than a treaty which is negotiated in a few weeks and signed in a day. Matrimony is a more exacting affair for both parties than a commercial contract." Others, advocates of Atlantic union, might not altogether agree with him when he writes that, "There is no magic formula which, when applied to Anglo-American relations, will place and keep them for all time upon a satisfactory footing"; they could point out that part at least of his prophecy, uttered in 1947,—"So, as I see it, in the case of the United States, more substantial than any treaty of alliance, *which we are unlikely to achieve*,* is an association of friendship and understanding",[3] —had already been falsified by 1949 when N.A.T.O. was born. All would agree that there may be grave Anglo-American differences in the future. But it is certain that greater efforts have never been made by two sovereign and independent nations to create the conditions in which such differences can be prevented from doing harm. And these positive efforts are supported by the long traditions of Anglo-American history, by the common language, by a kindred democracy, and by the strong emotional bonds of mutual friendship and dependence forged in the one hundred and forty years of Anglo-American peace.

---

[1] Q. Mowat, p. 162.   [2] *What I Saw in America,* p. 243.
* Author's italics.   [3] *Anglo-American Relations,* pp. 5-6.

CHAPTER SEVEN

THE DIPLOMATIC RELATIONSHIP

BEFORE we attempt very briefly to tell the story of Anglo-American diplomatic relations in the last chapter of the book, it would be wise to consider the general character of those relations; so often in diplomatic history the general shape of things, which alone is of cardinal importance, is lost to view in the confusion of manifold events. It is the plan of this chapter, therefore, to consider first, very briefly, the role of Canada in Anglo-American diplomatic history; then to analyse the essential constituent elements in British and American foreign policy in the last century and three-quarters; and finally to trace swiftly the salient features of Anglo-American diplomatic relations since 1783, so that the reader may have a clear outline in his mind.

I

"THE behaviour of nations", writes Brebner in *North Atlantic Triangle*, "bears close analogies to the emotional surges, the anomalies, and the self-defeating actions of individuals",[1] and though it is most dangerous in the historian, as in the political scientist, to press the analogy between the nation and the individual too far, it certainly has its uses. Indeed, as we have already observed, one can hardly refrain from regarding the Anglo-American relationship as a family one; the simile thrusts itself forward at every turn. As early as 1823, in reference to the parallel course pursued by the two countries in the events leading up to the declaration of the Monroe Doctrine, Canning remarked that "the force of blood again prevails", and that "the mother and the daughter stand together against the world".[2] The analogy is put in its extreme form by Geoffrey Gorer in *The Americans*: "Most Americans feel towards England as though it were a father—authoritarian, wicked, past its

[1] p. 242.

[2] Q. R. W. Seton-Watson, *Britain in Europe, 1789-1914* (Cambridge, 1945), p. 85.

174

prime, old-fashioned, passed and left behind, but still a father; they can never be indifferent to Britain as they can to the rest of the world. They are more sensitive towards Britain . . . just as one is more sensitive to the public behaviour of relations than to that of strangers."[1] There is some truth in this in a psychological sense, for most of the difficulties between the two arose, as between parent and child, from the existence of bonds of intimate physical contact in the beginning, and of necessary association later. The colonies were founded very largely by men and women from Britain, and there remained a very intimate relationship until the Revolution, a relationship of which their common tongue, common history and common literature still and continually remind both parties. Throughout the nineteenth century British interests in the American continent, and particularly the existence of a common frontier between Canada and the United States, forced the two nations, even after America had attained independence, to live in close contact, so that, until they were finally cleared out of the way, causes of friction were never lacking. An American can write, "The United States has had more diplomatic controversies, and more serious ones, with Great Britain than with any other nation."[2] Yet in fact there was no fundamental clash of interest between them, and though the controversies themselves were serious, the causes of them were all capable of amicable adjustment. They gained their bitterness, and they were so frequent, largely because there was much misunderstanding and much psychological tension between the United States and the mother country.

But, largely because it was, in a sense, a family relationship, it survived the period of bitterness and animosity following upon the Revolution. It even survived the War of 1812, and indeed did so partly because it was so "futile and unnecessary" a conflict.[3] The nineteenth century accomplished the task of applying soothing balm to the resentment of the United States and the injured pride of Britain: "Great Britain had to learn to accept the United States as an equal for the first time. . . . The United States had to go through a period of blustering behaviour and international irresponsibility before she could adapt herself to the power and weight in the world with which her enormous growth had endowed her." Slowly but with some sureness the mellowing process continued. Perhaps the Civil War, as John Morley claimed, was the turning point; certainly Brebner rightly asserts, "The somewhat reluctant respect for the United States which Great Britain acquired

---

[1] London, 1948, p. 191.   [2] Bemis, p. 405.
[3] Morison and Commager, I, p. 431.

between 1861 and 1871 was almost bound to persist, in spite of all kinds of friction, misunderstanding, and chauvinistic altercations. Its strength for survival lay, on the one hand, in recognition of the growing weight in the world of the American Republic, and, on the other, in a dim but increasing understanding of the complementary roles which the two countries might play in the Atlantic region and in the world as a whole."[1] By the turn of the century—in 1894—Mahan could write that "a common tongue and common descent are making themselves felt, and are breaking down the barriers of estrangement which have separated too long men of the same blood. There is seen here the working of kinship—a wholly normal result of a common origin, the natural affection of children of the same descent, who have quarrelled and have been alienated with the proverbial bitterness of civil strife, but who all along have realized—or at least have been dimly conscious—that such a state of things is wrong and harmful."[2] Diplomatic relations were by then on a fairly satisfactory basis, but the apprehension of these facts was still—it is the operative word in both passages—'dim'.

By the middle of the twentieth century realization of them was complete and explicit. During the nineteenth century the way had been prepared by that "remarkable series of arbitrations which successively narrowed and finally dissipated the subjects of controversy." Common interests and sentiments prevailed over diplomatic difficulties and divergent national policies, for all the diplomatic controversies between them since 1815 have been "peaceably settled. . . . Such common sense rests on the pervading fact that it has been well for these nations to put aside their own quarrels in the face of greater menaces."[3] Because the menaces became real and apparent to Britain first, and because the causes of dissension were much closer and more important to the Americans than to her people, the will for good relations grew more rapidly in Britain than in the United States. But in due time America reciprocated, and it became so close a *rapprochement* that it had more the air of a family reunion than an *entente cordiale* between two foreign powers; and in fact by 1949 a very special relationship existed between them, much broader and yet closer than any formal alliance, such as the North Atlantic Pact, would make it appear. It is not perhaps without a certain symbolic significance that in 1912 *Whitaker's Almanack* for the first time did not include its information about the United States under "Foreign Countries", but gave it a separate heading of its own, coming immediately after the British Commonwealth. This peculiar relation-

[1] Brebner, pp. 242-3, 244.

[2] *The Interest of America in Sea Power*, pp. 108-9.   [3] Bemis, p. 405.

ship is a very real, if indefinable, thing, and, as the British Ambassador in Washington pointed out early in 1951, the very fact that the divergence of British and American policy over the recognition of Communist China caused so much alarm was a measure of the closeness of it. The restoration of the sense of brotherhood between America and Britain is one of the most important facts in twentieth century history.

Certainly it is the most significant theme in the history of the Anglo-American relationship, and in its development the part played by Canada, "the coupling-pin of Anglo-American relations",[1] is of unique importance. She was in the beginning a counterweight to the thirteen colonies within the First British Empire, then a bone of contention between Britain and the United States, then a hostage in American hands for British good behaviour which balanced British command of the seas, and finally, as she herself grew in power, the most powerful catalytic agent in, and occasionally even, by a strange paradox, the chief victim of, Anglo-American friendship. The Quebec Act of 1774, which helped to alienate the thirteen colonies from the mother country, also helped to prevent the participation of Canada in the revolt, and the reorganization of 1791, combined with the interests of the Montreal fur traders, enabled her to gain strength and to preserve her territory and independence in the War of 1812. It was virtually certain from 1814 onwards that only force could have united her with her great neighbour: "In general, traditional dependence on the Mother Country and traditional fear and dislike of the United States, combined with a disinclination to change and an unwillingness or inability to shed familiar cultural garments, were quite naturally so strong that it would have required a profound cataclysm to have projected the colonists into the American Union."[2] It was in Quebec that this "curious but understandable culture complex" was strongest, but it affected Canadians everywhere. "As a highly intelligent people, surpassed by no nation anywhere, Canadians resented the greater force of American culture coming from mere power of territory, natural resources and infinitely greater population."[3]

This Canadian national sentiment was fostered by the firm inauguration of Canadian self-government in 1847, and exacerbated by the growth of outspoken American annexationist designs in the sixties and seventies. Canadians in this era of Little Englandism could not but contrast the enlightened readiness of the mother country to loosen her

[1] Ibid, p. 791.   [2] Brebner, p. 179.   [3] Bemis, p. 801.

bonds, with the anxiety of the United States to enmesh her in new ones, and even the adverse effects of British free trade upon the Canadian economy did little to lessen her mistrust of her southern neighbour, who had alleviated those effects by making the Reciprocity Treaty of 1854, but, under the rule of protectionist Republicans, refused to renew it in 1866. It was ironical that the post-Civil War period, which saw a distinct betterment of Anglo-American relations, also saw American-Canadian relations at their nadir, but it was a reflection of the fact that, as Canadian independence grew, so did direct British interest in disputes between Canada and the United States lessen.

> During the early days of the Dominion, a good many thoughtful Canadians were justified in doubting whether Great Britain rated Canadian rights above Anglo-American understanding. These Canadian misgivings had a long ancestry, beginning with the surrender of the mid-continent to the new United States in 1783, and coming down through other territorial and fisheries settlements to the unexpected loss of territory north of the Columbia River in the Oregon settlement of 1846. Canadian political leaders knew that British leaders like Gladstone, Granville, Cobden and Bright expected the New Dominion to become part of the United States.[1]

Their answer to this fear was the formation of the Canadian federation of 1867, which was the immediate product of mistrust of the United States, combined with the pressure of particular Canadian economic (chiefly railroad) interests.

From this time, as Canada's strength grew and as it became clear that annexationism lacked wide support among the American public, American-Canadian relations improved as fast as Anglo-American relations. The extraordinary intimate association of the Canadian and American peoples began to bear fruit in understanding, though some elements of mistrust remained, and the kinship of Canadians and Americans became very much closer and more marked even than that of Americans and Englishmen: "So unrestricted and so natural have been the freedom of movement and interplay of populations, that Canadians and Americans do not think of themselves as foreign to each other; rather they consider themselves independent of each other."[2] It still remained true, as late as the Alaskan boundary dispute of 1903, that Canadian interests were sometimes ground between the upper and nether millstones of American power and of the now eager British desire for the friendship of the United States; Canada was a "puny third

[1] Brebner, p. 182.   [2] Bemis, p. 791.

party to a grand settlement between two Great Powers". But it was better that a minor Canadian interest should suffer from the amity of the two powers, than that she herself should be utterly crushed by their enmity; and, beginning with Macdonald, Canadian statesmen adjusted themselves admirably to the new dispensation, and made a very good best of it. He and his successors "saw clearly that Anglo-American understanding must be the basic objective of any realistic Canadian foreign policy."[1] Though from time to time she showed her independence, as in her rejection of the Taft Reciprocity Treaty of 1911 and her support of Britain rather than the United States over the Korean crisis of 1950-2, Canada has done all in her power for the last three-quarters of a century to promote Anglo-American friendship. And she has been in an increasingly strong position to do this owing to the rapid growth of her power in the twentieth century and to the coming of Dominion Status. She showed the extent of her influence very plainly in World War II, for Roosevelt's clear guarantee of Canadian integrity in 1938 did but make explicit what had been implicitly recognized by Canadians since the beginning of the century; as early as 1902 Laurier had remarked that the Monroe Doctrine protected Canada against enemy aggression.[2] After the actual outbreak of hostilities, she formed an admirable bridge between neutral America and belligerent Britain, making easier, and even possible, such early forms of united effort as the American-Canadian Joint Defence Board, the naval co-operation in the Atlantic, and the smooth working of Lend-Lease.

Bemis sums it up:

> Canada . . . has always been in effect a hostage for the benevolent conduct of the British toward the United States and the Monroe Doctrine. At no time during the nineteenth century could the United States have withstood a challenge of the British navy on the seas; but at no time since, say 1850, certainly since 1866, could Great Britain have defended Canada against an overland movement by the United States on the long exposed flank of her Empire. . . . Canada has always been instinctively conscious of this position of hostage for the good conduct of Great Britain toward the United States. . . . If only for this reason—among many other pleasanter ones—she has become the natural link of friendship, geographically, politically, economically, and culturally, between the two great English-speaking powers.[3]

One of the most remarkable phenomena of Anglo-American history, as we have suggested earlier, is the way in which the United

---

[1] Brebner, pp. 183, 191.   [2] Ibid, p. 271.   [3] Bemis, pp. 793-4.

States in the twentieth century has gradually assumed the role in international affairs which Britain so long performed. She has taken up, with misgivings and reluctance, the burden of leading the independent nations against the threat of domination by any single aggressive and dictatorial power. We can, and shall, see many other likenesses in diplomatic policy between the two countries, but none is so startling as this.

We can see, for instance, how both powers, at different periods, suffered a revulsion from the Atlas-burden of prime responsibility for the freedom of mankind. In this respect the isolationism of Britain after the Napoleonic wars resembles closely that of the United States almost exactly a century later.

> The policy which the United States pursued toward Europe after the separate peace with Germany, Austria, and Hungary, following the rejection of the League of Nations, may be compared to that of Great Britain after the Napoleonic wars and the peace settlement of 1815. Great Britain refused to make of the Quadruple Alliance . . . a pediment for the Holy Alliance. . . . Unchallenged in her absolute control of the sea, and thus safe behind the English Channel, she preferred to stand aloof from the issues of continental politics as long as no one upset the balance of power. Similarly a century later the United States, safe behind the Atlantic, rejected Woodrow Wilson's ideal of internationalism and stepped back from Europe to its own continent after the defeat of Germany.[1]

Equally interesting is the similarity between Britain's acceptance of the League of Nations in 1919 and America's acceptance of the United Nations in 1945. As the Swiss historian Rappard once pointed out, the very term 'United Nations' is a tribute to the 'United States', and the same might possibly be said of the terms 'League of Nations' and 'British Commonwealth of Nations'. Certainly the analogy illustrates nicely the way in which the United States has tended to assume the diplomatic role of Great Britain during the middle years of the twentieth century. Partly because, in her insular position, she has, like Britain, few direct quarrels with other nations; partly because, her land-hunger having been sated by the acquisition of her continental territories, as had that of Britain by that of her colonial empire, she has no aggressive intentions; partly because, owing to her way of life and form of government, she desires peace rather than war, as Britain has done at most periods of her history—America has, again like Britain before her, assumed her new diplomatic functions with distaste.

[1] Ibid, p. 712.

The emotional reaction of English Tories against the British participation in the War of the Spanish Succession at the beginning of the eighteenth century is almost ludicrously like the attitude of American Republican isolationists in modern times, while the parallel between the Little Englanders of the Boer War, and the American opponents of Republican policy in the Philippines at the same period, could hardly be more exact. But, though taken up with reluctance, the burden has never been put down by either power until the day was over and the struggle won, though, alas, neither has yet been able to cross the Delectable Mountains and lead the nations into the Promised Land.

But, having this general picture in our mind's eye,—a picture in which the United States swiftly outgrows Great Britain and comes more and more to take her leading place in the council of the free nations, a picture in which Canada is at once an agent and a symbol of the ever-deepening and widening cordiality of Anglo-American friendship—let us examine a little more closely, before we proceed with our story, the pattern which emerges from the history of Anglo-American relations.

II

WE CAN most readily discern this pattern if we first appreciate that Great Britain had reached a certain political maturity by 1783. This was most especially true of her foreign policy; she was old, even then, in the ways and vicissitudes, the alarums and excursions of national diplomacy, and she had for many years past picked her path, not without success, through the tangled thickets of international affairs. But it was also true to some extent of other aspects of her national life. There were, certainly, radical changes to come in the next one hundred and fifty years : she was in the nineteenth century to fulfil the promise of the seventeenth, and become a democratic state; she was to overhaul her whole governmental machine and to pass through a period of *laissez-faire* economic policies; she was to acquire a vast new African empire; she was to become one of the most highly urbanized and industrialized communities in the world. But the main lines of her national development were already clearly determined by 1783.

She was already one of the dominating European powers, and was moving into a position almost of supremacy; indeed, French historians describe the eighteenth century itself as the period of the *"préponder-*

ance Anglaise", and she was to remain a Great Power, in so far as that vague classification has any meaning, well into the twentieth century. She was already unquestionably the greatest of colonial powers, and she remains so today, even after the liquidation of large portions of her empire. She was already the paramount naval power, having faced, without absolute disaster, in the last stages of the War of American Independence the combined maritime strength of France, Spain, Russia, America and Holland; and she remains today a formidable naval power, even though she has relinquished her naval supremacy to the United States. She had by 1783 comfortably taken the lead over Holland, her nearest rival, in the extent and importance of her commerce; her foreign trade is still vast, and she still is more dependent on it than any other nation in the world. Her population was to increase fivefold before 1950, but already the curve of her population graph had turned decisively upwards by 1783, and a swift movement of population from country to town had already begun. Finally, economic developments were already irresistibly under way which were to make her in the nineteenth century pre-eminently the greatest of industrial powers, the unique pioneer of industrialism on the national scale, and which were to keep her in some respects, even in mid-twentieth century, an industrial power of the greatest importance. The differences between the land ruled by the Younger Pitt and that ruled by Clement Attlee (and between the ways in which they ruled it) are very great, but they are not so great as those which separate Pitt from Cardinal Wolsey. Her peaceful, almost regular, growth after 1832 contrasts vividly with the turbulence of her development in the seventeenth century. In 1783 Englishmen looked back as far to Shakespeare as we look back to Dr. Johnson, and already, in Shakespeare's day, the English government could claim an older and more continuous and effective tradition than any other European institution, except perhaps the Papacy. By the final breach with the United States in that year Great Britain was already in many ways a mature political power, and the main lines of her development were already determined.

Nothing could be less true of the United States. As we have seen, her population was to increase between forty- and fifty-fold, and, from a mere coastal strip of inhabited territory, she was to become a great continental power bordering on the two main oceans of the world. From a people living by agriculture, shipping and commerce, they were to become the greatest industrial community the world has ever seen, producing by any reckoning far more manufactured products than all the rest of mankind put together. Though she has always been in some senses a democratic nation, she too had to undergo a serious process of democratization in the early nineteenth century, and she had, above all, in a supreme struggle, to throw off the dead hand of Negro slavery. Her constitution has in theory remained virtually unchanged since its foundation in 1789, but in practice it has altered enormously. Her history since 1783 equals in length and hugely exceeds in importance the absolute total of her history before that date. From a colony of Britain she has become unquestionably the most powerful state on earth, and one accused by her enemies of an imperialism more dangerous than any which has preceded it. The foreign policy of the United States has responded, and has adapted itself to these revolutionary changes in her life, in the same way that that of Britain has remained singularly unchanged just because her life has changed, comparatively, so little. This continuity of British policy between 1783 and the present day, and its contrast with the fundamental transformation of American policy in the same period, is the main fact in the history of Anglo-American diplomatic relations.

One would like to use the word 'consistency' to describe British policy over the years, except that it carries with it certain undesirable overtones; in particular, it implies the use of the word 'inconsistency' to describe the policy of the United States, a term which is not fitting, both because it has an air of denigration and because it is not altogether accurate. But if it is clear that the word is not used in the sense of what one might call day-to-day consistency—the changeless prosecution of a policy which never alters to meet new circumstances—but of the pursuit of policies which do not in fact change much because the interests on which they are based do not alter radically, it is perhaps an illuminating description. It is true that on the surface Great Britain could be very inconsistent on occasion, as for instance in the way in which she swung in the nineteenth century between the poles of isolation from and participation in European affairs, whereas the United States during the same period pursued a policy of avoiding entangling alliances with the utmost consistency. But, taking the full stretch of the years, and having some regard for the traditions which Britain had already established before 1783, it is clear that British foreign policy was, throughout, consistent in its pursuit of certain fundamaental objectives, and in the way it was guided by certain principles, whereas that of the United States completely altered in its objectives, its character and even its principles, between the Farewell Address of Washington and Roosevelt's Fourth Inaugural. Let us first consider British policy.

III

WITHIN ten years of the Treaty of Versailles of 1783 Great Britain entered the war against Revolutionary France. This struggle, in which the Younger Pitt became so reluctantly involved, and which, merging as it did into that against Napoleon, lasted with only one short break for more than twenty years, was the greatest struggle in the history of mankind to date. Improved cannon, better firearms, increased productive power, the coming of universal military service, all these things rendered it more destructive than any of its predecessors. It changed its character to some extent during its course since it ceased to be a war against a *soi-disant* democracy and became one against the increasingly tyrannical régime of Napoleon: but, in both its phases, it was from the British point of view essentially a war to prevent the conquest of Europe by France, a war to prevent the domination of the European continent by a single power. In this sense it was nothing new; it was just another war of a type which was traditional in British policy. It can certainly be asserted that the tradition began in the late sixteenth century, when England joined the Netherlands in their struggle to gain independence from Catholic Spain, and thus to prevent Philip II from moving closer to the establishment of an effective European hegemony, a design which was dramatically, or at least symbolically, frustrated by the defeat of the Armada. During the early seventeenth century England was largely preoccupied with her internal troubles, but after 1688 she is to be found, once more in collaboration with the Dutch, opposing the schemes of Louis XIV for the domination of Europe. After the accession of William III to the English throne, and even more after his death, effective leadership of the anti-French coalition passed into the hands of Britain, and it was largely the work of Marlborough that made possible in 1713 a reasonably successful conclusion to the War of the Spanish Succession, which checked French designs, if it did not render them impossible, for the future. During the eighteenth century Britain was involved in two major wars, both against France, the War of the Austrian Succession and the Seven Years' War, and was able in the latter to add greatly to her colonial empire.

In 1793 came the long French wars against what Pitt described as "a danger the greatest that ever threatened the world . . . a danger which has been resisted by all the nations of Europe, and resisted by none with so much success as by this nation, because by none has it been resisted so uniformly and with so much energy."[1] The nineteenth century saw only one major war in which Great Britain was involved, the Crimean, for she stood apart from the Franco-Prussian war between her traditional enemy and her traditional ally. But she was soon to find that old friend would become new enemy, and therefore old enemy new friend, so that in 1914 she was once again involved in fighting a war to prevent the conquest of Europe by a single power, in this case, Germany. This was a war beside whose bloodshed that of all previous wars paled into insignificance, but yet we find that by 1939 Great Britain is once more fighting for her life, and for that of Europe, if not of the world, against a revivified Germany more mighty in arms than ever before. Once more, though by a narrow margin, she was able, with the aid of her giant allies, who were forced into the struggle at a later stage by the direct and lunatic attacks of the enemy, to carry the war to a successful conclusion. Only she among the United Nations entered the war at the beginning and remained in it until the end, and from her shores alone was the great reconquest of Europe possible; in this sense, she was once more the foundation stone of the coalition which eventually frustrated the ambitions of Germany, Italy and Japan. Such a policy as this has now been pursued with remarkable consistency by Britain for four hundred years, and though the power whose supremacy she opposed has been different, her primary objectives have not changed. What have those objectives been?

The first and fundamental object of British policy, as of the policy of every nation, was, of course, national survival, and her very existence as a nation was threatened by Hitler, and probably by Napoleon, both of whom contemplated and planned, though they never attempted, actual invasions. At other times, though her life itself may not have been in quite such jeopardy, her existence as a great and independent power certainly was. In the midst of the protracted conflict with France, on 17 February, 1800, Pitt was asked in the House of Commons what were his war aims, and he replied, "In one word . . . it is *Security*".[2] On 13 May, 1940, Churchill, when asked the same question in the same place, echoed this reply, though in a characteristically pugnacious form, "You ask, What is our aim? I can answer in one word: *Victory*".[3] But whatever its precise form, the fundamental objective was continued existence as an independent power.

[1] Q. *Britain in Europe*, p. 17.   [2] Q. ibid, p. 17.
[3] Winston S. Churchill, *The Second World War*, II, (London, 1949), p. 24. Author's italics.

185

The second objective was a less fundamental, but none the less very important, modification of this, a modulation, one might call it, in a minor key, the well known and much abused policy of the balance of power. This phrase, which is so apt to arouse the ire of liberals and idealists, merely embodied the intention of preventing excessive power from falling into the hands of any single state, because this threatened the independence of the other states, Great Britain among them. This policy has been criticized, partly as unconstructive, and partly because it seemed to some an effort on the part of Great Britain to assure her own preponderant influence, by encouraging an even balance between the greatest powers or groups of powers; it has been held to result merely in the construction of two great blocs of mistrustful nations, whose very existence inevitably precipitates war. In fact the policy has no such object and has had no such result, for it is apparent that, in nearly all the great wars of the last three hundred years in which Britain has played a leading role, the major cause of conflict has been the desire of some great power or group of powers to establish their own supremacy. Britain's balance of power policy is in reality her "instinctive opposition to any bid for world power, from whatever quarter, and her no less marked preference for a certain equilibrium of forces on the European continent."[1] Britain's balance of power policy had certain specific manifestations, certain particular objects in view, the most important being a determination to prevent the Low Countries from falling wholly into the hands of a hostile, or even of any, Great Power; this object British governments have pursued with unswerving consistency from the Revolt of the Netherlands in the sixteenth century to the invasion of Belgium in 1914. It was here, where the pistol pointed to her heart, that she was most sensitive to any threat to the balance of power.

The third principle of British policy was that she sought no territorial gains in Europe; after the loss of Calais by Queen Mary, Britain never sought, even under the Hanoverian Kings, to make continental acquisitions, with the occasional exception of strategic bases such as Gibraltar. Indeed she instinctively avoided for many years even alliances or definite commitments to action there. When she entered wars, her traditional policy was to pursue for the most part colonial gains overseas. This meant that she tended to try and fight her battles in the colonies, where, through her pre-eminence at sea, she could most effectively bring her weight to bear. The Tory party in the Spanish Succession War first made this demand vocal, in their opposition to

[1] *Britain in Europe* p. 35.

186

Marlborough's later policy, and it was classically expounded and triumphantly vindicated by Chatham in the Seven Years' War; it was the policy which so struck the imagination of Macaulay when he wrote of Frederick the Great's attack upon Maria Theresa: "[I]n order that he might rob a neighbour whom he had promised to defend, black men fought on the coast of Coromandel, and red men scalped each other by the Great Lakes of North America."[1] The Younger Pitt has always been criticized by historians because he frittered away his forces in futile military ventures, but he certainly swept all the available French colonies into his net. Even in World War I Allenby's Palestine campaign was an effort in the same direction, while in World War II it was in North Africa that the "hinge of fate" turned.

But Great Britain has never been able in the course of these life and death struggles to neglect the European theatre altogether, for in World War I she made her main effort there, and the Peninsular War and the D-day campaign were both decisive in their day. Nevertheless she has always kept her actual contribution of armed forces as small as possible; Marlborough's British troops formed a surprisingly small part of his command, Wellington's army was by no means wholly British, and in 1944 Eisenhower's forces became increasingly American as the months passed. Whenever she could, Britain has preferred to fight her European battles, as opposed to those in the colonies and at sea, by the use of her political and financial power, by building up coalitions against the enemy, by subsidizing the armies of her allies. Upon the solid base of her island position she has attempted to build, and when they collapsed to build again, a succession of common fronts against the common enemy. The masterly diplomacy of Marlborough, the almost superhuman patience of Pitt and his successors in erecting successive European alliances against a triumphant France, Churchill's revival, even to the very phrase, of his ancestor's Grand Alliance; this has been the British path to victory. It has been by no means popular with other nations, for until World War II Britain herself remained immune from the worst ravages of war, and the taunt that she would fight to the last drop of blood of the last Frenchman came sometimes from deep in the European heart. But there can be no doubt that it was the best way to win, if indeed it was not the only way, for her population was never as great as that of her opponents, so that she could never match man for man, while her riches were often much greater and, combined with her island position, gave her her trump card—staying power.

Her fourth objective was always to retain effective control of the seas,

[1] Macaulay, *Critical and Historical Essays* (London, 1852), p. 780.

or at least to prevent control of them falling into the hands of another power. Not until the opening years of the twentieth century did she give up her effort to retain a navy equal to that of any two other powers; and only after World War I did she come to admit the equality, and in World War II the supremacy, of the United States Navy. To other powers, particularly the United States, the term Freedom of the Seas has had a quite different meaning, and Britain's traditional diplomatic role has brought her into frequent collision with America, the greatest of the neutral powers; the interest of the former was obviously in time of war to restrict as far as possible neutral commerce with the enemy, for economic warfare was her most potent weapon, whereas the interest of the latter was naturally the very reverse. To Britain, Freedom of the Seas meant freedom for the shipping of all countries to trade without restriction, except with Britain's enemies in time of war; to America, it tended to mean absolute freedom for the shipping of all nations in war as well as in peace. This question, which had been serious enough to be chiefly responsible for the outbreak of the War of 1812, became less important as the United States became less and less primarily a maritime power, and as in world affairs her interests became more and more allied to those of Britain. It is interesting, for instance, that in the Civil War the North advanced many traditional British arguments to support her blockade of the South, while in World War I America was content to acquiesce in practices after 1917 which she had condemned —at least in theory—before that date.

To Britain this maritime policy was absolutely vital. It was essential to the maintenance of her commerce, which was never during the years with which we are concerned, as it was to America, a comparative luxury. Already, by the time of the American Revolution, she had ceased to export grain, and during the Revolutionary and Napoleonic wars she became increasingly dependent on imports, not only of raw materials for industry, but, even more vital, of food. In every great war this problem of ensuring her flow of imports increased in severity, until in 1941 it assumed its most acute form; without question it was in both World Wars the most dangerous weapon which Germany could use against her. Strategically this means that Great Britain has always been, has always considered herself, and has always been considered by others, as primarily a naval power; she was so long before 1783 and, with the necessary addition of an air force, she is still so today. This has made her policy of building up coalitions against menacing powers —rather than fighting them, except at intervals, single-handed—even more obviously the right policy; her power of blockade and her capacity to continue her own indispensable commerce have again and again been the foundation of her victories.

Finally, though it is a difficult concept to express in words which will be equally accurate in 1783 and 1952, Great Britain has always stood in greater or less degree in her foreign policy for what may be called 'constitutional' government. One can perhaps say of the United States that she has always, since the formation of the Constitution, been a 'democratic' state, though, as we have pointed out, considerable qualifications must be made in the use of the term in the Federalist era. But one certainly cannot say so of Britain until the late nineteenth century, for Castlereagh and most of his contemporaries in the ruling class shuddered at such a notion. It is clear that during the war against Revolutionary France, Britain was not fighting for democracy as Jefferson knew it, since he would more probably have awarded that palm to the French themselves; yet even here the question is complex, for there is not so very much to choose between the repressive policy of Pitt and that of Washington in this era, particularly if it be remembered that England was less than thirty miles from France and America three thousand. But on the other hand, Great Britain certainly did stand for opposition to tyrannical and arbitrary, as well as aggressive, governments. It is possible at least to make out a case for the idea, as Churchill has done in his biography, that Marlborough's chief motive in the War of the Spanish Succession was to prevent future French aggressions, by imposing some sort of internal constitutional check on the power of the French monarchy. It is true that the democratic lustre of seventeenth century England became somewhat tarnished in the Britain of the Hanoverians, and that the governing class increasingly forgot that Locke had defended the Revolution of 1688 because it was popular, and remembered only that he had done so because it protected the sacred right of property: but it is also true that the English constitution in the eighteenth century was the cynosure of European (if not American) eyes, and that Englishmen still looked back, if without any intention of repeating the performance, to the Revolution of 1688 as the foundation of their liberties.

Certainly, in her everyday policy Britain has never refused to deal with absolute or arbitrary governments just because they were absolute or arbitrary. In 1936 Anthony Eden, in what Seton-Watson describes as "the true tradition of all his predecessors since Castlereagh and Canning,"[1] declared that it was "neither necessary nor desirable that our likes or dislikes for foreign forms of government should prejudice

[1] R. W. Seton-Watson, *Britain and the Dictators* (Cambridge, 1938), p. 266.

our international friendships or influence the course of our foreign policy."[1] This certainly echoes what Canning said in Parliament in 1823: "The general acquisition of free institutions is not necessarily a security for general peace", and Britain should retain an "essentially neutral" attitude, "not only between contending nations, *but between conflicting principles*."[2] As Seton-Watson sums it up, "This country has never insisted upon identity of political outlook as a basis of alliance and friendship".

"But", he goes on to say, ". . . it is quite clear that political affinities render co-operation easier."[3] Canning, for instance, prefaced the words quoted above with another sentiment: "No man can witness with more delight than I do, the widening diffusion of political liberty. . . . I would not prohibit other nations from kindling their flame at the torch of British freedom".[4] Others, such as Palmerston and Russell, would have gone a good deal further, and Gladstone declared in the famous Midlothian campaign that British foreign policy

> should always be inspired by love of freedom. . . . In the foreign policy of this country the names of Canning, of Russell and of Palmerston, will ever be honoured by those who recollect the erection of the Kingdom of Belgium and the union of the disjointed provinces of Italy. It is that sympathy—not with disorder, but on the contrary founded on the deepest and most profound love of order—which ought in my opinion to be the very atmosphere in which the Foreign Secretary of England ought to live and move.[5]

In the early nineteenth century Britain's hesitance to declare unrestricted support for liberal causes in time of peace was reflected in those mysterious and equivocal words which chase one another through the diplomatic records of the period, 'intervention' and 'nonintervention' in the affairs of Europe. The Concert of Europe after the Napoleonic Wars demanded intervention against democratic causes in certain countries, and Britain refused to intervene, but Palmerston and Russell tried to turn the tables on their opponents by fostering subsequent liberal movements, while still talking of non-intervention—a situation which was characteristically summed up by Talleyrand in his definition of 'non-intervention' as *"un mot métaphysique et moral qui signifie à peu près la même chose qu'intervention"*. In normal times the policy of Great Britain, whether calling for intervention or opposing it, could fairly be described in Granville's words as a policy by which the government would try to cultivate especially intimate relations "with

[1] Q. ibid, p. 266. [2] Q. ibid, p. 371. [3] *Britain in Europe*, p. 650.
[4] Q. *Britain and the Dictators*, p. 371. [5] Q. *Britain in Europe*, pp. 547-8.

the countries which have adopted institutions similar in liberality to our own."[1]

But the hesitancy disappeared altogether in time of war, when Britain was prepared to support any country, or movement in a country, which would further the cause. In 1808, for example, Sheridan in the Commons urged support for Spain against Napoleon, and Canning at once declared, "we shall proceed upon the principle that any nation of Europe which starts up with a determination to oppose a Power which is the common enemy of the nations, becomes instantly our essential ally."[2] Naturally, too, a preference was given to popular movements, and this became increasingly clear as the century progressed; by World War I she could wholeheartedly associate herself with Wilson's desire to make the world safe for democracy, and in World War II could readily participate in the framing of the Atlantic Charter. So strongly had she come, by 1939, to pursue this objective, that while in the throes of war with Germany she ran the temerous risk of becoming involved at the same time with Russia, by threatening to give way to the popular British demand to send unrestricted aid to Finland when she was attacked by the Soviet Union. This principle of supporting 'constitutional' forms of government, though it became stronger as she herself became increasingly democratic, has always been a part of British foreign policy from the eighteenth century onwards. Primarily Britain opposed France and Germany because they had aggressive designs, but she opposed them also because they were ruled by what she believed were despotic governments dangerous to liberty.

Great Britain, then, traditionally pursued five main objectives: her national survival, the balance of power, control of the seas, an overseas empire, and free government. She has pursued them, in some sort at least, since the sixteenth century, and throughout that time has been persistently active in European affairs. There were, it is true, periods of so-called isolation in her policy: an important one, for example, in the seventeenth century, a less notable one under Walpole in the early eighteenth, and another important one in the nineteenth. These phases were a natural reflection of her geographical position; as an island power, at once in and out of Europe, she alternated between "the wish for isolation and an extreme policy of interference," and these "apparent hesitations and half-measures . . . foreign observers have sometimes sought to explain . . . by farsighted and calculated policy."[3]

[1] Q. *Britain in Europe*, pp. 293-4. [2] Q. ibid, p. 25.
[3] *Britain and the Dictators*, p. 7.

This tendency to withdraw into her own shell, particularly after a crisis in which she had participated, confused foreigners, and gained for her the reputation embodied in the term "Perfidious Albion"; and her refusal to enter into binding commitments in time of peace merely added to this effect. Only by slow degrees did she accept the idea of permanent participation in any form of European political organization.

Castlereagh at first accepted the system of the European Concert of Powers, and wrote of it in 1817: "I am quite convinced that past habits, common glory and these occasional meetings, displays and repledges are among the best securities Europe now has for a durable peace", but within two or three years he found it necessary to protest against some of the doings of the reactionary European rulers, while Canning had already declared that regular conferences "with the great despotic monarchs . . . would really amount to a combination of governments against liberty." Later, when he had succeeded Castlereagh in power, he withdrew altogether from the Concert, arguing that the system of periodical meetings was "new and of very questionable policy, and that it will necessarily involve us deeply in all the politics of the Continent, whereas our true policy has always been not to interfere except in great emergencies and then with commanding force."[1] He put it more theatrically in the form, "Every nation for itself and God for us all."[2]

This participation in, followed by withdrawal from, European events was characteristic of nineteenth-century English policy. As Russell said, the "traditionary policy of this country is not to bind the Crown and country by engagements, unless upon special cause shown arising out of the special circumstances of the day".[3] Palmerston in particular tended always to follow his own path, agreeing with Russell that "it is very difficult to lay down any principles from which deviations may not frequently be made", or, as he put it in his more belligerent mood, "I hold with respect to alliances that England is a Power sufficiently strong, sufficiently powerful to steer her own course. . . . I hold that the real policy of England—apart from questions which involve her own particular interests, political or commercial—is to be the champion of justice and right, . . . giving the weight of her moral sanction and support wherever she thinks that justice is".[4] A return to isolation after the

[1] Q. *Britain in Europe*, pp. 52-3.

[2] Q. E. Halévy, *History of the English People, 1815-30* (London, 1926), p. 168.

[3] Q. *Britain in Europe*, p. 293.

[4] Q. P. Guedalla, *Palmerston* (London, 1926), pp. 280-1.

Crimean War was partly checked by Disraeli, who expressed the view in one of his last great speeches that, "If . . . one of the most extensive and wealthiest empires in the world, . . . from a perverse interpretation of its insular geographical position, turns an indifferent ear to the feelings and fortunes of continental Europe, such a course would, I believe, only end in its becoming an object of general plunder. *So long as the power and advice of England are felt in the councils of Europe, peace, I believe, will be maintained, and for a long period.* Without their presence war . . . seems to me inevitable."[1] There followed in the last two decades of the century, nevertheless, a period of marked isolationism under the leadership of Salisbury; indeed, with the exception of the Crimea, which, as a Near Eastern question, affected the Empire more than the mother country, the mid and late nineteenth century saw the high water mark of Britain's "splendid" isolation. This was largely because during much of this time she was without peer in Europe.

France had passed the peak of her relative strength, and Italy and Germany were only just coming into existence, while no European power had yet felt the full impact of the Industrial Revolution as Britain had, and therefore none could equal her in economic strength. Comparative figures of population, too, show that during these years she was stronger, relative to the other nations, than at any previous or subsequent period.

Population Figures in Millions

	1815-21	1870-2	1880-1	1890-1	1900-1	1910-1
France	30.4	36.1	37.6	38.3	38.9	39.6
Germany	(21)	41	45.2	49.4	56.3	64.9
U.K.	20.8	31.8	35.2	38.1	41.9	45.3
U.S.A.	9.6	38.5	50.1	62.6	75.9	91.7
Italy	—	—	28.4	30.3	32.4	34.6

[Figures are from R. C. K. Ensor, *England, 1870-1914*, pp. 102-3, 269, 498. They are based on census returns within the years indicated.]

In fact, between about 1830 and 1880 Britain was nearer to being the paramount power in the world than at any other era in her history.

But with the rapid growth of the German menace she became conscious of her isolation as an unhappy condition, so that, in the difficult years leading up to World War I, she set about the task of seeking friends, and, in the years after it, considered herself as very nearly irretrievably committed to European affairs. Thus, though it

[1] Q. *Britain in Europe*, p. 544.

might appear at first sight true to say of Britain's policy since 1783, "The desire for isolation, the knowledge that it is impossible—these are the two poles between which the needle of the British compass continues to waver",[1] in reality the periodic revulsions from participation in European affairs only serve, on a broader view, to emphasize the persistence of her habit of intervention whenever a crisis arose.

On the whole Britain remained remarkably constant to her tradition and her basic principles, and this applies as much to the years after World War I when her power had declined relative to that of the new rising nations, such as the United States, as it does to the earlier years. One is repeatedly reminded of this by the analogies which strike the eye between one period and another. Seton-Watson rightly claims that in 1914 the main lines of British policy showed "surprisingly little change since the days of Napoleon",[2] while the similarity between her situation in 1914 and in 1939 was, for the inhabitants of the country, too obvious to need emphasis.

Even more remarkable in some ways is the likeness between the part she played in the Napoleonic Wars and in World War II. In both she was, as an island power, the essential foundation of ultimate victory; in both, her determination to persist to the end made that victory possible. In both, she entered, although reluctantly, upon the struggle because she feared the overweening ambition of the enemy and because she desired security from aggression, and in both she found in the end that only the destruction of the personal dictatorships of her enemies could give her any hope of that security. In both, she was able to retain control of the seas and keep her own life lines open, though nearly the whole coastline of Europe fell under enemy influence, and though the enemy replied to blockade with counter-blockade. In both, she suffered early and frequent military disasters, and saw her allies destroyed with depressing swiftness. In both, she was able to watch the enemy make his first uneasy and temporary terms with Russia, while he conquered virtually the rest of Europe; to observe how he was forced to abandon his plans for a direct assault on England because he lacked control of the sea; to gaze fascinated as each dictator in turn—whether impelled by a similar megalomania, or by a remorseless but mysterious logic, which forces the master of a great national army in time of war to turn it to use on land when baulked by the sea—hurled himself in desperate and fatal folly upon that "cloud of power in the north". Well might the British have murmured in both cases, *"Quos Deus vult perdere prius dementat"*. Finally, in both cases, in conjunction—co-

[1] Ibid, p. 37.   [2] Ibid, p. 646.

operation would be perhaps too cordial a word—with a Russia advancing in massive numbers from the east, she was able to gain a foothold on one of the Mediterranean peninsulas, which sapped the strength of the enemy, and, eventually, with her allies to achieve a final victory. This particular parallel is merely the most impressive of many which illustrate the continuity and comparative changelessness of British policy between 1783 and the present day.

IV

THE policy of the United States, on the other hand, changed much in this time, for it underwent at least two fundamental transformations. At first, after the Revolution, the United States was primarily concerned with cutting the remaining political bonds which tied her to Europe, and particularly to Britain, but after the end of the War of 1812 her emancipation was complete, and, in increasingly self-conscious isolation, she devoted herself to the problems of expansion across her own continent. At the same time, the Monroe Doctrine, and, even more, the mid-century gloss upon it, which virtually prohibited any further European intervention in the Americas, consolidated this continental isolation and made it secure. But by the end of the century, with the closing of the frontier and the vast development of American wealth and power, she began to be conscious of her own strength, and, along with other things, her trade upon the two great oceans of the world began to break down this traditional isolation, first in Asia and then in Europe. The first clear sign of it was in the outburst of so-called American Imperialism in the Spanish-American War, but this was followed by the eventual and reluctant American intervention in World War I, and, after a period of renewed isolationism, in World War II. The latter seemed clearly to signify that the United States had entered world affairs to stay.

Thus American policy has undergone two radical changes; first a retirement from the political affairs of Europe, and then a return to them, or rather to the broader ones of the world as a whole. Both have been perfectly natural developments. It was obviously to be expected that, after establishing her independence in name, she should do so in fact, particularly with the whole world of the West to conquer, and with that powerful element present in the American people which tended to regard the political life of Europe as a sink of iniquity. It was equally obvious that, as the earth contracted under the influence of modern technology, and as the United States expanded, so she should come to play a leading part in international affairs. Furthermore, in a broad sense, it is apparent that the policies of the United States could not follow traditional lines, because no such lines existed; most of the objectives of American foreign policy which were established by 1900, as they are recounted by its historian, were in the very nature of things new objectives which had to be hammered out to deal with new situations.

It was in the eighteenth and nineteenth centuries that the essentials of American foreign policy were clearly defined and successfully achieved in the teeth of a hostile world: the winning and preservation of independence; the redemption of the territorial integrity of the United States within the boundaries laid down in the treaty of peace and independence; the westward expansion across North America to form a Continental Republic—the supreme achievement of American nationalism; the Freedom of the Seas; the Monroe Doctrine; commercial reciprocity accompanied by the conditional most-favored-nation formula; the breakdown of the commercial monopoly of the European colonies in the New World; wide-open occidental immigration, accompanied by the doctrine of the right of expatriation; voluntary arbitration. Only two of these fundamental policies remained challenged at the end of the nineteenth century; the right of expatriation and the Freedom of the Seas.[1]

With the cessation of large-scale immigration the former ceased to be of such importance as it had been, and after American participation in World War I little more was heard of the latter. Once her own position was securely established in this way, America began to become involved in the wider affairs of the world, where many of the problems followed the old lines, though some indeed were new; these wider problems required a change in American policy, but this change was in many ways a return to those very European entanglements, against which Washington and Jefferson had so strongly and, for a while, so successfully warned.

This process of withdrawal and return—it is in many ways a classic example of Toynbee's thesis—contrasts in marked fashion with the continuity of British policy. It means that the foreign policy of the United States can conveniently be considered under three main headings, emancipation from Europe, isolation, and emergence as a world power. Before considering this history in our eighth and last chapter,

---

[1] Bemis, p. 877.

let us glance swiftly at the general pattern of Anglo-American relations between 1783 and 1952.

The first period, that of American emancipation from Europe and especially from Britain, begins with the Revolution and can (in so far as precise dates mean anything in such a context) justly be said to end with the Treaty of Ghent in 1814, for by that time the United States had fairly well shrugged off the garments of European influence. The Revolution, which broke the back of the attachment, had swiftly become a possibility in the period following the end of the Seven Years' War in 1763, and had burst into reality in 1776: but when the flood subsided with the recognition of American independence by the Treaty of Versailles in 1783, it was found that many of the familiar landmarks of European association, though weakened, were still standing, and even that new European threats to the infant republic had come into existence. During the next thirty years they were very largely removed.

The avoidance by Washington of an entanglement of a permanent nature with France, by his proclamation in 1793 of the neutrality of the United States in the war between France and Britain, inaugurated the American tradition of neutrality in European struggles. Jay's Treaty of 1794 solved the major and immediate problems of Anglo-American relations which had been left unsettled in the Treaty of 1783, and made a living thing of the formal diplomatic intercourse which had been established between the two countries. Under President Adams, Federalist influence over the government continued to gain strength, and its conservative mistrust of French Jacobinism led not merely to increasing feeling against France, but to the beginnings of a better feeling towards Great Britain. In 1799 the United States found herself on the brink of actual hostilities with France, but Adams held back until he was succeeded in 1801 by Jefferson, who, as leader of the Republicans, was pro-French in sympathy. During his presidency a determined effort was made to apply the theory of American neutrality consistently, even if the embargo policy, which implemented it, proved materially harmful to America. This was a logical attempt to throw off impartially all the bonds of Europe, though it was sanguine in its idealism, but the complications arising from the great maritime interests of the eastern seaboard of the United States made its operation difficult. Though the Louisiana purchase opened up the West to America during Jefferson's Administration, Republican enthusiasm for France waned as Napoleon's pretensions to democratic government became transparently false. But this did not mean much increase in pro-British feeling (Tocqueville still said in 1830 that he could conceive of no hatred more poisonous than that which the Americans then felt for England); rather it gave strength to American isolationist sentiments. Actual war broke out between Britain and the United States in 1812, partly through rivalry in the West but largely because of the clash of maritime interests. Paradoxically, however, it did not embitter relations further, but seemed to have the ultimate effect of clearing the air. It ended in military stalemate, was terminated by a peace which ignored all the main issues between the two nations, and resulted in a vague realization on both sides that little was to be gained and much to be lost by active hostility. After this date there was never war between them again, and there was a slow but steady improvement in relations. The United States decisively turned her back upon Europe, in the way which Tocqueville so brilliantly illustrated by pointing out that in mid-eighteenth century an American meant by the phrase 'back-country' the wilderness of the West, because he was oriented to Europe, while by mid-nineteenth century he meant the eastern regions of the American continent, because he now faced instinctively West.

The second period, that of American isolation from the non-American world, lasted nearly as long as the century, and throughout it the American people were primarily occupied, as the Mexican War showed, in the tremendous task of opening up the Great West. This was the era of most significant growth in the internal life of the United States, which naturally left little time or energy for international affairs, particularly during the middle years of the century, when even interest in the West was for a while overlaid by intense absorption in the Civil War. It began appropriately with the inauguration of the Monroe Doctrine, which was from a continental point of view a public declaration of isolationism; and for the future of Anglo-American relations this act of fundamental agreement, though not co-operation, was a good augury. The two most serious border disputes between the two nations, in Maine and Oregon, which might have involved a struggle between them despite American isolation, were happily settled in the eighteen-forties. The Civil War raised serious problems in Anglo-American relations, which came to a head in the *Trent* and *Alabama* disputes, for the natural difficulties arising from the cleavage in the United States were made worse by an acute division of English sympathies and interests. The well-intended, if sometimes inefficient, British policy of neutrality did enable the obstacles to be surmounted, as was their aftermath, the *Alabama* claims. The settlement of these brought into salutary prominence the use of arbitration for the settlement of disputes between the two governments. As the years passed, the mistrust of the earlier period between the nations began to evaporate, and to be replaced, at first by indifference, and later by something approaching warmth. The Venezuela incident of 1895 showed how strong anti-British feeling in the United States could still be, though anti-American feeling in Britain was very much weaker, but it was perhaps the last severe flurry in the blizzard of Anglo-American misunderstanding. It was a fortunate thing—partly cause, partly coincidence—that this fruition of comradeship began just at the time of what Mahan described as the American "projection" of "our physical power . . . beyond the waters that gird our shores."[1] The same decade which saw the closing of the frontier, the symbol of American maturity, ended with the Spanish-American War, the symbol of the new American Imperialism, which was merely one manifestation, though an important one, of the emergence of America as a world power. This was what Mahan meant when he wrote in 1894, "Whether they will or no, Americans must now begin to look outward. The growing production of the country demands it. An increasing volume of public sentiment demands it."[2] These things meant the end of American isolationism as a permanent policy.

But it is not possible to put a date to the beginning of the third period, that of America's appearance as a world power, for not only were there times in the twentieth century when she reacted vigorously from it into isolationism, but there had already been signs of it well before 1898. The increased participation of the United States in world affairs had two phases or aspects; first, American Imperialism, and second, her assumption of a leading role among the Great Powers. But these both sprang from a common source, her great and increasing strength, and her recognition, albeit reluctant, of the power which it carried with it. This was appreciated in some quarters in England even sooner than in the United States, for as early as 1872 Disraeli pointed out that the New World was "throwing lengthening shades over the Atlantic" and creating "vast and novel elements in the distribution of power."[3] The first manifestation of this was in the imperial sphere; already, by the end of the Reconstruction period, America had begun to show a marked interest in the Pacific islands, and, even before the Civil War, her interest in such Caribbean territories as Cuba had been

[1] *The Interest of America in Sea Power*, p. 98.
[2] Ibid, pp. 21-2.   [3] Q. *Britain in Europe*, p. 502.

intense. This imperialism had a meteoric career, with the Spanish-American War and the acquisition of the Philippines, and partly inspired the building of the Panama Canal and the two-ocean navy, but the coming of Wilsonian Democracy led to a gradual reversal of the imperialist policy, and to its ultimate abandonment in the years between the world wars. These years, however, did not see any significant American withdrawal from international affairs, but rather the reverse, for under Wilson she became involved in the even broader issues of World War I. (In any case, irrespective of American internal politics, there was a tendency for wars, heretofore regarded as 'colonial' or 'imperial', to become increasingly interlocked with world events as a whole, so that the sequence of Spanish-American, Boer, Russo-Japanese and World Wars was not a surprising one. Thus an imperialist America probably could not long have avoided a major war.) The technical reason for her entry into World War I was the traditional American doctrine of the Freedom of the Seas, but behind this, though largely unrecognized, lay her fear of a disastrous disturbance of the balance of power in case of a German victory and her accompanying fear for the future of democratic government in such an event.

In 1919, at the height of victory and with a prestige and power in the world that she had never previously attained, she underwent in an especially severe form the disillusion with war, even successful war, which affected all the nations. She had not, it is true, suffered as severely as her allies, but she felt even more acutely that the suffering had not been worth while, and many of her people repudiated Wilson's League of Nations, in the belief that American re-entry into world affairs had been a grave error. After the Presidential election of 1920, isolationism became for a period the professed policy of a majority of the American people. In the long run, however, events proved that, even for the United States, no such policy was possible in a world of national and ideological rivalries. It came to pass in the end as Mahan had prophesied, "In this same pregnant strife the United States doubtless will be led, by undeniable interests and aroused national sympathies, to play a part, to cast aside the policy of isolation which befitted her infancy, and to recognize that, whereas once to avoid European entanglement was essential to the development of her individuality, now to take her share of the travail of Europe is but to assume an inevitable task, an appointed lot, in the work of upholding the common interests of civilization."[1]

[1] *The Interest of America in Sea Power*, p. 123.

It was not, in fact, in Europe that the first strain came, but in the Pacific, where America was by habit perhaps more sensitive and certainly less inhibited—between China and Japan; nevertheless, whether or not the United States would have taken firm action there, Britain would not, so that the political calamities which successively befell Europe in the nineteen-thirties were at first met in America by the uncompromising isolationist policy which reached its high-water mark in the neutrality legislation of 1937. This, in its efforts utterly to withdraw from contacts which might involve risk of war, harped back to Jefferson's embargo policy, and was as little able to stand the test of action, for, under the dynamic leadership of Roosevelt, American influence began once more to make itself felt in the world, and by the outbreak of World War II had become a potent moral and economic factor in the balance of power. The Cash and Carry law of November, 1939, frustrated in large part the practice of the neutrality legislation, and America's response to the overwhelming continental victories of Hitler in 1940, the Lease-Lend plan and "shoot at sight" orders to the U.S. Navy, utterly destroyed it. Pearl Harbour put full-scale American participation in the war beyond all doubt, and with it the part which the United States was in the future to play in world affairs. After she had pushed the war, along with her companion nations, to overwhelming victory in 1945, she became the corner-stone of the United Nations, and in 1949 entered wholeheartedly into the North Atlantic Treaty Organization. Her powerful and noble intervention in Korea in 1950 put the seal upon her leadership of the free peoples against a new enemy; after this, despite the minor resurgence in the persons of Taft and Hoover in 1951 of isolationist sentiment, there could be no serious doubt that America was in world affairs to stay.

The half-century which had seen this transformation had also witnessed the final blossoming of Anglo-American friendship; the great arbitrations of the late nineteenth century had prepared the way for a working-together in relatively minor matters in the early years of the twentieth, so that the foundations were laid for close co-operation in the world wars. Though in the inter-war years there were emotional and contentious problems, such as that of the war debts, at issue between the two countries, the peoples maintained an unprecedented and unprecedentedly cordial intercourse at all levels, so that, as Roosevelt indicated in 1939, the Americans could never in such a war be "neutral in thought." As it proceeded in fact, Anglo-American

201

unity, as personified not only in the close friendship of Roosevelt and Churchill but even more in the single personality of an Eisenhower, attained a completeness never before equalled between two sovereign allies. The rumblings of disagreement after 1949 only served to throw the fundamentals of agreement into more intense relief.

V

THUS indeed has the wheel turned full circle. The United States, from an erstwhile dependency of Great Britain in 1783, had become by 1947 the dispenser of Marshall Aid to an ailing parent. Throughout this period of transformation, British policy remained comparatively unchanged, while that of the United States effected a complete revolution, from eighteenth-century participation in European affairs, through a studied isolation, to renewed participation in world events, only now in the role of a principal, though a principal perhaps closer emotionally to her partner than she had ever been before, even in colonial days.

But it is not surprising that America should so largely have assumed the role which Britain had played in the past, for despite the radical alterations in American diplomacy, the policies of the two countries have always had much in common at the roots. We have already seen how important is the geographical basis of these similarities, and certain political affinities arise more or less directly from them. The insular position of both, in fact, is the basis of their diplomacy; the differences are largely matters of degree. We have seen, for instance, that both have a marked tendency towards an isolationist policy; that Britain in the nineteenth century showed, though to a lesser degree, the same reluctance as America to become embroiled in European affairs. It was merely that physical isolation was not so possible for her, and, in the same way, as the oceans narrowed in the twentieth century, so did the United States find herself less and less able physically to stand apart. In fact, the contrast between the policy of America in 1850 and in 1950 was not due to a change in her motives, but to a change in her circumstances; she was greater and the world was smaller, so that new policies were forced upon her if she was to maintain her traditional aims.

In reality, the success, and indeed the feasibility, of American isolationism had always depended in the nineteenth century upon the existence of a suitable balance of power in Europe, and, because Great Britain made a similar balance the prime objective of her foreign policy, this meant in practice that American isolationism was made possible only by the supremacy of the British Navy. As Bemis points out, the great successes of American diplomacy before 1898 "were due to taking advantage, without much deliberate calculation, of the wars, rivalries and distresses of Europe, in other words, to the balance of power in the Old World".[1] This unconscious dependence of the United States upon British preservation of the balance of power in Europe he more epigrammatically describes by writing, "Manifest Destiny might much better be described as Manifest Opportunity."[2] To the historian it is clear that this dependence of American isolation upon the British navy already existed at the time that the Monroe Doctrine was first enunciated, for, though Monroe's declaration was a unilateral one, it could never have had any reality had it not been known that the general aims of British and American policy were similar, for the United States had not yet the power to stop Britain from actions she might wish to take in the Western hemisphere. To the politically en-lightened and realistic American, this fact became clear as the twentieth century progressed; thus, "The intervention of the United States in the First World War in 1917 preserved the balance of power in Europe in favor of Great Britain and behind Great Britain in favor of the United States, which could always balance the exposed position of Canada against British seapower: the preservation of that balance was the real victory of the United States."[3] In 1940 the proposition, now a practical rather than a theoretical one, was crystal clear to the majority of Americans; if Britain had fallen, America might have been, at least for a time, without adequate defence against Germany, and this fact was epitomized in the exchange of the fifty American destroyers for the British bases for hemispheric defence. The balance of power was in fact shown to be what it always had been, as vital an objective of American policy as of British—only she was protected from the necessity of positive action before the twentieth century by the com-bination of her geographical isolation and British sea power.

Another basic similarity in the diplomacy of the two nations is a difficult and contentious one to elucidate. Both have been, as nations go, peace-loving in their policy. Bellicose leaders have held sway in their time in both states—Palmerston in the one and Theodore Roosevelt in the other—as have men ardently ready for war when war appeared inevitable—Winston Churchill in the one and Jackson in the other—but in neither has militarism, nor the desire for war as

[1] Bemis, p. 877.   [2] Ibid, p. 216   [3] Ibid, pp. 878-9.

such, held sway for long. The record of both has been occasionally questionable—in some of the Indian wars of the United States and some of the colonial wars of Great Britain for example. Indeed, the cynic, or the embittered European, may well suggest that it is just because their reputation in such spheres is doubtful, that their reputation elsewhere is good; they were fortunate to be so situated that their national desire for expansion could be satisfied in the empty lands of the American West, or of Africa and Australasia.

But the fact remains that in international affairs the record of Britain, and even more of the United States, is relatively good, partly because they expanded under the impulse of a vigorous nationalism in places where not much disturbance was caused to the balance of power and way of life of the civilized nations of the Western world. Seton-Watson writes:

> British policy may be said to have thrown its weight from time to time into the European scales in order to secure virtual immunity for her overseas designs. . . . What . . . has scarcely ever varied is the importance attached to naval power, both as a bulwark against invasion, as a protection to British carrying trade, and as a screen behind which colonial expansion could be conducted. . . . From this it follows that certain strategic routes of empire have always been specially in the mind of British statesmen . . . and . . . for two centuries and a half Mediterranean interests have also bulked very largely . . . in British calculations.[1]

This imperial preoccupation canalized British chauvinism in channels where it did less harm than that of France or Germany. Similarly, Bemis writes of America that, after 1823,

> The remaining years of the nineteenth century were to witness throughout the vacant western reaches of this continent a process of self-sustained expansion destined to make the United States a world power fronting on the two great oceans of civilization and ready to control a waterway between them. . . . Expansion expressed the pent-up forces of the developing national spirit in the United States. It has remained its principal and most successful manifestation.[2]

Such a power had little time for aggressive designs elsewhere while she was expanding in America, and not much desire to expand further when she had completed her continental development.

But important though these facts are in explaining the peaceful

[1] *Britain in Europe*, pp. 36-7.　　[2] Bemis, p. 215.

intention of these 'sated' powers, they are not adequate to the effect, for satiety alone does not seem to induce pacifism in nations. In trying to explain the peaceful policies of the two powers, it is hard to avoid the conclusion that their desire for peace is not unconnected with a democratic form of government, that political liberty and popular control of government tend on the whole to promote pacific policies. It is possible certainly to throw doubt on such a conclusion; to point, for instance, to the Mexican War, in the inauguration of which popular opinion in the United States played a powerful part. But, though there may be exceptions to the rule, it is, broadly speaking, true that the common people desire peace, for they are the ones who suffer most in war. They do not desire it at any price, and with their backs to the wall they will fight with valour, pertinacity and desperation; but their first instincts are pacific, and, in countries where they have some measure of control over their governments, there is a tendency to seek peace and ensue it.

But, whatever its cause, it is substantially true that the policies of Britain and the United States since 1783 have been for the most part peaceful. In truth the record of no other great power can match that of the United States in its honourable desire for peace; Bemis truly writes, "Manifest Destiny . . . was not based on militarism. . . . American expansion across a practically empty continent despoiled no nation unjustly, and . . . there is no American today who would want to see that expansion undone."[1] The record of Britain, too, is on the whole creditable; though perhaps more prepared for war when necessary than the United States, at least until very recent times, she has pursued a peaceful policy in more difficult circumstances with commendable perseverance, and though subject—with decreasing frequency—to fits of jingoism, the original sentiment remained true in its entirety *"We don't want to fight, but by Jingo if we do!"* For if there is one fact which emerges from the speeches and actions of successive Foreign Secretaries from Pitt to Grey, it is the paramount importance which they attached to Peace as the foremost British interest."[2] In their desire for peace, then, the policies of the two nations have had much in common, and have had it in common in an increasing degree as the years passed, for in the twentieth century the knowledge that both peoples desired peace above almost all else has constituted an ever more powerful bond between them.

In other ways also their policies have more in common than has

[1] Bemis, pp. 215-6. [2] *Britain in Europe,* p. 647.

always been realized. It has been usual, particularly—as was natural—among Anglophobe Americans, to contrast the iniquitous imperialism of Britain with the egalitarian idealism of the United States, rather in the same way that certain English liberals have been wont to point the finger of scorn at American policy towards the Negroes, who constitute a problem of which the average Englishman has neither knowledge nor experience. But even here the differences have been exaggerated at the expense of the similarities. We have seen how very alike the waves of late nineteenth-century imperialism in the two lands were, but Americans, seeing these things always through the eyes of Jefferson, have until very recently placed too little credence in the expressed intention of Britain to guide all her colonial dependencies towards complete self-government, and have insufficiently understood the nature and importance of the development of the Second British Empire as a free association of equal and independent member nations. In what may be called 'strategic imperialism' there has, in the last hundred years, been little to choose between them, and now there is nothing at all. Britain, at least since her acquisition of Gibraltar in 1704, and the United States, at least since an abortive effort by Secretary Marcy in 1854 to annex Hawaii, have both sought and obtained strategic bases for national defence, which are in a different category from colonial conquests. Britain was earlier off the mark in this pursuit, and, chiefly because of her extensive trade and empire, spread her network of national defence much wider, but before long it had become clear to the United States that such bases were also indispensable to her.

As powers slow to take up arms, they have both been equally slow to lay them down; unwilling to precipitate war, they have usually been ill prepared for it except in the basic strength of their position. They have, however, been seldom equalled and never surpassed in their ultimate capacity to win victories, for, relying upon their wealth and staying-power rather than upon their numbers, neither has ever been beaten in a great modern war, except Britain in the War of American Independence itself. In these respects also, their policies have been closely akin.

Both, finally, have usually had the cause of human liberty at heart. Both were, or came to be, democracies, and both have sought to promote constitutional or democratic systems of government, for their own sake and because they thought them more conducive to the peace of the world. In this they have grown ever closer together, particularly as it became apparent that the ascendancy which liberal ideas had established in the nineteenth century was not necessarily or automatically to be perpetuated in the twentieth. The totalitarian systems of Fascism and Communism drove the two greatest democracies into parallel courses of action; indeed, even in their weaknesses in the face of the enemy they were alike, for in a sense the appeasement policy of Chamberlain (and even more the isolationism of Beaverbrook and the *Daily Express*) was but the isolationist policy of Harding, Coolidge and Hoover writ small. The rejection by the United States of the American guarantee of French integrity, incorporated in Wilson's Versailles Treaty, led directly to the similar repudiation by Britain, since the guarantee of the latter had been made conditional on that of the former.

It is, then, by no means surprising that the United States should so largely have assumed Britain's role in international affairs; it is in fact natural that the cloak of Elijah should thus have fallen upon Elisha, that America in her power should have become the leader of the free nations. Of the five main objectives of traditional British policy, only that of imperialism is not equally now a major motive in American diplomacy, and even this has been in the past, and is still, in a strategic sense, not without its influence upon United States policy. All the others—national survival, the balance of power, control of the seas and free government—are important, indeed pre-eminently the most important, principles upon which America bases her actions in international affairs. Never perhaps before in history, has there been such correspondence, almost identity, of fundamental interests and intentions between two sovereign nations.

Thus the twentieth-century cordiality of Anglo-American relations is solidly based on a foundation of similar, even common, policies, and we may be conscious of this as we glance very briefly at the history of Anglo-American diplomatic relations.

CHAPTER EIGHT

ANGLO-AMERICAN RELATIONS[1]

I

THE diplomatic relationship of Great Britain and the United States, as sovereign and independent powers, had an unusual inauguration in the violence of the American Revolution. This bitter struggle inevitably left its mark upon both of them, and particularly upon the younger and thus more impressionable; indeed, it is not too much to assert that the trauma inflicted by it has not even now ceased to affect America's conduct, and for many years remained the mainspring of her political actions.

What were the principal effects of the American Revolution upon the future of Anglo-American relations? Briefly, the violent rupture gave to the relationship between the two peoples its unusual and peculiar quality. Their common origin, common tongue, kindred institutions, and strong mutual interests still remained; these provided a basis for political and social friendship almost unprecedented between two independent nations, and on this basis there was in the end built what, it is to be hoped, will be a permanent and unshakeable union. The foundations for this union always remained, but the tide of emotion by which they were overlaid in the bitter struggle for independence took many years to subside, leaving them still solid and clearly to be observed, though even yet washed by many a wave of ill-feeling. For at least half a century suspicion became the most apparent characteristic of Anglo-American relations, suspicion which once again burst into the flame of war in 1812. The British, whose pride had received a severe blow in 1783, took refuge in an even more marked and freely expressed contempt for Americans than existed for other "colonials"; most British criticism took the form of supercilious derision of American society and an openly expressed belief—and hope—that the American democratic and republican experiment would fail. Only

[1] For a full history of Anglo-American diplomatic relations, recourse may be had to my *Great Britain and the United States* (London, 1954).

with the coming of political and social reform, and of a new doctrine of colonial relationships, in Britain itself, did this attitude begin to disappear. The Americans reacted even more strongly. All their hatred of arbitrary government, all their dislike of aristocratic inequalities, all their animosity towards the ways of the Old World, became centred in their reaction against everything British. Anti-British sentiments became almost a *sine qua non* of American political success, and this spirit died even harder than did anti-Americanism in Britain.

Yet, despite all this, the basis of common interest remained and in some ways grew more solid. Geographically, though America might seek to draw in her garments from European contamination, she could not do so; as David Hartley wrote in 1783, "Great Britain and the United States must still be inseparable, either as Friends or Foes. This is an awful and important truth." Technical developments, following hard upon the heels of the Revolution, forced the two peoples into closer and closer proximity, for within twenty-five years of the Peace of Paris a steamship was plying upon American waters, and even before that date improvements in the design of vessels had ushered in the era of the swift Clipper ship. Socially and culturally this meant an ever-increasing measure of contact between the two peoples, and the more contact there was the harder it became to ignore the amount they had in common. Small wonder that the British and American minds were torn between feelings for and against each other. Anglo-American feeling has indeed something of the schizophrenic in it. It is remarkable, for instance, how little their emotions bore any relation to the gravity of particular issues; trivial questions like the Sackville-West letter of 1888 and General Butler's New Orleans order in the Civil War were to arouse more fury than many of the grave border disputes. Their common interests bound them indissolubly together, however much their surface sentiments might pull them apart. Of this peculiar relationship Canada remained a remarkable symbol; geographically and economically inseparable from the United States, she yet retained her political and cultural relationship with Britain. She remained at once a hostage for, and an agent of, Anglo-American understanding.

Once independence had been achieved, it was in its effect upon the psychology and the outlook of the two peoples that the Revolution was most important. In Britain, though there was suspicion on the surface, there was below that a marked increase of respect. She was not, after all, accustomed to disastrous defeats in war, such as she suffered in 1783; it was comforting to reflect that, though faced towards the end of the struggle by the most formidable array of European enemies ever ranged against her in her whole history, it was not really by them that she had been beaten, but by the Americans, who were her own flesh and blood. When all was said and done, it took a man of British stock to beat an Englishman. This grudging respect for America has in some senses always remained the characteristic English feeling towards her. It took time to work to the surface, but when, ultimately, it did so, it was accompanied by, and to some extent effected, a great revolution in British political thinking. No doubt the success of the American experiment did something to forward the cause of domestic democratic reform in England in mid-nineteenth century, but the grim and salutary lesson of the American Revolution directly revolutionized, though with a delayed action, the British concept of Empire. The idea of the free association of equal members of the British Commonwealth, which arose out of the movement in the eighteen-thirties and forties symbolized in the Durham Report, owed its inspiration to the English realization that any other course must ultimately lead to a repetition of the American disaster, as well as to a growing clarity of democratic purpose, which was to some extent derived from the American example, operating either directly or through France and her history. In a different way, the Revolution reinforced a lesson which England had already begun to learn, the lesson that the only way to avoid revolution is to promote evolution. The march of the British Dominions towards independent and equal membership of the Commonwealth was effected by gradual changes, by steps spread over a century of history. Thus, paradoxical as it might seem, the sudden breach effected by the Revolution produced in Britain a strengthening of this characteristically English belief, in the adaptation of existing institutions to new purposes, in preserving in order to reform.

The effect upon America was different, for it is not perhaps fanciful to claim that the clean break which the Revolution made exaggerated a tendency, already strong in the American people, to like fresh beginnings and radical solutions to political and social problems. It is easy for an Englishman to under-estimate the effect of the Revolution upon American history. It was to the Americans much more than just one event in a long history: it was the very birth of their nation. Englishmen see it as one almost inevitable step in the protracted development of the colonies, but, rather naturally, Americans are not so very conscious of its relationship to imperial history. Myths have their importance, even when they have little basis in reality, and the importance of the Revolution in American legend has obscured in the American mind the fact that the United States did not, in a kind of spontaneous political generation, spring fully armed and adult from the head of the mother country. When Lincoln talked of a new birth of freedom, he gave voice unmistakably to this American preconception, and he signified a very important fact about it, that it marked for them not only the birth of their country, but the birth of liberty also. For Americans the United States was from its inception inextricably involved in the human search for freedom; America and liberty were indeed born as twins and were nurtured in the same cradle. This effect of the Revolution was burned into the American soul by the fact that the fighting was done on American soil. Both in adversity and in success, the war was the crucible in whose white-heat American patriotism was born: on the anvil of Valley Forge the steel of Americanism was tempered.

But the steel was tempered, too, in the waters of success, for confidence followed upon triumph in the war; the gaining of the Mississippi boundary, for instance, when Congress would at a pinch have accepted one along the crest of the Appalachians, pointed forward to the American conquest of their continental domain. Even in the dangerous disillusion of peace, the Critical Years were terminated by the remarkable and unprecedented, yet solid, success of the formation of the Federal Constitution. These achievements gave to the development of the American attitude to the world its characteristic flavour. It gave it at home its belief in republicanism, in political democracy and, to some extent, radicalism; it gave it, in its policy towards the rest of the world, that revulsion from all things European, and most particularly at first, all things English, which was to find expression in the powerful forces of American isolationism. This went hand in hand with a great absorption of national effort in the rapid exploitation of the West, and the brushing aside of all obstacles thereto; Manifest Destiny in the West implied a maximum withdrawal from the affairs of Europe. Yet, oddly combined with this, was the strenuously idealistic tone of American foreign policy, which found expression, not only in impractical notions as far apart as Jefferson's embargo policy and the Kellogg Peace Pact, but also in great international ventures like the League of Nations and the United Nations. The desire for isolation was accompanied, often thwarted, and, in the end it seems, overlaid, by an almost Messianic sense of mission, a powerful urge to democratize the affairs of men. This development is clearly reflected in the history of Anglo-American relations. The deep-seated mistrust of Britain which followed the Revolution was, though very slowly, replaced by an appreciation of their common outlook and interests.

211

In this way the American Revolution set the tone of Anglo-American relations for many years. There was an inevitable bitterness and mistrust on both sides, though it was stronger and lasted longer in America. At the same time, it could not indefinitely obscure the wide basis of potential agreement between them, and there developed in the twentieth century an increasing measure of co-operation, which must remain a source of satisfaction, if only because it is a source of strength, to both parties. Yet, emotionally tinged as human thoughts are, Englishmen and Americans cannot be expected to regard the American Revolution in the same light. To the Englishman, conscious of the later free development of the other British colonies, it must seem, at best regrettable and at worst lamentable, that the folly of his ancestors was so great, or at least that their wisdom was so small, that they were unable to avoid the disruption of the First British Empire. He cannot but reflect how useful it might have been in this century to have constituted part of a great commonwealth of which the United States would have been a full, and by this time the dominating, member. The American must see the matter differently; to him the Revolution is too important, too integral, too glorious a part—the very foundation indeed —of his national history, for him to wish that it had never happened. And perhaps he is right, for even the Briton, when he reflects upon the fruitfulness of American independence, and the benefits which have arisen, and may yet arise, from free and friendly rivalry and competition between the two peoples, may doubt the wisdom of his regrets. It may be that Nathaniel Hawthorne was right when he wrote, "If England had been wise enough to twine our new vigour round her ancient strength, her power would have been too firmly established ever to yield, in its due season, to the otherwise immutable law of imperial vicissitude. The earth might then have beheld the intolerable spectacle of a sovereignty and institutions, imperfect, but indestructible."

II

The Treaty of Paris, which ended the War of American Independence by recognizing the full sovereignty of the United States, was finally signed on 3 September, 1783. In a sense it constituted a framework for the future development of Anglo-American relations, many of the difficulties of which were to arise from ambiguities in the treaty, or from changes affecting it. The first serious complex of Anglo-American problems after 1783, for instance, developed directly out of it. The

British Government refused to fulfil its undertaking to withdraw its troops from certain western posts in United States territory until the American Government had honoured its obligations concerning the debts owed by Americans to British creditors and the restoration of Loyalist property. The resulting tension in the West grew worse in the ensuing years, and an even more potent source of friction was added when the long French Revolutionary and Napoleonic Wars between France and Britain began early in 1793.

In this great European struggle, as in that of 1914-17 and to a less extent of 1939-41, the United States was the most important neutral maritime power, and in all three wars it was Britain's policy to restrict as much as possible, by the use of her great naval strength, the trade of all neutrals with her enemies. At first, in each case, the Anglo-American struggle which resulted was ostensibly waged over the international law of neutral maritime rights, but as each European war was prolonged and became more bitter, the actions of the belligerents became more ruthless and the legal arguments were increasingly abandoned in favour of naked reprisals. This brought ever more serious clashes between the belligerents and the United States, and in the French wars they were more severe with Britain than with France. By 1794 this Anglo-American tension was still embryonic but it had become sufficiently threatening to convince Washington of the necessity of making a positive bid for a firm settlement with Britain.

As a result, in that year, his envoy John Jay signed in London the treaty commonly called after him, which was probably the most unpopular treaty in American history. It was ratified in the Senate (although by the narrowest possible margin) largely owing to the dogged support of Washington, who was inclining more and more towards the pro-British views of Hamilton and the Federalists and against the rising tide of Jeffersonian Republicanism, which was at first very sympathetic to Revolutionary France. In fact, considering that Britain was engaged in a deadly struggle which rendered it very difficult for her to make concessions on neutral rights, the treaty was not as detrimental to American interests as has often been asserted. In the form in which it was finally ratified, it not only achieved the withdrawal of British troops from the Western posts, but also set a most fruitful precedent in Anglo-American relations (and international affairs in general) by establishing a joint commission which succeeded in settling a major ambiguity (one of the many concerning the boundaries of the United States with British North America) in the treaty of 1783. From this success there stemmed the long, and indeed unique, history of

Anglo-American arbitrations in the years to come. Furthermore, a not illiberal, though limited, trade treaty was signed. Jay was, however, unable to extract any real concessions at all in the sphere of neutral rights, so that this problem remained as a source of increasing difficulty in the immediate future.

But at first—so strong were the anti-French feelings of the Federalists —the United States very nearly became involved in war with the other European protagonist, France; but after this had been averted by President Adams, Jefferson's accession to the Presidency in 1801 set in train a prolonged deterioration in Anglo-American relations. Republican efforts to bring Britain to terms by economic sanctions—various forms of economic self-denying ordinance, restricting her trade with one or both belligerents, were tried out in vain—only made matters worse, and tension was steadily intensified by British refusals to relinquish the practice of impressing seamen (when it was claimed that they were British) from American merchant ships on the high seas for service in the Royal Navy. When in 1807 the local British commander rashly and stupidly, as well as unwarrantably, seized some British deserters from the American naval vessel *Chesapeake* by force, at the cost of a number of American casualties, war was barely averted, and American emotions were increasingly aroused on the impressment issue. Sincere efforts on the part of Monroe, the American minister in London, in 1807, and Erskine, the British minister in Washington, in 1809, to stop the rot, were repudiated by Jefferson and Canning respectively; and when tension once more developed in the West, where American ambitions to conquer Canada waxed strongest, Congress declared war, on the recommendation of President Madison, on 18 June, 1812.

Despite the American victory at New Orleans in 1815, the War of 1812 was militarily quite inconclusive. Partly as a result of this and partly of the ending of the European war, which had been the cause of most of the Anglo-American disagreements, the Treaty of Ghent, which terminated hostilities in 1814 on the basis of the *status quo ante bellum*, did not even mention either impressment or neutral rights. The former was never again to be employed, but the latter were to play a long and vital part in the history of Anglo-American relations. Three joint commissions were set up under the treaty in an effort to resolve the six major remaining ambiguities in the Canadian-American boundary; three of these were settled by 1822, but three still persisted. A dispute over American fishing rights off the coasts of British North America, which had been a source of difficulty since 1783, was settled in 1818, when the second of two Anglo-American commercial treaties supplemental to the Treaty of Ghent was signed. The actual provisions of these economic agreements were much less important than the fact that in 1822 Britain began to move in the direction of free trade, which finally became her declared national policy more than a quarter of a century later. This made possible what American trading interests had long desired, a virtually unrestricted commercial intercourse between the United States and the British Empire, particularly those parts of it bordering on the Atlantic.

In a sense the Treaty of Ghent closed the first chapter in American foreign policy. The years since 1783 had been largely spent by the United States in endeavouring to rid herself of the toils of Europe, and particularly of Britain, thus freeing herself to turn her back on the Old World and attend to her own affairs. Western ambitions in the War of 1812 had heralded a new era, when the United States was to be almost exclusively preoccupied in acquiring and developing the great continental domain which lay to the West. Because Canada was ever-present on the northern flank of her westward march, America's relations with Britain remained closer, and also more difficult, than with any other country. But the War of 1812, "futile and unnecessary" though it was, left no permanent scars, and gave the two nations a decent respect for one another's strength; because it was a stalemate and was soon ended, it checked any tendency to the further deterioration of Anglo-American relations. In this sense it did not form too unsatisfactory a basis for the relationship in the ensuing century of American isolation.

III

The determination of the United States to isolate herself from European affairs and to devote her resources to the opening up of the Great West was, in effect, the subject of a remarkable affirmation with the enunciation of the Monroe Doctrine, for this solemn executive declaration postulated that the wars of Europe were no concern of the United States, and, conversely, warned the powers of Europe against interference in American affairs. But it was much more than an isolationist *pronunciamiento,* for the doctrine threw the mantle of the Republic's power and protection over the whole Western Hemisphere. Primarily directed against France, Spain and Russia, and originally suggested by Britain as a joint action, John Quincy Adams insisted that it must be a unilateral American venture, even though it could only be made good by British naval power. Thus the United States, by acting alone though in the knowledge of British complaisance, asserted her freedom of action, while recognizing and to the best of her ability guaranteeing the independence of the Latin American colonies which had thrown off the yoke of Spain. Even the aged Jefferson had advised accepting Britain's offer of alliance, but on 2 December, 1823, quite independently, Monroe sent his famous message to Congress, dissociating the United States from European affairs except when her rights were threatened, pointing out that the political systems of Europe and America were different, and declaring that, although with "the existing colonies or dependencies of any European power we have not interfered and shall not interfere", "we should consider any attempt on their part to extend their system to any portion of this hemisphere as dangerous to our peace and safety".

Britain did not formally accept the Monroe Doctrine but she acquiesced in it in practice, and this acquiescence alone made its effective maintenance possible before the rise of American naval power in the twentieth century. In fact little was heard of it, once the immediate effects of the message had died down, until it was reaffirmed by President Polk in 1845. But the determination of Adams that the United States should pursue an independent course ensured that it was not until the end of the nineteenth century that a continuous Anglo-American co-operation entered once more into the realms of possibility.

The years between 1823 and 1860 in Anglo-American relations were primarily concerned with the settlement of the chief boundary disputes between the two countries, with commercial competition and friction, and with rivalries in Latin-America which centred chiefly on the question of a possible Isthmian canal. The Administrations of Jackson between 1829 and 1837 saw the decisive steps taken towards liberalizing trade between the United States and the British Empire in America, as well as the growth of a better feeling between the two governments than had existed since the days of Washington, for during the Presidency of his predecessor, John Quincy Adams, feeling had run very high with Canning on these commercial issues. But the crisis which arose in 1837, and lasted till the signing of the Webster-Ashburton Treaty in 1842, was much more severe than that of 1824-7 and dispersed much of the goodwill that Jackson and Prime Minister Wellington had created.

The root of the trouble was the disagreement over the Maine-New Brunswick boundary, which was coming to a head as settlement built up in the disputed area from both the American and British sides of the border. But the whole crisis became much more menacing with the outbreak in 1837 of armed rebellion against British rule in Canada. American (and particularly Irish-American) sympathy for the rebels took practical form when one of the Canadian insurgent leaders fled across the Niagara river and established his headquarters on American soil, whereupon a party of Canadian volunteers entered the United States on a foray, killing an American in the process. The Federal government acted with restraint—even obtaining new neutrality legislation from Congress in 1838—and, though Palmerston did not show the same caution, under the more conciliatory Aberdeen, who succeeded him in 1841, negotiations were opened in Washington by Alexander Baring, Lord Ashburton, and he was determined to reach an agreement. In this he was successful, for the final treaty settled not only the Maine boundary, but also another border dispute in the area of the Great Lakes, thus fixing once and for all the Canadian-American boundary from the Atlantic Ocean to the Rocky Mountains.

Within three years of the Webster-Ashburton Treaty, Texas, which had established its independence of Mexico in 1836, had been annexed by the United States, and in the very next year came the Mexican War. The expansionist programme on which President Polk had been elected in 1844 had demanded not only Texas, but Oregon as well. This disputed territory, stretching from the Rockies to the Pacific, had, by an Anglo-American treaty of 1818, been declared "free and open" to Americans and British alike, and a number of efforts to end this temporary "joint occupation" by a compromise fixing the boundary along the 49th parallel had failed. A really sharp crisis with Britain resulted from Polk's election, but in the end, with the Mexican War on his hands, he consented to accept the continuation of the 49° prairie boundary to the sea and the inclusion of Vancouver Island in British territory. Thus in 1846 the last serious Anglo-American dispute about the borders of the continental United States was settled, and within two years, by the Treaty of Guadalupe Hidalgo, the United States, having added 1,204,896 square miles to her existing 1,792,223, had reached almost her present boundaries in the south as well as the north. She had fulfilled with astonishing rapidity what many of her people called her Manifest Destiny.

These prodigious gains of territory from Mexico, added to her acquisition of Florida thirty years before, were, not unnaturally, the cause of some misgivings in the minds of British statesmen, and not only somewhat sharpened Anglo-American commercial rivalry but also focused attention on the interest of both governments in the possibility of an Atlantic-Pacific canal in Central America. From this situation there emerged the Clayton-Bulwer Treaty of 1850, a highly unsatisfactory, very complex and deliberately ambiguous agreement, which was to be a source of Anglo-American misunderstanding for half a century. The difficulties revolved at first around the status of the British colonies of the Bay Islands and British Honduras and of the British protectorate over the Indians of the Mosquito coast, the bombardment of whose capital by order of the American Government in 1854 might well have had very grave consequences if the hands of the British had not been tied by the Crimean War. With the ending of this war, during which the attempts of the British Minister in Washington to recruit troops for service in the Crimea had resulted in his dismissal by President Pierce, the atmosphere improved markedly, and a *modus vivendi* was reached over Central America in 1860. In the future, American dissatisfaction with the Clayton-Bulwer Treaty was to concentrate on its neutralization of the Isthmus and its internationalization of any future canal: Britain on the other hand was slowly coming to realize that America was destined to be a great power whether she liked it or not and to apprehend dimly, yet with increasing force, that it was very much better to be her friend than her enemy. Thus in the end an exclusively American canal was to prove possible, while in 1860 the outlook for Anglo-American relations was in some ways more auspicious than at any time since 1783.

The Civil War set them back very seriously, perhaps through no real fault of either party. British sympathies in the war, it is true, were divided and changeable, but the policy of the British Government never actually altered from that laid down in the Proclamation of Neutrality issued on 13 May, 1861, recognizing the belligerency of both North and South. The clearest evidence of this was the failure of the South to obtain that full British recognition of the Confederate government on which it had set its heart, let alone the British intervention for which it hoped. It is true also that in allowing the construction and indirect sale to the South of the commerce raider *Alabama,* which did so much damage to Northern shipping, Britain overstepped the strict limits of neutrality as now understood, but the concept of neutrality was not then so clearly defined either in British or international law, while in the end the prevention by the British Government of the similar sale of the Laird "rams" to the Confederacy put British policy back on the rails again. These incidents caused acute tension, but it was no more acute than that caused by the Union's seizure of two Confederate diplomats from the British ship *Trent* earlier in the war; here it was the United States which, largely under the influence of Seward, showed its good sense and good will by releasing the envoys. In the diplomatic sphere (as opposed to the military, where the Northern armies had to invade and conquer the South) it was the Confederacy which was forced to take the initiative by trying to obtain European recognition, if not active aid; the North had to maintain the diplomatic *status quo*. The South failed because the weapon in which it had puts its faith—cotton—was not sufficiently effective; its denial to the mills of Britain by the Northern blockade (and even by deliberate Southern policy) did not produce the clamour for intervention by the British people which optimistic Southerners confidently anticipated, partly because of the existence of unusually large cotton stocks in Britain, partly because of the development of alternative sources of supply, partly because of the war boom in other industries than cotton, and partly because of sympathy for the cause of the North among the labouring classes, who were most hard hit by the shortage.

At the very beginning of the war, Britons had mostly taken the unsophisticated view that the struggle was about slavery, and the generally strong British opinion on that subject led to widespread sympathy with the North. But when Lincoln consistently declared that it was in fact about the Union and not about slavery, British ideas changed. A certain upper class element gave free rein to its sympathy for a kindred oligarchical society in the South, and to its pleasure in the apparent failure of the great democratic experiment across the Atlantic. On the other hand, radical and working-class opinion reacted very favourably to Lincoln's assertions that the North was fighting for the cause of democracy. In the end, under the leadership of Bright, such sentiments as these played an important part in the growing movement for Parliamentary reform in Britain, and the victory of the North was very influential in the genesis of the Reform Bill of 1867. But for a period the issue was confused, even for men as liberal as Gladstone, by the South's plea that it was in fact a nation rightly struggling to be free—a cry which aroused, as it did over Italy, Hungary and Poland, an instinctive response in the hearts of Englishmen. But probably most influential of all in moulding British opinion in the end was Lincoln's Emancipation Proclamation of 1862 for, despite its shortcomings, it made it increasingly clear that the struggle was one to free the slaves after all; and on this issue there was no division of public opinion in Britain. Thus vocal sympathy for the South faded as the victory of the North approached.

But public opinion in mid-nineteenth century Britain was one thing, government policy still another. The dominant British figure in these years was Palmerston, and, for all his understanding of English opinion, he was at bottom very much a realist, who set the tone of British Government deliberations by keeping his eye more on the military situation than upon the state of British popular feeling. Whenever there was serious danger of British involvement, precipitate action was in the end prevented by the obstinate military perseverance of the North. Britain's leaders were wise enough in the event to see that intervention which would aid the South would be a disaster if the North won the war, and thus it was that, though Britain was unpopular for a spell in both North and South after the war, Anglo-American relations were not disastrously damaged by it.

Northern animosity found expression in the post-war years in the most energetic of all the American movements to annex Canada, one rendered very formidable by the vast Union armies still in being, but when it became clear that such an idea now commanded very little support among Canadians, who in fact expressed their opposition most forcibly by establishing the new Canadian Confederation in 1867, American good sense asserted itself and the movement died away. Feelings still found vent, however, in the American claim for damages arising out of the depredations of the *Alabama* during the war, depredations made possible in the view of the American Government by defects in Britain's attitude of neutrality. This issue dominated Anglo-American relations for seven years after the end of the war, and swept along in its path less important questions such as the perennial one of Canadian fisheries and the one arising from the Fenian raids of armed Irish bands across the border from the United States into Canada. A comprehensive treaty signed in Washington in 1871 settled nearly all the matters in dispute, and, in what was now becoming an established Anglo-American tradition, sent the *Alabama* case to arbitration. The Geneva award of 1872, which dismissed the more extreme American claims at the suggestion of the American representative, C. F. Adams, assessed the damages to be paid by Britain at $15,500,000. To their credit, under the influence of Gladstone, the British Government accepted the award, so that it marked a triumph of that policy of concession and conciliation which alone has worked well between the two peoples.

Thus Anglo-American relations entered in 1873 upon twenty-two quiet years, which were very fruitful in the steady growth of social contacts and mutual confidence. The diplomatic issues of this period—international sealing, the Sackville-West incident, the fisheries once more—were hardly more than trivial. The Isthmian question did begin to move again into the public eye, but it did not come into full focus until the turn of the century. The Venezuela incident of 1895-6 alone, at the end of the era, showed that the embers of American anglophobia could very readily be fanned into flame. The long-standing border dispute between Venezuela and Britain's colony of Guiana only became of importance when the second Cleveland Administration decided that Britain's alterations in her boundary claims amounted to a violation of the Monroe Doctrine; but when this unexpected belligerence (not uncharacteristic of Olney, the Secretary of State) was greeted by Lord Salisbury with excessively deliberate sang-froid, the situation began to look ominous. Salisbury, however, then grasped the seriousness of the position and powerful voices were raised on both sides of the Atlantic —though particularly perhaps in Britain—against the mere possibility of a fratricidal war, so that a satisfactory diplomatic solution was found without undue delay. Nevertheless, the incident constituted in some respects a salutary lesson, for at bottom the situation of which it was a symptom arose from the developing power of the United States and from her increasing involvement in the affairs of the world, both in Europe and in the Pacific area. As the young giant began to emerge from isolation, great changes in the world were to be necessary; on her successful adaptation to these vast movements, the future fate of Britain was in large degree to depend. It was perhaps as well that she should be sharply reminded, at the outset of this era, of the passions still latent beneath the seemingly smooth surface of Anglo-American relations.

IV

The first steps of the United States on to the world stage at the end of the nineteenth century took the form of what has been called "the great aberration" of American imperialism. They were impelled more by internal pressures upon the formation of her foreign policy than by those external forces which were to become dominant in the period of World War I. Both, however, were at bottom manifestations of the same process, which Henry Adams noted when, in 1904, he reached Washington, "where the contrast of atmosphere astonished him, for he had never before seen his country think as a world-power." But in Anglo-American history these years are not only important because they saw gigantic shifts in the structure of international power, but also because they witnessed a dramatic increase in the cordiality and warmth of Anglo-American relations; this new Anglo-American understanding must, as L. M. Gelber writes, "take first rank" among "the decisive events of modern history". This fact has not always been grasped since by United Kingdom historians, and this has encouraged a Eurocentricity of outlook among educated Britons which has been rendered even more marked by their ignorance of American history and affairs. Fortunately for Britain, her statesmen in this era, partly because of the expansive effect of the still-living Imperial idea, took larger views, and put its proper, its supreme, value, on "the rise of Anglo-American friendship".

These critical years at the turn of the century were ones of apparent complexity, but beneath the choppy waters of Anglo-American diplomacy the tide ran strongly and swiftly towards agreement. In both countries, emerging from a traditional isolation, which, of course, went much deeper in the United States than in Britain, long-term political, social and sentimental trends worked towards it, and in both, sharp, immediate, international difficulties placed a premium on mutual friendship. The United States, venturing suddenly on a decisive scale into imperialist enterprise, was surprised, even shocked, by the hostility of the great powers of Europe, and correspondingly fortified by the friendliness of Britain, which not only took the form in the Spanish-American War of a benevolent neutrality very vexing to most of Europe, but extended to a widespread sympathy for the kindred colonial adventures of the other "Anglo-Saxon" nation. Britain was less surprised by the hostility of the powers a year later, in the remarkably analogous circumstances of the Boer War, but she was even more grateful for the resolute sympathy of the American Government because she was more conscious of the danger of her isolated position in the world. Indeed, the primary impulse towards an Anglo-American *entente* unquestionably came from Britain, and this was largely so because of her uneasiness at the international situation in which she found herself. Fear of Germany led her not merely to rapprochement with France and to actual alliance with Japan, but to a close, if intangible, understanding with the United States, for which twenty years later she was unhesitatingly to sacrifice the Japanese agreement. It is less often realized that a similar fear impelled America in the same direction, and was chiefly responsible for the remarkable rise of the United States Navy from its negligible strength in 1890 to a position second only to Britain's in 1906. Under the influence (equally potent on both sides of the Atlantic) of Admiral Mahan, who not only pointed a prophetic finger at the danger from Germany but also asserted that "in unity of heart among the English-speaking races lies the best hope of humanity in the doubtful days ahead", both nations came to regard it as axiomatic during these years that their navies could only be complementary and never hostile to one another. This was much more important to Britain than to the United States, and it, above all else, made possible the vital strategic redistribution of British forces which preceded World War I and which made so great a contribution to her victory in it.

Britain veritably laid siege in these years to the citadel of American confidence, and almost all the leading English statesmen went repeatedly on record in favour of co-operation with the United States. There, too, though many hung back, powerful personalities and groups reacted cordially to British advances. The flowering of Anglo-American friendship in this, probably the most vital, period of its development was also due to the increasing similarities of predilection, interest and outlook between the two peoples. This symbiosis was to continue and to gain strength in the future.

Thus in the Spanish-American War, which broke out in 1898, Britain, in benevolent neutrality, held the ring for the United States, and her sea power made the intervention of any hostile European power virtually impossible. Her diplomats fumbled a little at the very beginning, but by the time that hostilities ceased, she was positively pressing the American Government to take the Philippines, as well as Puerto Rico, from Spain; as Kipling urged the American people, in famous words,

"Take up the White Man's burden—
Ye dare not stoop to less—
Nor call too loud on Freedom
To cloke your weariness."

John Hay, who was American ambassador in London from 1897 until the next year, when he was translated to be Secretary of State in Washington, never forgot this manifestation of British goodwill; and on his friend Henry Adams it made so profound an impression that this bringing of "England into an American system" seemed to him for the first time in his life some evidence of a "possible purpose working itself out in history". When the Boer War began in 1899 Hay repaid British friendship by determining that no American action harmful to Britain should result, and he accordingly kept the anti-colonial and pro-Boer sympathies of many of his countrymen under control—the most vital contribution he could make to the British cause.

In another sphere, too, the Secretaryship of Hay was to see a marked American effort to align her policy with that of Britain, combined with a striking willingness on the part of the United States Government to take the international initiative, in a way hardly conceivable before the Spanish-American War. Traditional British policy towards China had largely consisted of preventing action by any other power which would interfere with free commercial intercourse with the Chinese—what came to be called the Open Door policy. British approaches to the United States in 1898 suggesting joint action in this area had been politely put off by Washington, then very preoccupied with Spain (rather as had Canning's approaches to Monroe three-quarters of a century before), and in 1899 Hay independently sent his first Open Door Note to the major powers, calling for assurances of non-intervention in China (rather as Monroe had spoken out alone in 1823) in the knowledge of British sympathy. In 1900 he went further, independently once more, in the second Open Door Note which called on the powers to preserve the territorial integrity of China. But public opinion in years to come in America was to lag behind that of government, and it was not for a very long time that the United States was to show itself willing to use force in support of its policies in the Far East, so that practical possibilities of Anglo-American co-operation in that sphere evaporated.

In these matters Anglo-American relations pointed forward to the future, when their problem was increasingly to be that of aligning their attitudes towards third parties, and no longer that of solving direct disputes between themselves: this was a very marked advance. Thus Britain's unwise association with Germany, in an effort to extract their just debts from Venezuela in 1902-3, did not assume the aspect of an Anglo-American clash over the Monroe Doctrine, partly because in a sense the action had been "cleared" with the American Administration beforehand, but even more because Britain hastily withdrew when she saw the vigour of American reaction against Germany's intervention. Two issues remaining in these years, which came by the processes of diplomacy to be linked, were, however, direct Anglo-American disputes, the Isthmian question and the Alaska boundary conflict. The United States refused to play the game desired by Canada—bartering British concessions in Central America against American concessions in Alaska—and once this was clear, the United States was bound to get its way on both issues, for Britain rightly realized that good Anglo-American relations were far more valuable both to her and to Canada than any particular Canadian interest. This was to leave some soreness in Canada, but before long Canadians themselves reasserted their belief that Canada could only live in circumstances of British-American friendship—the fundamental axiom of Canadian foreign policy.

With the rise of American power and the growth of American imperialism the determination of the United States to build and to control an Isthmian canal alone and unaided had become steadily stronger, and the provisions of the ill-starred Clayton-Bulwer Treaty neutralizing and internationalizing any future canal became more and more unpopular in the United States. In the changed circumstances of British strategy and of Anglo-American friendship a new Isthmian treaty was signed between the two powers in 1900, but there could be no better illustration of America's new power and Britain's complaisance that the Senate in effect insisted on another treaty, which did not neutralize the canal, but gave the United States a unique police function in its vicinity. This was the Hay-Pauncefote Treaty of 1901, which cleared the way for the building of the Panama Canal exclusively by the United States. Similarly, Theodore Roosevelt, who had now become President, in effect refused to compromise the Alaska boundary dispute with Canada, since he believed, with some justice, that the Canadian case was a very weak one. In 1903 in a supposedly judicial settlement, which was in fact partly the result of great political pressure, the British Chief Justice (who held the balance between the Canadians and Americans on the arbitral tribunal) came down in favour of the United States. Thus was settled virtually the last territorial dispute between the British Empire and the United States; for nearly a century their manifold problems, many of them arising from the Treaty of 1783, had been settled by a mixture of negotiation and abitration. Efforts in these years before World War I to generalize and institutionalize these arbitration arrangements were not very successful, but the century of achievement, and the habit formed thereby, were none the less important for the future.

V

The goodwill between the two countries which was the outcome of this and other factors in these years was to survive in remarkable fashion the vicissitudes of the next half-century. Two minor differences in the next decade, over Mexican policy and over the Panama Canal tolls, were readily surmounted by the mutually sympathetic Democratic and Liberal governments after 1913. But the first real test was the outbreak of World War I in 1914, and it was as well that in that centennial year of the Treaty of Ghent Anglo-American friendship was on a solider foundation than at any time since Independence, for the Great War reproduced in some ominous ways the circumstances of the Napoleonic struggle, with the difference that the United States was now not only the second naval power but also the strongest nation in the world, although it was still Britain's interest to reduce American trade with her enemies as much as possible. It is true that in the Civil War the Union, as the chief naval belligerent and the blockading power, facing Britain as the leading trading neutral, had seen the other side of the coin, but efforts in the years since 1865 to narrow or close the gap between the two points of view on neutral rights had failed when, ironically and unusually, the House of Lords refused to accept the Declaration of London in 1911, just as the United States had refused to accept the Declaration of Paris on the same subject in 1856. Thus Anglo-American friction over the "freedom of the seas" began as soon as the war broke out in 1914.

Fundamentally, two things determined that this never brought the two countries to the breaking point. The first was the stupidity and brutality of German policy; thus whenever Germany let things take their course, the constant clash of Anglo-American maritime tension augmented, but at each Anglo-American crisis the Imperial German Government took, or permitted, some action which shocked American opinion and in this way automatically lowered the temperature of Anglo-American relations. So it was at bottom, as Wilson declared it was, the German programme of unrestricted submarine warfare, with its toll of civilian lives, which forced the President into war. The second factor which prevented a breach was that, in contrast with the situation a century before, a far better understanding between Britain and America made it possible to avoid fatal mistakes. Thus many Americans had a real sympathy for the Allied cause, as opposed to what they regarded as the autocratic militarism of the Central Powers, while Britain was now very sensitive to the strength and importance of the United States and framed her policies accordingly. Wilson was probably expressing his inner personal conviction when he said to Joseph Tumulty, "England is fighting our fight", and Asquith was certainly expressing his when he declared, "At bottom the two people surely understand one another and have unbreakable bonds of sympathy. No serious breach is conceivable. Mr. Page, after any policy or plan is thought out on its merits my next thought always is how it may affect our relations with the United States. That is always a fundamental consideration." Henry Cabot Lodge struck to the heart of the matter when he said in a Senate debate on the British blockade and the German submarine campaign that "his heart was more moved by the thought of a drowned baby than an unsold bale of cotton", and it was the German announcement on 31 January, 1917, of the renewal of unrestricted submarine warfare that led directly to the American declaration of war on 6 April, despite the fact that Anglo-American relations had been worse in the previous six months than at any time during the war.

For there had been serious Anglo-American differences in the three preceding years, differences arising not only from the blockade, as it was loosely called, but also from the attitude of the American Government to the fundamental issues of the war. Wilson's own position varied between his austere appeal to the American people in 1914 to "be impartial in thought as well as in action" and his readiness to undertake in 1916 that the United States would probably enter the war if Germany would not accept his mediation on terms to be previously agreed with the Allies. When, in depression at the carnage and in his desire for the sake of civilization as a whole to arrange a "peace without victory", he declared in December, 1916, that "the objects which the statesmen of the belligerents on both sides have in mind are virtually the same, as stated to their own people and to the world", British opinion was profoundly disturbed. There were, as a result, those who believed that even when America entered the war, she would still only do so half-heartedly: they proved to be quite wrong. Not only did she throw all her might into the scale but in addition Anglo-American co-operation, particularly at sea, became very close. No more, for example, was heard of the error of British ways of blockade, though the doctrine of the Freedom of the Seas was still to be a bone of contention between the statesmen of the coalition in the making of the peace.

Yet despite this decisive American contribution to the winning of the war, Wilson still maintained a certain aloofness from the Anglo-French cause; he called the United States, for instance, an Associated rather than an Allied power. In his fundamentally moral approach to politics he felt that America's hands were cleaner than those of the European powers, inheritors as they were of such iniquitous diplomatic traditions as a belief in the balance of power; but this instinctive and not uncharacteristically American preconception could not but appear upon occasion pharisaical to his European colleagues. Thus, from the start, his famous Fourteen Points speech of January, 1918, launching his conception of a peace which should inaugurate a new moral order in international affairs by its generous rectitude and its institution of a League of Nations, had a mixed reception in Britain, as indeed it did also in his own country. The more realistic—or cynical, according to the point of view—of the Europeans were determined to restrain Wilson's idealism in the interests of security, if not of retribution. In this way the actual Treaty of Versailles of 1919 became a compromise between the ruthless practicality of Clemenceau and the lofty and sanguine moralism of Wilson, and, as Lloyd George acted in some sense as a buffer between these two, so British public opinion on the whole occupied an intermediate position between the mass of French opinion on the one hand and pro-League opinion in the United States on the other.

For the American people were far from unanimous in supporting Wilson's insistence on the fullest United States participation in the League of Nations. A fundamental division over foreign policy had become apparent in 1918 when Wilson led the Democrats to fight the Congressional elections on strict party lines, and from this time forward domestic opposition to the whole moralistic conception of international affairs, for which Wilson stood, increased. But the President, already ailing and soon to be grievously stricken, would accept no compromise, and demanded from his supporters in the Senate unswerving insistence on the League, the whole League, and nothing but the League. The struggle which ensued was a protracted one, and, as the Republican Henry Cabot Lodge, Wilson's chief opponent, had realized, the longer it went on the more isolationist American opinion tended to become. Thus it was not until March, 1920, that the Treaty, with and without amendments—the so-called reservations—finally failed to obtain the requisite two-thirds majority in the Senate, and that all real hope of American participation in the League of Nations disappeared. The sweeping Republican victory in the Presidential election of 1920 confirmed the increasing American withdrawal from the affairs of Europe. This reversion to isolationism left a deep mark on the European attitude to America, but it was somewhat less traumatic in the case of Britain than in that of France, for it was not entirely unexpected; what is more, it followed so closely the pattern of traditional British behaviour that it met with a kind of grudging British comprehension. Indeed there were groups in Britain who still yearned after the same kind of isolationism, which had been practised by Britons in previous eras; and in fact when the United States refused to ratify its guarantee to France against German attack, the British Government, which had quietly made theirs conditional on the American, also withdrew their specific guarantee. Many, indeed most, British statesmen were to remain excessively sceptical of American intervention in the affairs of Europe when these began to deteriorate rapidly in the 1930s and when, with the accession of Franklin D. Roosevelt to the Presidency, there was more possibility of it, but in many ways Britain slipped back readily into the familiar pattern of Anglo-American relations which had developed in the previous two decades.

And though the Republican administrations of the twenties ostentatiously dissociated themselves from the affairs of the League of Nations, the United States took the lead in convening the Washington naval conference of 1921, from which there emerged—vital and formidable step for Britain—a recognition of the equality of Britain and America in capital ships, and the effective abandonment of the Anglo-Japanese alliance, at the request of the United States, in favour of the very vague and generalized provisions of the Four and Nine Power Treaties. The painful process of recognizing American naval equality in lesser spheres, such as that of cruisers, was not completed by Britain until the London Naval Conference of 1930; and efforts in 1931 to concert Anglo-American opposition to Japanese aggression in Manchuria failed, partly because of the sceptical incompetence of the British Foreign Secretary, Sir John Simon, and partly because of the inability of Secretary of State Stimson to make any real headway against the pacifist convictions of President Hoover and the isolationist mood of the American people. Mutual recriminations at this same time on the subject of German reparations and Allied war debts came to a head when, in the first throes of the Great Depression, Britain, along with all the other debtor nations except Finland, began to make only token repayments. After Congress had passed the Johnson Act in 1934, prohibiting American loans to any government in default on a debt to the United States, Britain finally ceased payments altogether. Despite the numerous commercial treaties negotiated by Secretary of State Hull, including one with Britain in 1938, the depression enhanced the American absorption with domestic affairs, but British financial intimacy with—indeed dependence on—the United States was very clear at the height of the British economic crisis in August, 1931. Roosevelt's torpedoing of the London Economic Conference of 1933, however, which was in fact due to his economic convictions, was seen in Britain as yet another manifestation of American isolationism.

This American mood did indeed appear to deepen as the rise of Hitler and the growing obstreperousness of Mussolini accelerated the drift to war in Europe. The Nye committee's investigation of the

American munitions industry which began in 1934, and the thesis of its isolationist members—that it was at bottom the desire of America's financiers to protect their investments, which caused the American entry into World War I—led to a clamour for the passage of neutrality legislation to prevent the recurrence of this catastrophe. The result was the Neutrality Act of 1935, which was replaced by an even more isolationist measure in 1937; this prohibited the export of arms or ammunition to belligerents, gave the President power to put an embargo on certain war materials, forbade the sale of these except for cash and prohibited their carriage in American vessels, made it unlawful to arm American merchant ships, and absolutely prohibited American travel upon belligerent vessels. By this unprecedented self-denying ordinance America in effect renounced her international rights and surrendered most of her international influence; but in fact the President and the State Department had struggled hard to prevent the passage of the legislation in this form, and more and more, as the situation worsened in Europe, the President tried to drag a reluctant legislature and people towards a realization of some of the basic facts of international life. Despite increasingly strenuous efforts, epitomized in his Chicago "quarantine" speech of October, 1937, and his secret and rejected offer to Chamberlain to call a conference in Washington in January, 1938, he made little progress before the outbreak of war between Britain and Germany on 3 September, 1939.

VI

The President's Proclamation of Neutrality on 5 September, however, unlike that of Wilson twenty-five years before, contained the phrase "without interfering with the free expression of opinion and sympathy", and, from the first, feeling against the dictatorships ran high among the American people. Before long the Neutrality Act was modified to allow belligerents to buy arms for "cash and carry" them away in their own ships, and when in the spring of 1940 almost the whole of Western Europe fell before the German armies pro-Allied sentiment became rapidly so pronounced that on 10 June Roosevelt could declare that we "will extend to the opponents of force the material resources of this nation". Once American opinion was convinced that Britain would not yield or be rapidly conquered, the President's policy of sending all aid short of war gradually made headway. In September, fifty over-age American destroyers were in effect exchanged for United States ninety-nine year leases of a number of defence bases in British possessions in the Caribbean. After the President's re-election in the autumn for an unprecedented third term, he grappled with a fundamental Anglo-American problem, the exhaustion of Britain's dollar assets in the United States in face of her ever expanding demand for arms and war materials. The result was the Lend-Lease Act of 1941, which was to be the supreme economic instrument of victory. During the ensuing year the United States edged closer and closer to war with Germany, so that by September she had not only occupied Greenland and Iceland and given orders to her navy to shoot German submarines on sight, but had actually signed, in the Atlantic Charter, an Anglo-American declaration of aims in a war which ostensibly she had not yet entered. The question of when and to what extent she would do so was rendered hypothetical by the Japanese attack on Pearl Harbour three months later, and Germany's consequent declaration of war on the United States.

There now followed an exceedingly close integration of the Anglo-American war effort and a high degree of popular co-operation, probably surpassing in completeness any previous co-ordination of war policy between two sovereign peoples. Not merely was the example set by the close personal relationship between Roosevelt and Churchill at the summit, but it was followed by the establishment of the Combined Chiefs of Staff Committee for the joint prosecution of the war; in the European theatre, under the united command of General Eisenhower, it penetrated to all levels of the Allied armies. The common law marriage of 1940-1 became a full matrimonial relationship in 1942. This is not to say that there were no serious Anglo-American disagreements during the war, but simply that they were exceptions to the general rule. One of them was the dispute over the timing and importance of the so-called Second Front in North-West Europe; another was the unhappy "Battle of the Generals", British and American, during that same campaign; yet another was that over the recognition of General de Gaulle's government of France. As the war moved to a close, indeed, the future of liberated peoples, such as those of Italy and Greece, led to differences of considerable gravity. There was, too, a persistent undercurrent of misunderstanding about the nature and future of the British Empire and Commonwealth, made more ominous by the President's strong views on British colonialism and the equally powerful and contrary convictions of the Prime Minister; but though it showed itself, for example, over India, it never became sufficiently strong to cause a first-rate crisis. These divergences, however, did but throw into clearer relief the unparalleled Anglo-American co-operation and cordiality in these years of war, which seemed in a sense to form an altogether fitting climax in the long drama of Anglo-American relations.

But though life may be dramatic, international life is not drama, for it has no final curtain, and as was perhaps inevitable the closeness of the relationship diminished as the war approached its end. One potential threat to Anglo-American co-operation was what Sir James Grigg once called in a considerable overstatement, Roosevelt's obsession with the idea derived "from de Tocqueville by way of Henry Adams . . . to the effect that the only two nations or groups who would count after the war were Russia and America". In truth, Roosevelt's real, and really dangerous, obsession was that by personal goodwill and charm at the summit he could reach a satisfactory settlement with Stalinist Russia. So out of touch with reality was this belief that it never became an actual threat to Anglo-American unity; the ineluctable facts of history dictated that basic understanding between Britain and the United States would be firmer and more enduring than any between America and the Soviet Union. And, despite Yalta, it is clear that in the last weeks before his death Roosevelt was realizing this and moving steadily, and indeed swiftly, to the same position of opposition to Communist international policies which was so strongly held by his successor, President Truman.

Indeed, the dominant fact in the history of Anglo-American relations since 1945, as in that of international relations as a whole, has been the "cold war" between the free world led by America on the one hand and the Communist world dominated by the Soviet Union, latterly in conjunction with the People's Republic of China, on the other. Whenever, as is the way of wartime allies when peace comes, Britain and America showed signs—at times very dangerous—of drifting apart, the situation was usually saved by some Communist action or threat which drove them together again. One of the Anglo-American difficulties in fact was that the two governments and peoples came to rely perhaps too much on the force of Russian intransigence to cement their alliance, and so at times paid their mutual relationship far too little attention, particularly in view of the wholehearted part played, after the war, by the United States in international affairs. Thus, for instance, the economic difficulties of Britain, and later of Europe, were overcome to a considerable extent by means of American assistance, embodied in the Anglo-American loan of 1946 and the magnificently generous Marshall Plan which was launched in 1947—and much

American support for these derived from fear of Communist Russia. A more direct result of Russian pressure was the formation of NATO which began in 1948, partly on Canadian and British initiative, and the establishment of American atom bomber, and later nuclear rocket, bases in Britain. The Berlin air lift was a remarkable example of the speed with which in practice Anglo-American military co-operation could be restored in face of a Communist threat.

Not all the divergences between Britain and America were immediately or easily rectified. The intimate collaboration, for instance, which had produced the extraordinary and overwhelming achievement of the atomic bomb during the war, was progressively disbanded, and all the more swiftly and absolutely when it began to seem to the United States (despite the defects in her own record which were soon to become apparent) that Britain's security regulations to prevent leakages to Russia were dangerously lax, and when the late Senator Joseph R. McCarthy of Wisconsin began his virulent, but happily short-lived, "red hunting" campaign in American political life. So, too, British public opinion found it as difficult to accept the fact of America's absolute naval superiority after World War II as it had found it to accept that of her equality after World War I. This sensitivity was also apparent in some Britons' resentment against the dependence of their country on a United States now so obviously superior to Britain in political and economic strength. But broadly speaking, as far as Europe was concerned, there was never any fundamental Anglo-American difference of opinion: Russian obduracy could be relied upon, even down to the renewed Berlin crisis of 1958-9, to make good the deficiencies in Anglo-American accord.

Potentially more serious was the rift which appeared between them in the Far East when Britain precipitately granted *de jure* recognition in January, 1950, to the victorious Communist government in Pekin. However little the United States could be held responsible for the defeat of Chiang Kai-Shek's Nationalist regime, American public opinion was deeply disturbed by the enormous alteration in the world's balance of power which was dramatized by the announcement in the next month of the Sino-Soviet pact. Before British-American policies could be realigned, perhaps by a reluctant American recognition of the facts of the matter (although this would have run contrary to the Hoover-Stimson tradition of non-recognition, which had its roots in Wilsonian international moralism), the North Korean invasion of South Korea was launched in June, 1950. The magnificently courageous lead given by President Truman resulted in United Nations condemnation of the aggression, and in military support for the South Koreans. When by the end of the year United Nations forces had not only crossed the 38th Parallel which divided the two countries, but were crushing all the resistance that lay between them and the Yalu River border of Manchuria, the massive intervention of Red China flung them swiftly back, and produced a situation of ultimate military stalemate. The only way out of this impasse satisfactory to the United States seemed for a time to be a full-scale war with China, which the United Nations Commander-in-Chief, General MacArthur, appeared to favour; fear of this in some British quarters greatly disturbed Anglo-American relations until in April, 1951, the President dismissed the General from his command. But even when this particular fear had subsided, and even, too, when an armistice on the compromise line of the 38th Parallel had, after infinitely protracted negotiation, been signed in 1953 by the new Republican administration, many Britons remained apprehensive about the possibly explosive effects of what they regarded as the rigidity of American Far Eastern policy. This continued to be based on a refusal to recognize Communist China, or to consent to her admission to the United Nations (which British critics considered "unrealistic"), and on a determination to keep Formosa in the friendly hands of the Chinese Nationalists, for primarily strategic reasons, despite the war of nerves conducted in the area from time to time by the Pekin government. Though there were signs of a change in American public opinion in 1958, this Anglo-American difference remained unresolved at the end of that year.

But happily, by that date, the gravest Anglo-American breach of all —the most serious, it seemed at the time, since World War I or even since the Venezuela crisis of 1896—had been remarkably, indeed astoundingly, repaired. This, the Suez crisis of 1956, had arisen, with terrifying suddenness, out of the tangled complexities of Middle Eastern politics, on which there had never been evolved a firm, joint Anglo-American policy.[1] Initially after World War II American support for Israel had conflicted with British support for certain of the Arab kingdoms, a situation complicated by Anglo-American oil rivalries. In 1956, when Britain, partly as a result of American insistence, had evacuated the Suez Canal Zone, and when President Nasser had begun to import arms from behind the Iron Curtain, the American Administration decided that it could not continue to promise financial support for Egypt's project of an Aswan High Dam; Washington's announcement

---

[1] I wrote as early as 1952, "Only through Anglo-American unity can the Middle East become an asset rather than a burden to the free world."

to this effect on 19 July was followed a week later by President Nasser's emotional proclamation of the nationalization of the Suez Canal. The effect on Britain, the chief user of the Canal (which had so long been regarded as the life-line of the British Empire), was such that from the first the British Government made no secret of its readiness to use force to remedy this breach by Egypt of what Britons regarded as her international undertakings; France, in the midst of the Algerian war, was even more militant. From this beginning arose the gravest Anglo-American crisis of this generation, for the British use of military force brought a direct clash with the United States Government, partly because of America's apparently firmer belief in the pacific obligations of member states to the United Nations.

The tragedy arose from many deep-rooted sources. One was long pent-up British resentment of American strength and certain American attitudes, particularly that of anti-colonialism; while this often arose from American ignorance of the true nature of the British Empire and Commonwealth in mid-twentieth century, British opinion was sometimes correspondingly blind to the wisdom of America's desire to encourage the rapid development of new nationalisms in Asia and Africa and thus to cultivate their friendship. The refusal of the Eisenhower Administration to countenance the Anglo-French use of force in the settlement of this international dispute seemed to many Britons hypocritical, and lacking in proper feeling for a close ally, in view of America's undoubted willingness to use armed strength in defence of her own vital interests; America's correct observation that she had never since World War II taken the initiative, as Britain was now helping to do, in the use of military force was countered by Britons with the statement that the American Administration (like most Americans, traditionally insensitive to the Middle East) simply did not appreciate that the Suez Canal was literally a vital British concern—though subsequent events were to show that in fact Britain could get along well enough without it. The prolonged procrastination of Secretary of State Dulles, which appeared to most Americans a wise postponement of the use of force, appeared to the British Government a disingenuous attempt to prevent Britain from asserting her just international rights. But in the event, when France and Britain invaded the Suez Canal Zone, ostensibly to prevent the spread of war as a result of an Israeli attack on the Sinai peninsula, it became clear that the British Government had made a very grave error, in entirely misjudging the reaction of the United States Government and also of most of world opinion, including that of Canada. Because she deliberately failed to inform the United States beforehand, Britain had to use her very first veto in the Security Council on an American cease-fire motion, and found her actions condemned in the Assembly by 64 votes (including America's) to 5. This made the plea of her government that she was avoiding appeasement of the Munich type by using force on behalf of the international community patently unconvincing. The situation was not improved by military dawdling, and the consequent fact that, under political and economic pressure from the United States and independent threats from Russia, a cease-fire was accepted before the military objectives had been attained. Serious failures of leadership in America as well as Britain, and the fact that the United States very shortly, under the Eisenhower Doctrine, undertook to oppose the spread of Communism in the Middle East by armed force, which Britain declared she had been doing all along, do not absolve the British Government from the blame for a colossal blunder.

This did not consist in the invasion of Egypt as such, but in the fact that the British Government allowed their foreign policy to become obsessed with a relatively small sector of the international scene, for the Middle East cannot now compare in importance to Britain with the American relationship. The Atlantic Ocean, and not the Suez Canal, is the true heart of Britain's world. Any British Government which loses sight of this fact, even for a brief spell, has committed the most fatal of mistakes. Ever since the great readjustment of her international relations which began with the Anglo-American rapprochment of 1898, England has always tended to go astray when she has neglected the primacy of Anglo-American friendship. This cardinal folly of Sir Anthony Eden in 1956 might well have seemed irreparable.

Yet in fact it has been repaired in an astonishing fashion. Although himself bearing part of the collective responsibility of the Eden Cabinet for the egregious error, Prime Minister Macmillan has, with very great patience, single-mindedness and skill, set himself to restore the sense of Anglo-American interdependence. He has had, with American help, extraordinary success in the last two years, as may be instanced by the recent restoration (in 1958) of effective Anglo-American exchange of atomic information, and even more dramatically, by the joint Anglo-American intervention, at the request of the governments concerned, in Jordan and the Lebanon. I myself, in line with many other confident prophets, had written in 1952 that, peering into the future, it did indeed "seem certain beyond a peradventure that the unity of the British and American peoples would endure". There were times in the last weeks of 1956 when I felt inclined to rue the prediction, but now, after the

236

passage of two healing years, I must confess to even greater confidence. I cannot but ask myself whether the Anglo-American relationship, if it could survive the Suez crisis, can not survive anything?

INDEX

INDEX

tion, 31; politics, 31; economic life, 32; geographical development, 34-5; island position, 36-8; population, 39; population density, 40; urbanization, 41; armed forces, 42-9; concentration on navy, 42-3, 46; diplomatic policy, 51-2; assumes Britain's diplomatic rôle, 52, 179-81; growth of economy, 62-4; becomes creditor, 64; importance of British trade, 68-71; domination of world's economy, 70; tariff history, 75-8; industrial production 1860-1913, 81; British investment in, 84-8; British financial dependence on, 86-8, 88-94; repudiation of debts in 19th century, 93-4; migration with GB, 96-108; social impact on GB, 110-3; 'materialism' of, 133-4, 166-70; education, 134; linguistic fertility, 135-7; immaturity in 19th century, 147-8; confidence in future, 149-50; of 20th century, like GB of 19th, 171-3; GB a 'father', 174-5; changes in foreign policy, 182-3; basic policy, 195-202; protected by British Navy, 202-3.
United States Bank: 91, 93.
United States Navy: two-ocean, 38; national expenditure on, 43-7; interchange of ideas with British, 47; Chap. VIII, passim.
University of London: 121.
University of Michigan: 121.
University of North Carolina: 121.
University of Virginia: 141.
U.S.S.R.: See Russia.

VALLEY FORGE: 211.
Van Buren, President: 106.
Vancouver Island: 217.
Veblen, Thorstein: 152.
Venezuela dispute, 1895: 17, 20, 199, 221.
Venezuela incident, 1902-3: 224.
Versailles, Treaty of, 1783: 212.
Versailles, Treaty of, 1919: 228.
Victorianism: 132.
Vigne, Godfrey T.: 159.
Visitors, to each other: 109.

WALPOLE, Sir Robert: 191.
Walsh, Robert, Jr.: 146.
Wansey, Henry: 159.
War of 1812: 144-5, 175, 198, 208, 214, 215.
War of the Spanish Succession: 181.
Ward, Artemus: 139.
Ward, Mrs. Humphrey: 168.

Washington: 217, 221, 224.
Washington, President: 100, 142, 213, 216.
Washington Treaty, 1921: 229.
Washington, Treaty of, 1871: 220.
Waugh, Evelyn: 170.
Wealth of Nations: 72.
Webb-Pomerone Act, 1918: 62.
Webster, Daniel: 113-4, 143.
Webster, Noah: 127.
Webster-Ashburton Treaty, 1842: 216, 217.
Wedgwood, Josiah: 72.
Weld, Isaac: 159.
Wellington, Duke of: 216.
Wells, H. G.: 161-2.
West, Benjamin: 141.
West German Federal Republic: See Germany.
West Indies: 50; cotton produced in, 60.
Western Hemisphere: 49.
Western posts: 52.
Westminster Review: 146.
Westward Movement, the: 50, 198.
Whistler, J. A. McNeill: 141.
White, Joshua R.: 146.
White, Richard Grant: 127.
Whitman, Walt: 138, 152.
Wilberforce, William: 121, 123.
Wilson, President: tariff policy, 77, 117, 191; reasons for entering war, 226-7; and League of Nations, 228; aloofness from GB, 227; Fourteen Points, 228; and isolationism, 228.
Wilsonian Democracy: 125.
Wireless: 112.
With Malice Toward Some: 155.
Witherspoon, John: 137.
Wolseley, Viscount: 47.
Woods, John: 159.
Woolf, Virginia: 139.
Woollens: 75, 76, 77.
Working Classes in the United States, The: 161.
Workingmen's Association: 122.
World War I: US participation, 200; Chap. VIII, passim.
World War II: 75; US participation, 201; Chap. VIII, passim.
Wortley, Lady Emmeline Stuart: 161.
Wrecker, The: 136.
Wright, Frances: 121.

YALTA CONFERENCE: 232.
Yalu River: 234.
Young Men's Christian Association: 121.

247